D0057403

Business Glossary
English-Spanish/Spanish-English

General Editor
PH Collin

Spanish Editor
Lourdes Melcion

PETER COLLIN PUBLISHING

First Published in Great Britain 1995

Reprinted 1999

published by
Peter Collin Publishing Ltd
1 Cambridge Road, Teddington, Middlesex, TW11 8DT

Business Glossary Text
© Copyright P.H. Collin 1995

British Library Cataloguing in Publications Data

A Catalogue record for this book is available from the British Library

ISBN 0-948549-54-8

Text computer typeset by PCP
Printed and bound in Finland by WSOY

Cover illustration by Gary Weston

Preface

This glossary is for any business person or traveller who needs to deal with a foreign business language. It contains over 5,000 essential business terms with clear and accurate translations.

How to use this glossary

This glossary is arranged in two main sections. The first list English terms with a Spanish translation, the second half list Spanish terms with equivalent English translation.

Throughout the Business Glossary we have used a number of abbreviations:

adj	adjetivo	adjective
adv	adverbio	adverb
f	femenino	feminine
fpl	femenino plural	feminine plural
m	masculino	masculine
mf	masculino o femenino	masculine or feminine
mpl	masculino plural	masculine plural
n	nombre	noun
v	verbo	verb

Prefacio

Este glosario tiene como objetivo facilitar la comunicación a toda persona que se relacione o viaje por asuntos de negocios. Contiene más de 5.000 términos básicos de negocios con sus correspondientes traducciones.

Como usar este glosario

El glosario se divide en dos secciones. La primera contiene una selección de términos ingeleses traducidos al español y la segunda los términos españoles con su equivalente en inglés.

En la elaboración del glosario se han utilizado las siguientes abreviaturas:

adj	adjetivo	adjective
adv	adverbio	adverb
f	femenino	feminine
fpl	femenino plural	feminine plural
m	masculino	masculine
mf	masculino o femenino	masculine or feminine
mpl	masculino plural	masculine plural
n	nombre	noun
v	verbo	verb

English-Spanish
Inglés-Español

Aa

A1 de primera clase

abandon abandonar *o* renunciar a

abandon an action desistir de una acción

abatement disminución (f)

abroad (en el) extranjero (m)

absence ausencia (f)

absent ausente

absolute monopoly monopolio (m) absoluto

abundance abundancia (f)

accelerated depreciation amortización (f) acelerada

accept (v) aceptar

accept a bill aceptar una letra

accept delivery of a shipment aceptar la entrega de mercancías

accept liability for something aceptar la responsabilidad de algo

acceptable aceptable *o* admisible

acceptance aceptación (f)

acceptance of an offer aceptación (f) de una oferta

acceptance sampling muestreo (m) de aceptación

access (n) acceso (m)

accessible accesible

accommodation address dirección (f) postal

accommodation bill pagaré (m) *o* efecto (m) de favor

according to según

account cuenta

account executive ejecutivo (m) de cuentas

account for justificar *o* responder de

account in credit cuenta (f) con saldo positivo *o* cuenta acreedora

account on stop cuenta (f) bloqueada

account: on account a cuenta

accountant contable (mf)

accounting contabilidad (f)

accounts department departamento (m) de contabilidad

accounts payable cuentas (fpl) a pagar *o* por pagar

accounts receivable cuentas (fpl) a cobrar *o* por cobrar

accrual acumulación (f)

accrual of interest acumulación (f) de interés

accrue acumularse *o* devengar

accrued interest interés (m) acumulado

accumulate acumular *o* acumularse

accurate exacto, -ta *o* correcto, -ta

accusation (n) acusación (f)

accuse (v) acusar

acknowledge receipt of a letter acusar recibo de una carta

acknowledgement acuse (m) de recibo

acquire adquirir

acquisition adquisición (f)

across-the-board general

act (v) actuar

act (v) *[do something]* tomar medidas

act of God fuerza (f) mayor

acting interino, -na *o* en funciones

acting manager director (m) en funciones

action acción (f)

action *[lawsuit]* acción (f) legal

action for damages demanda (f) por daños y perjuicios

active (adj) activo, -va

activity (n) actividad (f)

actual real *o* efectivo, -va

actuals cifras (fpl) reales

actuarial tables tablas (fpl) actuariales *o* tablas de mortalidad

actuary actuario, -ria

ad valorem ad valorem

ad valorem tax impuesto (m) ad valorem

add añadir

add on 10% for service añadir el 10% por el servicio

add up a column of figures sumar una columna de cifras

addition suma (f) *o* adición (f)

additional adicional *o* suplementario, -ria

additional charges cargos (mpl) adicionales

additional premium sobreprima (f)

address (n) dirección (f) *o* señas (fpl)

address (v) dirigir

address a letter *or* **a parcel** poner las señas *o* la dirección

address label etiqueta (f) (de señas)

address list lista (f) de direcciones

addressee destinatario, -ria

adequate adecuado, -da

adjourn aplazar *o* diferir

adjourn a meeting aplazar una reunión

adjudicate in a dispute arbitrar un litigio

adjudication adjudicación (f)

adjudication tribunal tribunal (m) de justicia

adjudicator árbitro (mf) *o* juez (mf)

adjust ajustar *o* reajustar

adjustment ajuste (m) *o* reajuste (m)

administration administración (f)

administrative administrativo, -va

administrative body *or* **authority** órgano (m) administrativo

administrative expenses gastos (mpl) administrativos

admission entrada (f) *o* ingreso (m)

admission charge precio (m) de entrada

admit admitir

advance (n) *[loan]* anticipo (m)

advance (n) *[progress]* avance (m)

advance (v) *[lend]* anticipar

advance (v) *[progress]* avanzar

advanced (adj) anticipado, -a *o* adelantado, -a

advance booking reserva (f) anticipada

advance on account anticipo (m) a cuenta

advance payment pago (m) anticipado

advertise anunciar *o* publicar

advertise a new product anunciar un nuevo producto

advertise a vacancy anunciar una vacante

advertisement anuncio (m)

advertiser anunciante (mf)

advertising publicidad (f)

advertising agency agencia (f) de publicidad

advertising budget presupuesto (m) de publicidad

advertising campaign campaña (f) publicitaria

advertising manager jefe (m) de publicidad

advertising rates tarifas (fpl) publicitarias

advertising space espacio (m) publicitario

advice note nota (f) de aviso

advise *[suggest]* aconsejar

advise *[tell what happened]* informar

advise against desaconsejar *o* disuadir

adviser *or* **advisor** asesor, -ra *o* consejero, -ra

affidavit acta (f) notarial

affiliated afiliado, -da *o* filial

affiliation (n) afiliación (f)

affirmative afirmativo, -va

afford permitirse un gasto *o* tener tiempo

after-sales service servicio (m) posventa * de post-venta

after-tax profit beneficios (mpl) netos de impuestos

agency agencia (f)

agenda orden (m) del día

agent *[in an agency]* agente (mf)

agent *[representative]* representante (mf)

AGM (= annual general meeting) junta general anual

agree *[accept]* aceptar

agree *[approve]* acordar

agree *[be same as]* corresponder *o* coincidir

agree to do something aceptar hacer algo

agree with *[be same as]* corresponder *o* coincidir con

agree with *[of same opinion]* estar de acuerdo

agreed acordado, -da *o* convenido, -da

agreed price precio (m) acordado *o* precio convenido

agreement convenio (m) *o* acuerdo (m) *o* contrato (m) *o* pacto (m)

agricultural agrícola *o* agropecuario, -ria *o* agrario, -ria

aim (n) objetivo (m) *o* propósito (m)

aim (v) proponerse *o* aspirar a

air aire (m)

air freight flete (m) aéreo *o* carga (f) aérea

air freight charges *or* **rates** tarifas de carga aérea

air letter aerograma (m)

air terminal terminal (f) de aeropuerto

airfreight (v) enviar por carga aérea

airline línea (f) aérea

airmail (n) correo (m) aéreo

airmail (v) enviar por correo aéreo

airmail sticker etiqueta (f) de correo aéreo

airport aeropuerto (m)

airport bus autobús (m) del aeropuerto

airport tax tasas (fpl) de aeropuerto

airport terminal terminal (f) del aeropuerto

airtight packaging embalaje (m) hermético

all expenses paid todos los gastos pagados

all-in todo incluido

all-in price precio (m) todo incluido

all-risks policy póliza (f) a todo riesgo

allocate asignar

allocation of funds provisión (f) de fondos

allow permitir

allow *[accept]* aceptar

allow *[give]* conceder *o* dar

allow for dejar un margen *o* tener en cuenta

allow 10% for carriage dejar un margen del 10% para el porte

allowance for depreciation cuota (f) de depreciación

alphabetical order orden (m) alfabético

alter modificar

alteration modificación (f)

alternative (adj) alternativo, -va

alternative (n) alternativa (f)

amend enmendar

amendment enmienda (f)

American (adj) americano, -na *o* estadounidense

American (n) americano, -na *o* estadounidense (mf)

amortization amortización (f)

amortize amortizar

amount *[of money]* importe (m) *o* cantidad (f)

amount owing importe (m) debido

amount paid importe (m) pagado

amount to ascender a

analyse *or* **analyze** analizar

analyse the market potential analizar las posibilidades del mercado

analysis análisis (m)

annexe anexo (m)

announce anunciar *o* comunicar

announcement anuncio (m) *o* declaración (f)

annual anual

annual accounts cuentas (fpl) anuales

annual general meeting (AGM) junta general anual

annual report informe (m) anual

annually anualmente

answer (n) contestación (f) *o* respuesta (f)

answer (v) contestar *o* responder

answer a letter contestar una carta

answer the telephone contestar el teléfono

answering machine contestador (m) automático

answering service servicio (m) de contestación

antedate antedatar

anticipate anticipar *o* prever

apartment apartamento (m)

apologize disculparse *o* presentar excusas *o* pedir perdón

apology disculpa (f) *o* excusa (f)

appeal (n) *[against a decision]* apelación (f)

appeal (n) *[attraction]* atractivo (m) *o* interés (m)

appeal (v) *[against a decision]* apelar

appeal to (v) *[attract]* atraer *o* interesar

appear parecer

appendix apéndice (m)

applicant for a job candidato, -ta a un puesto de trabajo

application aplicación (f)

application *[request]* solicitud (f)

application for a job solicitud (f) de trabajo

application form impreso (m) *o* formulario (m) de solicitud

apply (v) aplicar

apply for *[ask for]* solicitar

apply for a job solicitar un trabajo

apply in writing solicitar por escrito

apply to *[affect]* referirse a

appoint nombrar

appointment *[job]* empleo (m)

appointment *[meeting]* cita (f) *o* compromiso (m)

appointment *[to a job]* nombramiento (m)

appointments book agenda (f)

appointments vacant ofertas (fpl) de trabajo

appreciate *[how good something is]* apreciar *o* valorar

appreciate *[increase in value]* subir (en valor)

appreciation *[how good something is]* apreciación (f) *o* aprecio (m) *o* valoración (f)

appreciation *[in value]* aumento (m) *o* subida (f)

apprentice aprendiz, -za

appropriate (adj) apropiado, -da

appropriate (v) *[funds]* asignar *o* consignar

approval aprobación (f)

approval: on approval a prueba

approve the terms of a contract aprobar los términos de un contrato

approximate aproximado, -da

approximately aproximadamente

arbitrate arbitrar

arbitrate in a dispute arbitrar un litigio *o* en una disputa

arbitration arbitraje (m)

arbitration board *or* **arbitration tribunal** comisión (f) *o* tribunal (m) de arbitraje

arbitrator árbitro (mf)

area área (f)

area *[of town]* distrito (m) *o* zona (f)

area *[region]* región (f) *o* zona (f)

area *[subject]* campo (m)

area code código (m) postal *o* territorial

area manager director, -ra regional

argument discusión (f) *o* argumento (m)

arrange *[meeting]* organizar

arrange *[set out]* ordenar *o* disponer *o* acomodar

arrangement acuerdo (m) *o* acomodo (m) *o* arreglo (m)

arrangement *[system]* plan (m)

arrears atrasos (mpl)

arrival llegada (f)

arrivals llegadas (fpl)

arrive llegar

article artículo (m)

article *[clause]* cláusula (f)

articles of association estatutos (mpl) *o* escritura (f) de constitución

articulated lorry *or* **articulated vehicle** camión (m) con remolque

as per advice según nota de expedición

as per invoice según factura

as per sample según muestra

asap (= as soon as possible) lo antes posible

ask *[inquire]* preguntar

ask *[request]* pedir

ask for solicitar *o* pedir

ask for a refund exigir el reembolso

ask for further details *or* **particulars** pedir más detalles

assembly asamblea (f) *o* reunión (f)

assembly *[putting together]* montaje (m)

assembly line cadena (f) de montaje

assess valorar *o* evaluar

assess damages fijar los daños

assessment valoración (f)

assessment of damages valoración (f) de daños

asset activo (m)

asset value valor (m) de activo

assets and liabilities activo (m) y pasivo (m)

assign asignar

assign a right to someone adjudicar un derecho a alguien

assignee cesionario, -ria

assignment asignación (f)

assignment *[work]* tarea (f)

assignor cedente (mf)

assist asistir *o* ayudar

assistance asistencia (f) *o* ayuda (f)

assistant ayudante (mf) *o* auxiliar (mf)

assistant manager subdirector, -ra

assisted: computer-assisted asistido por ordenador

associate (adj) asociado, -da *o* afiliado, -da

associate (n) socio, -cia

associate company compañía (f) afiliada

association asociación (f)

assurance seguro (m) (de vida)

assurance company compañía (f) de seguros

assurance policy póliza (f) de seguros

assure someone's life asegurar la vida de alguien

attach adjuntar *o* sujetar

attack atacar

attend *[meeting]* asistir

attended asistido, -da

attend to ocuparse de

attention atención (f)

attorney apoderado, -da *o* procurador, -ra

attract atraer

attraction atractivo (m)

attractive salary salario (m) interesante

auction (n) subasta (f)

auction (v) subastar

auction rooms sala (f) de subastas

audit (n) auditoría (f) *o* intervención (f) *o* revisión (f) de cuentas

audit (v) auditar *o* intervenir

audit the accounts revisar las cuentas

auditing auditoría (f)

auditor auditor, -ra *o* censor, -ra *o* interventor, -ra

authenticate autentificar *o* legalizar

authority autoridad (f)

authorization autorización (f)

authorize autorizar

authorize payment autorizar el pago

authorized autorizado, -da

availability disponibilidad (f)

available disponible *o* asequible

available capital capital (m) disponible

average (adj) medio, -dia *o* mediano, -na

average (n) promedio (m)

average (n) *[insurance]* avería (f)

average (v) calcular el promedio

average price precio (m) medio *o* precio corriente

avoid evitar

await instructions esperar instrucciones

award (n) premio (m)

award (v) conceder *o* adjudicar *o* otorgar

award a contract to someone adjudicar un contrato a alguien

Bb

back (n) dorso (m) *o* reverso (m)

back orders pedidos (mpl) pendientes

back payment pago (m) atrasado

back tax impuesto (m) atrasado

back up (v) respaldar *o* apoyar

back up (v) *[computer file]* archivar *o* guardar

backdate antedatar

backer garante (m)

backhander soborno (m)

backing respaldo (m) *o* apoyo (m) financiero

backlog acumulación (f) de trabajo atrasado

backup (adj) *[computer]* de reserva

backup copy copia (f) de reserva *o* de seguridad

backwardation margen (m) de cobertura

bad buy mala compra (f)

bad debt deuda (f) morosa *o* incobrable

bag saco (m) o bolsa (f)

bail someone out obtener la libertad de alguien bajo fianza

balance (n) equilibrio (m)

balance (n) *[accounts]* balance (m) o saldo (m)

balance (v) equilibrar

balance (v) *[accounts]* cuadrar o saldar

balance brought down *or* **brought forward** saldo (m)

balance carried down *or* **carrried forward** saldo (m) a cuenta nueva

balance due to us saldo (m) a (nuestro) favor

balance of payments balanza (f) de pagos

balance of trade balanza (f) comercial

balance sheet balance (m) general o de situación

ban (n) prohibición (f)

ban (v) prohibir

bank (n) banco (m)

bank (v) ingresar o depositar

bank account cuenta (f) bancaria

bank balance estado (m) de cuenta

bank base rate tipo (m) base de interés bancario

bank bill (GB) letra (f) bancaria o giro (m) bancario

bank bill (US) billete (m) de banco

bank book libreta (f) de ahorros

bank borrowings préstamos (mpl) bancarios

bank charges gastos (mpl) bancarios

bank credit crédito (m) bancario

bank deposits depósitos (mpl) bancarios

bank draft giro (m) bancario

bank holiday fiesta (f) oficial

bank loan préstamo (m) bancario

bank manager director, -ra de banco

bank mandate orden (f) de pago

bank statement extracto (m) de cuentas

bank transfer transferencia (f) bancaria

bankable paper efecto (m) negociable

banker banquero, -ra

banker's draft giro (m) bancario

banker's order orden (f) de domiciliación (bancaria)

banking banca (f)

banking hours horario (m) bancario

banknote billete (m) (de banco)

bankrupt (adj) en bancarrota o en quiebra o insolvente

bankrupt (n) quebrado (m)

bankrupt (v) arruinar

bankruptcy quiebra (f) o insolvencia (f) o bancarrota (f)

bar chart gráfico (m) de barras

bar code código (m) de barras

bargain (n) *[cheaper than usual]* ganga (f)

bargain (n) *[deal]* trato (m) o negocio (m)

bargain (n) *[Stock Exchange]* venta (f) en la bolsa

bargain (v) negociar o regatear

bargain offer oferta (f) de ocasión

bargain price precio (m) de ocasión o precio irrisorio

bargaining negociación (f)

bargaining position postura (f) negociadora

bargaining power poder (m) de negociación

barrier barrera (f)

barter (n) trueque (m)

barter (v) trocar

bartering trueque (m) o cambio (m) en especie

base (n) base (f)

base (v) basar

base (v) *[in a place]* radicar o establecer

base year año (m) base

basic (adj) básico, -ca

basic (adj) *[most important]* fundamental

basic discount descuento (m) básico

basic tax impuesto (m) básico

basis base (f)

batch (n) *[of orders]* serie (f) o remesa (f) o partida (f)

batch (n) *[of products]* lote (m)

batch (v) agrupar

batch number número (m) de lote

batch processing procesamiento (m) por lotes

bear (n) *[Stock Exchange]* bajista (mf)

bear (v) *[carry]* llevar

bear (v) *[interest]* devengar o rendir

bear (v) *[pay for]* pagar (costes)

bear market mercado (m) bajista

bearer portador, -ra

bearer bond título (m) al portador

begin empezar *o* comenzar

beginning comienzo (m)

behalf: on behalf of en nombre de

belong to pertenecer

below abajo

benchmark punto (m) de referencia

beneficiary beneficiario, -ria

benefit (n) beneficio (m) *o* subsidio (m)

benefit from (v) beneficiarse de

berth (n) amarradero (m)

berth (v) atracar

best (adj) lo mejor

best (n) (el, la) mejor

best-selling car coche en gran demanda

bid (n) oferta (f)

bid (n) *[at an auction]* oferta (f) *o* puja (f)

bidder postor (m) *o* licitador (m)

bidding ofertas (fpl) *o* subasta (f) *o* licitación (f)

big (adj) grande

bilateral (adj) bilateral

bill (n) (US) billete (m)

bill (n) *[draft]* letra (f)

bill (n) *[in a restaurant]* cuenta (f)

bill (n) *[in Parliament]* proyecto (m) de ley

bill (n) *[invoice]* factura (f)

bill (v) facturar

bill of exchange letra (f) de cambio

bill of lading conocimiento (m) de embarque

bill of sale contrato (m) de venta

billing facturación (f)

billion mil millones (mpl)

bills for collection letras (fpl) por cobrar

bills payable letras (fpl) a pagar

bills receivable letras (fpl) a cobrar

binding obligatorio, -ria *o* vinculante

black economy economía (f) sumergida

black list (n) lista (f) negra

black market mercado (m) negro

blacklist (v) poner en la lista negra

blame (n) culpa (f)

blame (v) culpar *o* echar la culpa

blank (adj) en blanco

blank (n) blanco (m) *o* espacio (m) en blanco

blank cheque cheque (m) en blanco

blister pack embalaje (m) de plástico tipo burbuja

block (n) *[building]* manzana (f)

block (n) *[of shares]* paquete (m)

block (v) bloquear

block booking reserva (f) en bloque

blocked currency moneda (f) bloqueada

blue chip acción (f) de primera categoría

blue-chip investments inversiones (fpl) en valores seguros

board (n) *[group of people]* consejo (m) (de administración)

board (v) abordar *o* embarcarse

board meeting reunión (f) del consejo de administración

board of directors junta (f) directiva

board: on board a bordo

boarding card *or* **boarding pass** tarjeta (f) de embarque

boardroom sala (f) de juntas

bona fide de buena fe

bond (n) bono (m) *o* título (m)

bonded warehouse depósito (m) aduanero

bonus prima (f) *o* bonificación (f)

bonus issue emisión (f) gratuita

book (n) libro (m)

book (v) reservar

book sales ventas (fpl) registradas

book value valor (m) contable

booking reserva (f)

booking clerk taquillero, -ra

booking office taquilla (f) *o* despacho (m) de billetes

bookkeeper contable (mf)

bookkeeping contabilidad (f)

boom (n) auge (m) *o* 'boom' (m)

boom (v) prosperar *o* aumentar

boom industry industria (f) próspera *o* en pleno auge

booming próspero, -ra *o* floreciente

boost (n) estímulo (m) *o* impulso (m)

boost (v) estimular *o* impulsar

border frontera (f)

borrow pedir *o* tomar prestado

borrower prestatario, -ria

borrowing préstamo (m)

borrowing power capacidad (f) de endeudamiento

boss (informal) jefe, -fa *o* amo (m)

bottleneck atasco (m) *o* embotellamiento (m)

bottom fondo (m)

bottom line saldo (m) final *o* total

bought ledger libro (m) mayor de compras

bought ledger clerk encargado (m) del libro de compras

bounce *[cheque]* devolver por falta de fondos

box number número de apartado de correos

boxed set juego completo en caja de presentación

boycott (n) boicot (m)

boycott (v) boicotear

bracket (n) *[tax]* categoría (f) *o* clase (f)

bracket together agrupar

brake (n) freno (m)

branch (n) sucursal (f) *o* rama (f)

branch manager director (m) de sucursal

branch office sucursal (f)

brand marca (f)

brand image imagen (f) de marca

brand loyalty fidelidad (f) a la marca

brand name marca (f) *o* nombre (m) comercial

brand new completamente nuevo, -va

breach of contract violación (f) de contrato

breach of warranty violación (f) de garantía

break (n) descanso (m)

break (v) *[contract]* infringir *o* incumplir

break an agreement romper un acuerdo

break down (v) *[itemize]* desglosar *o* detallar

break down (v) *[machine]* estropearse *o* averiarse

break down (v) *[talks]* romperse

break even (v) cubrir gastos

break off negotiations romper las negociaciones

break the law infringir la ley

breakages roturas (fpl) *o* desperfectos (mpl)

breakdown (n) *[items]* desglose (m)

breakdown (n) *[machine]* avería (f)

breakdown (n) *[talks]* ruptura (f) *o* interrupción (f)

breakeven point punto (m) muerto

bribe (n) soborno (m)

bribe (v) sobornar

brief (v) informar *o* dar instrucciones

briefcase cartera (f) *o* maletín (m)

bring traer

bring a civil action constituirse parte civil

bring in producir

bring out lanzar al mercado

British británico, -ca *o* inglés, -esa

brochure folleto (m) publicitario

broke (informal) sin dinero *o* arruinado, -da

broker agente (mf) *o* intermediario, -ria

brokerage *or* **broker's commission** corretaje (m) *o* comisión (f)

brown paper papel (m) de estraza

bubble pack embalaje (m) de plástico tipo burbuja

budget (n) presupuesto (m)

budget (n) *[government]* presupuesto (m) del Estado

budget (v) presupuestar

budget account *[in bank]* cuenta (f) presupuestaria

budgetary presupuestario, -ria

budgetary control control (m) presupuestario

budgetary policy política (f) presupuestaria

budgeting preparación (f) de presupuestos

build construir

building society sociedad (f) hipotecaria *o* de crédito hipotecario

built-in incorporado, -da

bulk volumen (m)

bulk buying compra (f) a granel

bulk shipments envíos (mpl) a granel

bulky voluminoso, -sa

bull *[Stock Exchange]* alcista (mf)

bull market mercado (m) alcista

bulletin boletín (m)

bullion oro (m) *o* plata (f) en lingotes

bureau de change agencia (f) de cambio

bureaucracy burocracia (f)

bus autobús (m)

business negocios (mpl)

business *[company]* empresa (f) *o* negocio (m)

business *[discussion]* asunto (m)

business address dirección (f) comercial

business call visita (f) de negocios

business card tarjeta (f)

business centre centro (m) comercial

business class clase (f) preferente (en aviones)

business equipment equipos (mpl) de oficina

business hours horas (fpl) de oficina

business letter carta (f) comercial

business lunch almuerzo (m) de negocios

business premises local (m) comercial

business school escuela (f) empresarial

business strategy estrategia (f) comercial

business transaction transacción (f) *o* trámite (m)

business trip viaje (m) de negocios

business: on business por asuntos de negocios

businessman hombre (m) de negocios

businesswoman mujer (f) de negocios

busy ocupado, -da

buy (v) comprar *o* adquirir

buy back volver a comprar *o* rescatar

buy for cash comprar en efectivo *o* al contado

buy forward comprar a futuros

buyer *[for a store]* encargado, -da de compras

buyer *[person]* comprador, -ra

buyer's market mercado (m) de compradores

buying compra (f)

buying department departamento (m) de compras

by-product subproducto (m) *o* producto (m) derivado

Cc

cable address dirección (f) telegráfica

calculate calcular

calculation cálculo (m)

calculator calculadora (f)

calendar month mes (m) civil

calendar year año (m) civil

call (n) *[for money]* demanda (f) de pago

call (n) *[phone]* llamada (f)

call (n) *[Stock Exchange]* demanda (f) *o* petición (f) de pago (de acciones)

call (n) *[visit]* visita (f)

call (v) *[meeting]* convocar (una reunión)

call (v) *[phone]* llamar (por teléfono)

call off a deal suspender *o* anular un acuerdo

call on (visit] visitar

call rate frecuencia (f) de visitas de un representante

callable bond obligación (f) redimible

campaign campaña (f)

cancel cancelar *o* suspender *o* anular

cancel a cheque anular un cheque

cancel a contract rescindir *o* anular un contrato

cancellation cancelación (f) *o* anulación (f)

cancellation clause cláusula (f) de rescisión

cancellation of an appointment cancelación (f) de una cita

cancelled cancelado, -da

candidate candidato, -ta *o* aspirante (mf)

canvass solicitar votos

canvasser persona (f) que busca clientes *o* solicita votos

canvassing búsqueda (f) de clientes *o* solicitación (f) de votos

canvassing techniques técnicas (fpl) de sondeo

capable capaz *o* competente

capable of capaz de

capacity capacidad (f)

capacity *[ability]* aptitud (f)

capacity *[output]* rendimiento (m)

capacity utilization empleo (m) de la capacidad

capital capital (m)

capital *[heritage]* patrimonio (m)

capital account cuenta (f) de capital

capital assets bienes (mpl) de capital

capital equipment bienes (mpl) de equipo

capital expenditure gastos (mpl) de capital

capital gains plusvalía (f)

capital gains tax impuesto (m) sobre las plusvalías

capital goods bienes (mpl) de capital

capital loss pérdidas (fpl) de capital *o* minusvalías (fpl)

capital-intensive industry industria con alto coeficiente de capital

capitalist (n) capitalista (mf)

capitalization capitalización (f)

capitalization of reserves capitalización (f) de las reservas

capitalize capitalizar

capitalize on aprovechar

captive market mercado (m) cautivo

capture acaparar

carbon copy copia (f) carbón

carbon paper papel (m) carbón

carbonless sin papel carbón

card *[business card]* tarjeta (f)

card *[material]* cartulina (f)

card *[membership]* carnet (m)

card *[postcard]* postal (f) *o* tarjeta (f) postal

card index (n) fichero (m)

card-index (v) pasar información a un fichero

card-index file fichero (m) de tarjetas

card-indexing paso (m) de información a un fichero

cardboard cartón (m)

cardboard box caja (f) de cartón

card phone teléfono (m) de tarjeta

care of (c/o) para entregar a

cargo carga (f)

cargo ship barco (m) de carga

carnet *[document]* carnet (m)

carriage porte (m) *o* transporte (m)

carriage forward porte (m) debido

carriage free franco de porte

carriage paid porte (m) pagado *o* franco a domicilio

carrier empresa (f) de transportes *o* transportista (mf)

carrier *[vehicle]* vehículo (m) de transporte

carry llevar *o* transportar

carry *[a motion]* aprobar

carry *[have in stock]* tener en existencia

carry *[yield]* producir

carry forward pasar a cuenta nueva

carry on a business llevar un negocio

carry out *[fulfil]* cumplir

carry over a balance pasar a cuenta nueva

cartel cartel (m)

carton cartón (m)

carton *[box]* caja (f) de cartón

case (n) *[box]* caja (f)

case (n) *[suitcase]* maleta (f)

case (v) *[put in boxes]* poner en una caja *o* embalar

cash (adv) en efectivo *o* al contado

cash (n) *[money]* dinero (m) efectivo

cash a cheque cobrar un cheque

cash account cuenta (f) de caja

cash advance anticipo (m) de caja a cuenta

cash and carry autoservicio (m) mayorista

cash balance saldo (m) de caja

cash book libro (m) de caja

cash card tarjeta (f) de cajero automático *o* tarjeta de dinero

cash deal transacción (f) en efectivo

cash deposit imposición (f) en efectivo

cash desk caja (f)

cash discount descuento (m) por pago al contado

cash dispenser cajero (m) automático

cash float fondo (m) de caja

cash flow flujo (m) de caja *o* 'cash flow' (m)

cash flow statement estado (m) de flujo de caja

cash in hand efectivo (m) en caja

cash offer oferta (f) en metálico

cash on delivery (c.o.d.) cobro (m) a la entrega *o* contra reembolso

cash payment pago (m) en efectivo

cash price precio (m) al contado

cash purchase compra (f) al contado

cash register caja (f) registradora

cash reserves reservas (fpl) de caja

cash sale venta (f) al contado

cash terms pago (m) al contado

cash transaction operación (f) al contado

cash voucher vale (m) de caja

cashable cobrable

cashier cajero, -ra

cashier's check (US) cheque (m) de administración

casting vote voto (m) de calidad

casual work trabajo (m) eventual

casual worker trabajador, -ra eventual *o* temporero, -ra

catalogue catálogo (m)

catalogue price precio (m) de catálogo

category categoría (f)

cater for abastecer

caveat emptor por cuenta y riesgo del comprador

ceiling techo (m) *o* límite (m)

ceiling price precio (m) tope *o* precio máximo autorizado

cellular telephone teléfono (m) celular *o* móvil

central central

central bank banco (m) central

central purchasing centralización (f) de las compras

centralization centralización (f)

centralize centralizar

centre centro (m)

CEO (= chief executive officer) jefe (m) ejecutivo *o* director (m) general

certificate certificado (m)

certificate of approval certificado (m) de aprobación

certificate of deposit certificado (m) de depósito

certificate of guarantee certificado (m) de garantía

certificate of origin certificado (m) de origen

certificate of registration certificado (m) de registro

certificated titulado, -da *o* diplomado,-da

certificated bankrupt quebrado (m) rehabilitado

certified accountant censor jurado de cuentas

certified cheque cheque (m) conformado

certified copy compulsa (f) *o* copia (f) auténtica *o* certificada

certify certificar

cession cesión (f)

chain cadena (f)

chain store tienda (f) de una cadena *o* sucursal (f)

chairman presidente, -ta

chairman and managing director presidente y director gerente

Chamber of Commerce Cámara (f) de Comercio

change (n) cambio (m)

change (n) *[cash]* dinero (m) suelto *o* moneda (f) suelta

change (n) *[in a shop]* vuelta (f)

change (v) cambiar

change hands cambiar de dueño

change machine máquina (f) de cambio

channel (n) canal (m)

channel (v) dirigir *o* encauzar

channels of distribution canales (mpl) de distribución

charge (n) coste (m) *o* precio (m) *o* cargo (m)

charge (n) *[in court]* acusación (f) *o* cargo (m)

charge (n) *[on account]* débito (m)

charge (v) cargar

charge (v) *[in court]* acusar

charge (v) *[price]* cobrar

charge a purchase cargar una compra en cuenta

charge account cuenta (f) abierta *o* cuenta de crédito

charge card tarjeta (f) de crédito

chargeable (to) a cargo de

charges forward gastos (mpl) a cobrar a la entrega

chart (n) gráfico (m), gráfica (f)

charter (n) flete (m) *o* alquiler (m)

charter (v) fletar *o* alquilar

charter an aircraft fletar un avión

charter flight vuelo (m) chárter

charter plane avión (m) chárter

charterer fletador, -ra

chase perseguir

chase *[an order]* apremiar

cheap barato, -ta

cheap labour mano de obra barata

cheap money dinero (m) *o* crédito (m) barato

cheap rate tarifa (f) reducida

check (n) *[examination]* control (m) *o* comprobación (f)

check (n) *[stop]* freno (m)

check (v) *[examine]* comprobar *o* cotejar

check (v) *[stop]* parar *o* contener

check in *[at airport]* facturar el equipaje

check in *[at hotel]* registrarse

check-in (counter) *[at airport]* mostrador (m) de facturación

check-in time horario (m) de presentación en el aeropuerto

check out *[of hotel]* pagar la cuenta y marcharse

checkout *[in supermarket]* caja (f)

check sample muestra (f) de inspección

cheque cheque (m)

cheque (guarantee) card tarjeta (f) de crédito

cheque account cuenta (f) corriente

cheque book talonario (m) de cheques

cheque number número (m) de cheque

cheque stub matriz (f) de un talonario

cheque to bearer cheque (m) al portador

chief (adj) principal *o* jefe

chief clerk jefe (m) de oficina

chief executive jefe (m) ejecutivo

choice (adj) escogido, -da *o* selecto, -ta

choice (n) *[choosing]* elección (f) *o* selección (f)

choice (n) *[items to choose from]* surtido (m)

choice (n) *[thing chosen]* preferencia (f)

choose elegir

Christmas bonus paga (f) extraordinaria de Navidad

chronic crónico, -ca *o* endémico, -ca

chronological order orden (m) cronológico

c.i.f. (= cost, insurance and freight) cif (coste, seguro y flete)

circular (n) *or* circular letter circular (f)

circular letter of credit carta (f) de crédito general

circulation circulación (f) *o* difusión (f)

circulation *[newspaper]* tirada (f)

city centre centro (m) de la ciudad

civil law derecho (m) civil

civil servant funcionario, -ria

claim (n) reclamación (f) *o* demanda (f) *o* reivindicación (f)

claim (v) exigir *o* reclamar *o* reivindicar

claim (v) *[suggest]* alegar *o* pretender

claimant demandante (mf)

claims department departamento (m) de reclamaciones

claims manager director, -ra de reclamaciones

clarify (v) aclarar *o* clarificar

class (n) clase (f) *o* categoría (f)

classification clasificación (f)

classified ads *or* advertisements anuncios (mpl) por palabras

classified directory directorio (m) comercial

classify clasificar

clause cláusula (f)

clawback devolución (f) (de impuestos)

clear (adj) claro, -ra

clear (v) aclarar * clarificar

clear (v) *[stock]* liquidar existencias

clear a cheque tramitar el pago de un cheque

clear a debt liquidar una deuda

clear profit ganancia (f) neta

clearance certificate certificado (m) de aduana

clearance of a cheque tramitación (f) del pago de un cheque

clearing *[paying]* liquidación (f) *o* pago (m) de una deuda

clearing bank banco (m) comercial

clerical de oficina

clerical error error (m) de copia *o* error de oficina

clerical staff personal (m) de oficina

clerical work trabajo (m) de oficina

clerk oficinista (mf) *o* empleado, -da de oficina

client cliente (mf)

clientele clientela (f)

climb subir *o* aumentar

clinch cerrar un trato

clipping service servicio (m) de recortes de prensa

close (n) *[end]* cierre (m)

close (v) *[after work]* cerrar

close a bank account cerrar una cuenta bancaria

close a meeting clausurar *o* levantar una sesión

close an account cerrar una cuenta

close down cerrar

close to cercano, -na *o* próximo, -ma

closed cerrado, -da

closed circuit TV circuito cerrado

closed market mercado (m) cerrado

closing (adj) final *o* al cierre

closing (n) cierre (m)

closing balance saldo (m) final

closing bid oferta (f) final

closing date fecha (f) tope *o* fecha límite

closing price precio (m) al cierre

closing stock existencias (fpl) finales

closing time hora (f) de cierre

closing-down sale liquidación (f) total por cierre

closure clausura (f) *o* cierre (m)

c/o (= **care of**) para entregar a

co-creditor coacreedor, -ra

co-director codirector, -ra

co-insurance coaseguro (m)

co-operate cooperar

co-operation cooperación (f)

co-operative (adj) cooperativo, -va

co-operative (n) cooperativa (f)

co-opt someone nombrar por coopción

co-owner copropietario, -ria

co-ownership copropiedad (f)

COD *or* **c.o.d.** (= **cash on delivery**) cobro a la entrega *o* contra reembolso

code código (m)

code of practice normas (fpl) de conducta

coding codificación (f)

coin moneda (f)

cold call visita (f) comercial sin cita previa

cold start empezar un negocio a cero

cold storage almacenaje (m) frigorífico

cold store almacén (m) frigorífico

collaborate colaborar

collaboration colaboración (f)

collapse (n) hundimiento (m) *o* derrumbamiento (m)

collapse (v) hundirse *o* derrumbarse

collateral (adj) colateral

collateral (n) garantía (f)

collect (v) *[fetch]* recoger

collect (v) *[money]* cobrar

collect a debt cobrar una deuda

collect call (US) llamada (f) a cobro revertido

collection recogida (f)

collection *[of money]* cobro (m)

collection charges *or* **collection rates** cobro (m) por recogida

collective colectivo, -va

collective ownership propiedad (f) colectiva

collective wage agreement convenio (m) salarial colectivo

collector cobrador, -ra *o* recaudador, -ra

commerce comercio (m)

commercial (adj) comercial

commercial (n) *[TV]* emisión (f) publicitaria *o* anuncio (m)

commercial attaché agregado, -da comercial

commercial college escuela (f) superior de comercio

commercial course curso (m) comercial

commercial directory guía (f) comercial

commercial district distrito (m) comercial

commercial failure quiebra (f) comercial

commercial law derecho (m) mercantil

commercial traveller representante (mf)

commercial undertaking empresa (f) comercial

commercialization comercialización (f)

commercialize comercializar

commission *[committee]* comisión (f) o comité (m)

commission *[money]* comisión (f)

commission agent comisionista (mf)

commission rep representante (mf) a comisión

commit *[crime]* cometer

commit funds to a project asignar fondos a un proyecto

commitments compromisos (mpl)

commodity mercancía (f)

commodity exchange lonja (f) o bolsa (f) de contratación o de comercio

commodity futures materias primas cotizadas en el mercado de futuros

commodity market lonja (f) o bolsa (f) de contratación

common *[frequent]* corriente o frecuente

common *[to more than one]* común o público, -ca

common carrier empresa (f) de transporte público

Common Market Mercado Común Europeo

common ownership propiedad (f) colectiva

common pricing fijación (f) colectiva de precios

communicate comunicar o comunicarse

communication comunicación (f)

communication *[message]* comunicado (m)

communications comunicaciones (fpl)

community comunidad (f)

commute *[exchange]* conmutar

commute *[travel]* viajar diariamente al trabajo

commuter viajero diario o viajera diaria

companies' register registro (m) de compañías

company compañía (f) o sociedad (f)

company director director, -ra de una empresa

company law ley (f) de sociedades anónimas

company secretary secretario, -ria de una empresa

comparability posibilidad (f) de comparación

comparable comparable

compare comparar o cotejar

compare with comparar con

comparison comparación (f)

compensate compensar o indemnizar o resarcir

compensation compensación (f)

compensation for damage indemnización (f) por daños y perjuicios

compete (with) competir (con)

competent competente

competing (adj) competitivo, -va

competing firms empresas (fpl) rivales

competing products productos (mpl) en competencia

competition competencia (f)

competitive competitivo, -va

competitive price precio (m) competitivo

competitive pricing fijación (f) de precios competitivos

competitive products productos (mpl) competitivos

competitively priced con precio competitivo

competitiveness competitividad (f)

competitor competidor, -ra

complain (about) quejarse

complaint queja (f)

complaints department oficina (f) de reclamaciones

complementary complementario, -ria

complete (adj) completo, -ta

complete (v) completar *o* acabar

completion finalización (f)

completion date fecha (f) de cumplimiento

completion of a contract firma (f) de un contrato

compliance conformidad (f) *o* acuerdo (m)

complimentary de favor

complimentary ticket entrada (f) de favor

compliments slip saluda (m) *o* tarjeta (f) de saludo

comply with obedecer

composition *[with creditors]* acomodamiento (m)

compound interest interés (m) compuesto

comprehensive completo, -ta *o* global

comprehensive insurance seguro (m) a todo riesgo

compromise (n) compromiso (m) *o* acuerdo (m)

compromise (v) transigir

compulsory obligatorio, -ria

compulsory liquidation liquidación (f) forzosa

compulsory purchase expropiación (f) forzosa

computer ordenador (m)

computer bureau oficina (f) de informática

computer department departamento (m) de informática

computer error error (m) de ordenador

computer file archivo (m) *o* fichero (m)

computer language lenguaje (m) informático *o* de ordenador

computer listing listado (m) de ordenador

computer printer impresora (f)

computer printout copia (f) impresa (de ordenador)

computer program programa (m) de ordenador

computer programmer programador , -ra de ordenadores

computer programming programación (f) de ordenador

computer services servicios (mpl) de informática

computer system sistema (m) informático

computer terminal terminal (m) de ordenador

computer time tiempo (m) invertido por el ordenador

computer-readable legible por ordenador

computer-readable codes códigos (mpl) legibles por ordenador

computerize informatizar

computerized informatizado, -da *o* informático, -ca

concealment of assets encubrimiento (m) de activos

concern (n) *[business]* negocio (m) *o* empresa (f)

concern (n) *[worry]* preocupación (f) *o* inquietud (f)

concern (v) *[deal with]* concernir

concession *[reduction]* desgravación (f)

concession *[right]* concesión (f) *o* agencia (f) exclusiva

concessionaire concesionario, -ria

conciliation conciliación (f)

conclude *[agreement]* concluir

conclusion conclusión (f)

condition condición (f)

condition: on condition that a condición de que

conditional condicional

conditions of employment condiciones (fpl) de empleo

conditions of sale condiciones (fpl) de venta

conduct negotiations llevar negociaciones

conference *[large]* congreso (m)

conference *[small]* asamblea (f) *o* conferencia (f)

conference phone teléfono (m) de conferencias

conference room sala (f) de conferencias

confess confesar

confidence confianza (f)

confidential confidencial

confidential report informe (m) confidencial

confidentiality confidencialidad (f)

confirm confirmar

confirm a booking confirmar una reserva

confirm someone in a job confirmar a alguien en su puesto de trabajo

confirmation confirmación (f)

conflict of interest conflicto (m) de intereses

conglomerate conglomerado (m)

congress congreso (m)

connect conectar *o* relacionar

connecting flight vuelo (m) de correspondencia

connection vínculo (m) *o* relación (f) *o* enchufe (m)

consider considerar

consign consignar

consignee consignatario, -ria

consignment *[sending]* consignación (f) *o* envío (m) *o* expedición (f)

consignment *[things sent]* envío (m) *o* remesa (f)

consignment note nota (f) de expedición *o* nota de envío

consignor remitente (mf) *o* consignador, -ra

consist of constar de

consolidate consolidar

consolidate *[shipments]* agrupar

consolidated consolidado, -da

consolidated shipment envío (m) agrupado de mercancías

consolidation agrupación (f)

consortium consorcio (m)

constant constante *o* invariable *o* continuo, -nua

consult consultar

consultancy asesoría (f)

consultancy firm asesoría (f) *o* consultoría (f)

consultant asesor, -ra *o* consejero, -ra

consulting engineer técnico (m) asesor *o* técnica (f) asesora

consumables bienes (mpl) de consumo

consumer consumidor, -ra

consumer credit crédito (m) al consumidor

consumer durables bienes (mpl) de consumo duraderos

consumer goods bienes (mpl) de consumo

consumer panel equipo (m) de consumidores

consumer price index índice (m) de precios al consumo (IPC)

consumer protection protección (f) al consumidor

consumer research investigación (f) sobre el consumo

consumer spending gastos (mpl) del consumidor *o* de consumo

consumption consumo (m)

contact (n) contacto (m)

contact: useful contact enchufe (m)

contact (v) contactar

contain contener

container *[box, tin]* recipiente (m) *o* envase (m)

container *[for shipping]* contenedor (m)

container port puerto (m) de contenedores

container ship buque (m) de contenedores *o* portacontenedores

container terminal terminal (f) de contenedores

containerization contenerización (f)

containerization *[shipping]* transporte (m) en contenedores

containerize poner en contenedores

containerize *[ship in containers]* transportar en contenedores

content significado (m)

contents contenido (m)

contested takeover oferta (f) de adquisición disputada *o* rebatida

contingency eventualidad (f) *o* contingencia (f)

contingency fund fondo (m) para imprevistos

contingency plan plan (m) de emergencia

continual continuo, -nua

continually continuamente

continuation continuación (f)

continue continuar *o* proseguir

continuous continuo, -nua

continuous feed alimentación (f) continua

continuous stationery papel (m) continuo

contra account cuenta (f) compensada

contra an entry anotar una contrapartida *o* un contraasiento

contra entry contrapartida (f) *o* contraasiento (m)

contract (n) contrato (m)

contract (v) contratar

contract law derecho (m) de contratos *o* de obligaciones

contract note contrato (m) de Bolsa

contract of employment contrato (m) de empleo

contract work trabajo (m) a contrata

contracting party parte (f) contratante

contractor contratista (mf)

contractual contractual

contractual liability responsabilidad (f) contractual

contractually según *o* por contrato

contrary contrario, -ria

contrast (n) contraste (m)

contribute contribuir *o* cotizar

contribution contribución (f) *o* colaboración (f)

contribution of capital contribución (f) de capital

contributor contribuyente (mf)

control (n) *[check]* control (m)

control (n) *[power]* control (m) *o* mando (m)

control (v) controlar

control a business controlar *o* dirigir un negocio

control key tecla (f) de control

control systems sistemas (mpl) de control

controlled economy economía (f) dirigida

controller *[who checks]* inspector, -ra

controller (US) contable (mf) jefe

controlling (adj) dominante

convene convocar

convenient cómodo, -da *o* conveniente

conversion conversión (f)

conversion of funds apropiación (f) indebida de fondos

conversion price *or* **conversion rate** precio (m) de conversión *o* tasa (f) de conversión

convert convertir

convertibility convertibilidad (f)

convertible currency moneda (f) convertible

convertible loan stock valores (mpl) convertibles en acciones

conveyance transmisión (f) del título de propiedad

conveyancer notario, -ria especialista en escrituras de trapaso

conveyancing transmisión (f) de títulos de propiedad

cooling off period (after purchase) periodo (m) de reflexión

cooperative society sociedad (f) cooperativa

copartner socio, -cia

copartnership coparticipación (f)

cope arreglárselas *o* hacer frente (a)

copier fotocopiadora (f)

copy (n) copia (f)

copy (n) *[book, newspaper]* ejemplar (m) *o* número (m)

copy (v) copiar

copying machine multicopista (f)

corner (n) *[inside angle]* rincón (m)

corner (n) *[outside angle]* esquina (f)

corner (n) *[monopoly]* monopolio

corner shop tienda (f) de barrio *o* de la esquina

corner the market acaparar el mercado

corporate image imagen (f) pública de una empresa

corporate name razón (f) social

corporate plan plan (m) de trabajo de una empresa

corporate planning planificación (f) empresarial

corporate profits beneficios (mpl) de la empresa

corporation corporación (f) *o* sociedad (f) mercantil

corporation tax impuesto (m) de sociedades

correct (adj) correcto, -ta

correct (v) corregir *o* rectificar

correction corrección (f) *o* rectificación (f)

correspond with someone escribir a alguien

correspond with something corresponder a algo

correspondence correspondencia (f)

correspondent *[journalist]* corresponsal (mf)

correspondent *[who writes letters]* correspondiente (mf)

cost (n) costo (m) *o* coste (m)

cost (v) costar *o* valer

cost accountant contable (mf) de costes

cost accounting contabilidad (f) de costes

cost analysis análisis (m) de costes

cost centre centro (m) de costes

cost factor factor (m) del coste

cost of living coste (m) de vida

cost of sales coste (m) de ventas

cost plus costo (m) más honorarios *o* porcentaje (m) de comisión

cost price precio (m) de coste

cost, insurance and freight (c.i.f.) coste, seguro y flete *o* cif

cost-benefit analysis análisis (m) coste-beneficio

cost-cutting reducción (f) de costes

cost-effective rentable

cost-effectiveness rentabilidad (f)

cost-of-living allowance subsidio (m) de carestía de vida

cost-of-living bonus plus (m) de carestía de vida

cost-of-living increase aumento (m) de sueldo por coste de vida

cost-of-living index índice (m) del coste de vida

cost-push inflation inflación (f) de costes

costing cálculo (m) de costos

costly costoso, -sa

costs costas (fpl)

counsel abogado, -da

count (v) *[add]* contar *o* calcular

counter mostrador (m) *o* ventanilla (f)

counter staff personal (m) de atención al público

counter-claim (n) reconvención (f)

counter-claim (v) presentar una reconvención

counter-offer *or* **counterbid (n)** contraoferta (f)

counterfeit (adj) falso, -sa *o* falsificado, -da

counterfeit (v) falsificar dinero

counterfoil matriz (f) (de un talonario)

countermand revocar

countersign refrendar

country país (m)

country *[not town]* campo (m)

country of origin país (m) de origen

coupon cupón (m)

coupon ad cupón (m) de anuncio

courier *[guide]* guía (mf) de turismo

courier *[messenger]* mensajero, -ra

court tribunal (m) *o* juzgado (m)

court case proceso (m) *o* causa (f) *o* juicio (m)

covenant (n) pacto (m) *o* convenio (m)

covenant (v) pactar

cover (n) cubierta (f) *o* funda (f)

cover (n) *[insurance]* cobertura (f)

cover (v) cubrir

cover a risk cubrir un riesgo

cover charge *[restaurant]* (precio del) cubierto (m)

cover costs cubrir gastos

cover note póliza (f) provisional *o* nota (f) de cobertura

covering letter carta (f) adjunta *o* explicatoria

covering note carta (f) adjunta *o* explicatoria

crane grúa (f)

crash (n) *[accident]* choque (m) *o* colisión (f)

crash (n) *[financial]* 'crack' (m)

crash (v) chocar

crash (v) *[fail]* quebrar

crate (n) cajón (m)

crate (v) embalar

credit (n) crédito (m)

credit (v) abonar *o* acreditar

credit account cuenta (f) de crédito

credit agency agencia (f) de informes comerciales

credit balance haber (m) *o* saldo (m) acreedor *o* a favor

credit bank banco (m) de crédito

credit card tarjeta (f) de crédito

credit card sale venta (f) con tarjeta de crédito

credit ceiling techo (m) crediticio

credit column columna (f) del haber

credit control control (m) de crédito

credit entry abono (m)

credit facilities facilidades (fpl) de crédito

credit freeze congelación (f) de créditos

credit limit límite (m) de crédito

credit note nota (f) de abono *o* nota (f) de crédito

credit policy política (f) crediticia

credit rating clasificación (f) crediticia

credit side haber (m)

credit-worthy solvente

credit: on credit a crédito

creditor acreedor, -ra

cross a cheque cruzar un cheque

cross off *or* **cross out** tachar

cross rate tipo (m) de cambio cruzado

crossed cheque cheque (m) cruzado

crowd multitud (f)

cubic cúbico, -ca

cubic measure medida (f) de volumen *o* de capacidad

cum coupon con cupón de interés

cum dividend con dividendo

cumulative acumulativo, -va

cumulative interest interés (m) acumulativo

cumulative preference share acción (f) preferente acumulativa

currency moneda (f)

currency conversion conversión (f) de divisas

currency note billete (m) de banco

currency reserves reservas (fpl) de divisas

current actual *o* corriente

current account cuenta (f) corriente

current assets activo (m) circulante

current cost accounting contabilidad (f) de costes actuales

current liabilities pasivo (m) circulante *o* obligaciones (fpl) a corto plazo

current price precio (m) actual

current rate of exchange tipo (m) de cambio actual

current yield rendimiento (m) corriente

curriculum vitae (CV) curriculum (vitae) (m)

curve curva (f)

custom clientela (f)

custom-built *or* **custom-made** hecho a medida *o* a la orden

customer cliente (mf)

customer appeal atractivo (m) para los clientes

customer loyalty fidelidad (f) a un establecimiento

customer satisfaction satisfacción (f) del cliente

customer service department departamento (m) de atención al cliente

customs aduana (f)

Customs and Excise Aduanas y Arbitrios

customs barriers barreras (fpl) arancelarias

customs broker agente (mf) de aduanas

customs clearance despacho (m) aduanero *o* de aduanas

customs declaration declaración (f) de aduana

customs declaration form impreso (m) de declaración de aduana

customs duty derecho (m) de aduana

customs entry point puesto (m) aduanero

customs examination inspección (f) aduanera

customs formalities formalidades (fpl) aduaneras

customs officer *or* **customs official** aduanero, -ra *o* funcionario, -ria de aduanas

customs receipt recibo (m) de aduana

customs seal precinto (m) de aduana

customs tariff arancel (m) aduanero

customs union unión (f) aduanera

cut (n) recorte (m) *o* rebaja (f)

cut (v) recortar

cut down on expenses reducir gastos

cut price (n) precio (m) reducido

cut-price (adj) a precio reducido

cut-price goods mercancías (fpl) a precio reducido

cut-price petrol gasolina a precio reducido

cut-price store tienda (f) de rebajas

cut-throat competition competencia (f) encarnizada

CV (= curriculum vitae) curriculum (vitae) (m)

cycle ciclo (m)

cyclical cíclico, -a

cyclical factors factores (mpl) cíclicos

Dd

daily diario, -ria

daisy-wheel printer impresora (f) de rueda de margarita

damage (n) daño (m)

damage (v) dañar

damage survey inspección (f) de daños

damage to property daños (mpl) materiales

damaged dañado, -da *o* tarado, -da *o* deteriorado, -da

damages daños (mpl) y perjuicios

data datos (mpl)

data processing elaboración (f) *o* proceso (m) de datos

data retrieval recuperación (f) de datos

database base (f) de datos

date (n) fecha (f)

date (v) fechar

date of receipt fecha (f) de recepción

date stamp fechador (m)

dated *[with date]* con fecha de

dated *[old]* anticuado, -da

day día (m)

day *[working day]* jornada (f)

day shift turno (m) de día

day-to-day cotidiano, -na *o* diario, -ria

dead (adj) *[person]* muerto, -ta *o* fallecido, -da

dead account cuenta inactiva

dead loss siniestro (m) *o* pérdida (f) total

deadline fecha (f) tope *o* plazo (m) límite (m)

deadlock (n) punto (m) muerto

deadlock (v) estar en punto muerto

deadweight peso (m) muerto

deadweight cargo carga (f) por peso muerto

deadweight tonnage toneladas (fpl) de peso muerto

deal (n) transacción (f) *o* negocio (m) *o* trato (m)

deal in (v) comerciar (en) *o* negociar (en)

deal with an order servir un pedido

deal with someone tratar *o* comerciar con alguien

dealer comerciante (mf) *o* tratante (mf)

dealing *[Stock Exchange]* operaciones (fpl) en bolsa

dear caro, -ra

debate debate (m) *o* discusión (f)

debenture bono (m) *o* pagaré (m) de interés fijo

debenture holder obligacionista (mf)

debit (n) débito (m) *o* debe (m)

debit an account adeudar *o* cargar en cuenta

debit balance saldo (m) deudor

debit column columna (f) del debe

debit entry asiento (m) de débito *o* adeudo

debit note nota (f) de adeudo

debits and credits debe y haber

debt deuda (f)

debt collection cobro (m) de morosos

debt collection agency agencia (f) de cobro de morosos

debt collector cobrador (m) de morosos

debtor deudor, -ra *o* prestatario, -ria

debtor side debe (m)

debts due deudas (fpl) a pagar

decentralization descentralización (f)

decentralize descentralizar

decide decidir *o* optar

decide on a course of action optar por una línea de conducta deciding decisivo, -va

deciding factor factor decisivo

decimal (n) decimal (m)

decimal point punto (m) decimal

decision decisión (f)

decision maker persona (f) que toma las decisiones

decision making toma (f) de decisiones

decision-making body órgano (m) decisorio

decision-making processes procesos (mpl) decisorios

deck cubierta (f)

deck cargo carga (f) en cubierta

declaration declaración (f)

declaration of bankruptcy declaración (f) de quiebra

declaration of income declaración (f) de renta

declare declarar o confesar

declare goods to customs declarar mercancías en la aduana

declare someone bankrupt declarar a alguien en quiebra

declared declarado, -da

declared value valor (m) declarado

decline (n) baja (f) o descenso (m)

decline (v) [fall] disminuir

decontrol liberalizar o suprimir controles

decrease (n) descenso (m) o reducción (f) o disminución (f)

decrease (v) disminuir o reducir

decrease in price bajada (f) de precio

decrease in value disminución (f) de valor

decreasing (adj) decreciente

deduct deducir o descontar

deductible deducible

deduction deducción (f)

deed título (m) o escritura (f)

deed of assignment escritura (f) de cesión

deed of covenant escritura (f) de convenio

deed of partnership escritura (f) de sociedad

deed of transfer escritura (f) de transferencia

default (n) incumplimiento (m)

default (v) incumplir

default on payments incumplir los pagos

defaulter deudor, -ra

defect defecto (m) o tara (f)

defective [faulty] defectuoso, -sa

defective [not valid] defectivo, -va

defence defensa (f) o protección (f)

defence counsel abogado (m) defensor

defend defender o proteger

defend a lawsuit defenderse en juicio

defendant demandado, -da o acusado, -da o parte demandada

defer aplazar o diferir

defer payment diferir el pago

deferment aplazamiento (m)

deferment of payment aplazamiento (m) de pago

deferred diferido, -da o aplazado, -da

deferred creditor acreedor (m) diferido

deferred payment pago (m) aplazado

deficit déficit (m)

deficit financing financiación (f) del déficit presupuestario

deflation deflación (f)

deflationary deflacionista

defray [costs] pagar o sufragar

defray someone's expenses costear los gastos de alguien

del credere prima (f) al comisionista

del credere agent agente (mf) del credere

delay (n) demora (f) o retraso (m)

delay (v) demorar o retrasar

delegate (n) delegado, da

delegate (v) delegar

delegation delegación (f)

delete suprimir

deliver entregar o repartir

delivered price precio (m) de entrega

delivery entrega (f) o reparto (m)

delivery date fecha (f) de entrega

delivery note albarán (m)

delivery of goods reparto (m) de mercancías

delivery order orden (f) de expedición

delivery time plazo (m) de entrega

delivery van furgoneta (f) de reparto

deliveryman recadero (m)

demand (n) demanda (f)

demand (n) *[for payment]* reclamación (f) *o* requerimiento (m) de pago

demand (v) exigir *o* reclamar

demand deposit depósito (m) a la vista

demonstrate demostrar *o* mostrar (el funcionamiento de algo)

demonstration demostración (f) *o* prueba (f)

demonstration model modelo (m) de prueba

demonstrator exhibidor, -ra

demurrage gastos (mpl) de demora

department departamento (m) *o* sección (f)

department *[in government]* Departamento (m) de Estado *o* ministerio (m)

department *[in shop]* sección (de tienda)

department store grandes almacenes (mpl)

departmental departamental

departmental manager jefe, -fa de departamento *o* de sección

departure *[going away]* salida (f)

departure *[new venture]* novedad (f)

departure lounge sala (f) de embarque

departures salidas (fpl)

depend on depender de

depending on según

deposit (n) *[in bank]* depósito (m) *o* ingreso (m) *o* imposición (f)

deposit (n) *[paid in advance]* depósito *o* señal (f) *o* entrada (f)

deposit (v) depositar *o* ingresar

deposit account cuenta (f) de depósito *o* cuenta a plazo

deposit slip recibo (m) (de depósito)

depositor depositante (mf) *o* impositor, -ra

depository *[place]* almacén (m)

depot almacén (m) central *o* centro (m) de transporte

depreciate *[amortize]* amortizar *o* depreciar

depreciate *[lose value]* depreciarse *o* perder valor

depreciation *[amortizing]* amortización (f) *o* depreciación (f)

depreciation *[loss of value]* depreciación (f) *o* pérdida (f) de valor

depreciation rate coeficiente (m) *o* tasa (f) de amortización

depression depresión (f) *o* crisis (f) económica

dept (= department) dpto. (= departamento)

deputize for someone sustituir a alguien

deputy delegado, -da *o* adjunto, -ta *o* suplente (mf)

deputy manager subdirector, -ra *o* director, -ra adjunto, -ta

deputy managing director director, -ra general adjunto, -ta

deregulation liberalización (f) *o* desregulación (f)

describe describir *o* exponer

description descripción (f)

design (n) diseño (m)

design (v) diseñar *o* proyectar

design department departamento (m) de diseño

desk escritorio (m) *o* mesa (f) de despacho

desk diary agenda (f) de mesa (de despacho)

desk-top publishing (DTP) autoedición (f) *o* publicación (f) asistida por ordenador

despatch (= dispatch)

destination destino (m)

detail (n) detalle (m)

detail (v) detallar

detailed detallado, -da

detailed account cuenta (f) *o* factura (f) detallada

determine determinar

Deutschmark marco (m) alemán

devaluation devaluación (f) *o* desvalorización (f)

devalue devaluar *o* desvalorizar

develop *[build]* construir

develop *[plan]* desarrollar

developing country país (m) en vías de desarrollo

development desarrollo (m)

device aparato (m) *o* dispositivo (m) *o* estratagema (f)

diagram diagrama (m)

dial (v) marcar

dial a number marcar un número

dial direct marcar directamente

dialling acto (m) de marcar

dialling code prefijo (m)

dialling tone señal (f) de línea

diary agenda (f)

dictate dictar

dictating machine dictáfono (m)

dictation dictado (m)

differ diferir *o* ser distinto

difference diferencia (f)

differences in price diferencias (fpl) de precio

different distinto, -ta *o* diferente

differential (adj) diferencial

differential tariffs tarifas (fpl) diferenciadas

difficult difícil

difficulty dificultad (f)

digit dígito (m)

dilution of equity dilución (f) del capital

dimensions dimensiones (fpl)

direct (adj) directo, -ta

direct (adv) directamente

direct (v) dirigir

direct cost coste (m) directo

direct debit domiciliación (f) bancaria

direct mail venta (f) por correo

direct mailing envío (m) de publicidad por correo

direct selling venta (f) directa

direct tax impuesto (m) directo

direct taxation imposición (f) directa

direct-mail advertising publicidad (f) por correo

direction dirección (f)

directions for use instrucciones (fpl) *o* modo de empleo

directive directriz (f) *o* directiva (f) *o* instrucción (f)

director director, -ra *o* consejero, -ra

directory directorio (m)

disagreement desacuerdo (m)

disburse desembolsar

disbursement desembolso (m)

discharge (n) *[of debt]* pago (m) *o* descargo (m)

discharge (v) *[employee]* despedir

discharge a debt pagar una deuda

disclaimer renuncia (f) *o* abandono (m) de responsabilidad

disclose revelar *o* divulgar

disclose a piece of information revelar una información

disclosure divulgación (f) *o* revelación (f)

disclosure of confidential information revelación (f) de información confidencial

discontinue suspender *o* interrumpir

discount (n) descuento (m) *o* rebaja (f)

discount (v) descontar

discount house *[bank]* banco (m) de descuento

discount house *[shop]* tienda (f) de rebajas

discount price precio (m) de descuento

discount rate tipo (m) *o* tasa (f) de descuento

discount store tienda (f) de rebajas

discountable descontable

discounted cash flow (DCF) cash flow actualizado *o* flujo de caja descontado

discounter banco (m) de descuento

discredit (v) desacreditar

discrepancy discrepancia (f) *o* diferencia (f)

discuss discutir

discussion discusión (f) *o* debate (m)

dishonour deshonorar

dishonour a bill devolver una letra

disk disco (m)

disk drive disquetera (f)

diskette disquete (m) *o* diskette

dismiss an employee despedir a un empleado

dismissal despido (m)

dispatch (n) *[goods sent]* envío (m)

dispatch (n) *[sending]* despacho (m) *o* envío (m)

dispatch (v) enviar *o* consignar *o* despachar *o* expedir

dispatch department oficina (f) de expedición

dispatch note nota (f) de expedición *o* de envío

display (n) exposición (f) *o* exhibición (f)

display (v) exhibir *o* exponer

display case vitrina (f)

display material material (m) de exposición

display pack embalaje (m) de exposición

display stand or display unit estantería (f) o vitrina (f) de exposición

disposable desechable o de usar y tirar

disposal venta (f)

dispose of excess stock deshacerse de o vender las existencias sobrantes

dissolve disolver

dissolve a partnership disolver una sociedad

distress merchandise efectos (mpl) embargados (vendidos a bajo precio)

distress sale venta forzosa o remate (m)

distributable profit beneficios (mpl) distribuibles

distribute distribuir o repartir

distribution distribución (f) o reparto (m)

distribution channels canales (mpl) de distribución

distribution costs costes (mpl) de distribución

distribution manager jefe, -fa de distribución

distribution network red (f) de distribución

distributor distribuidor, -ra

distributorship distribución (f) exclusiva

district distrito (m)

diversification diversificación (f)

diversify diversificar

dividend dividendo (m)

dividend cover cobertura (f) del dividendo

dividend warrant cheque (f) en pago de dividendos

dividend yield rentabilidad (f) del dividendo

division [part of a company] sección (f) o departamento (m)

division [part of a group] división (f) o sucursal (f)

do hacer

do business with comerciar con

dock (n) muelle (m) o dique (m)

dock (v) [remove money] deducir o descontar del sueldo

dock (v) [ship] entrar en dársena o atracar

docket lista (f) del contenido de un paquete

doctor's certificate parte (m) de baja

document documento (m)

documentary documental

documentary evidence pruebas (fpl) documentales

documentary proof prueba (f) documentada

documentation documentación (f)

documents documentos (mpl)

dollar dólar (m)

dollar area zona (f) del dólar

dollar balance reserva (f) en dólares

dollar crisis crisis (f) del dólar

domestic interior o nacional

domestic market mercado (m) interior o nacional

domestic production producción (f) interior o nacional

domestic sales ventas (fpl) nacionales

domestic trade comercio (m) interior

domicile domicilio (m)

door puerta (f)

door-to-door de puerta en puerta o a domicilio

door-to-door salesman vendedor, -ra a domicilio

door-to-door selling venta (f) a domicilio

dossier expediente (m)

dot-matrix printer impresora (f) matricial

double (adj) doble

double (v) duplicar o duplicarse

double taxation doble imposición (f)

double taxation agreement acuerdo (m) de doble imposición

double-book reservar la misma plaza a dos personas

double-booking doble reserva (f)

down abajo

down payment entrada (f) o depósito (m) o pago (m) inicial

down time tiempo (m) muerto

down-market dirigido, -da a un mercado popular

downside factor factor (m) de riesgo (en una inversión)

downtown (adv) en el centro de la ciudad *o* hacia el centro

downtown (n) centro (m) de la ciudad

downturn descenso (m)

downward hacia abajo

dozen docena (f)

drachma *[Greek currency]* dracma (m)

draft (n) *[money]* letra (f) *o* giro (m)

draft (n) *[rough plan]* borrador (m) *o* proyecto (m)

draft (v) hacer un borrador *o* redactar

draft a contract redactar un contrato

draft a letter redactar una carta

draft plan *or* **draft project** anteproyecto (m)

draw *[a cheque]* girar

draw *[money]* sacar

draw up preparar *o* redactar

draw up a contract preparar *o* redactar un contrato

drawee librado, -da

drawer librador, -ra

drawing account cuenta (f) corriente

drive (n) *[energy]* energía (f) *o* empuje (m)

drive (n) *[part of machine]* motor (m)

drive (v) *[a car]* conducir

driver conductor (m) *o* chófer (m)

drop (n) caída (f) *o* baja (f)

drop (v) descender *o* bajar *o* caer

drop in sales caída (f) de las ventas

due *[awaited]* que está por llegar

due *[owing]* debido, -da *o* vencido, -da

dues *[orders]* pedidos (mpl) por servir

dull átono, -na

duly *[in time]* oportunamente

duly *[legally]* debidamente

dummy producto (m) ficticio

dummy pack embalaje vacío *o* ficticio

dump bin caja (f) de artículos sueltos para la venta

dump goods on a market practicar el 'dumping'

dumping 'dumping' (m)

duplicate (n) duplicado (m) *o* copia (f)

duplicate (v) copiar *o* duplicar

duplicate an invoice copiar una factura

duplicate of a receipt duplicado (m) de una factura

duplicate receipt factura (f) por duplicado

duplication duplicación (f)

durable goods bienes (mpl) duraderos

duty *[obligation]* obligación (f)

duty *[tax]* impuestos (mpl) *o* arancel (m)

duty-free libre de impuestos

duty-free shop tienda (f) libre de impuestos

duty-paid goods mercancías (fpl) con impuestos aduaneros pagados

Ee

e. & o.e. (errors and omissions excepted) salvo error u omisión

early pronto *o* temprano

earmark funds for a project asignar fondos a un proyecto

earn (v) ganar

earn (v) *[interest]* devengar

earning capacity escala (f) de rendimiento

earnings ingresos (mpl)

earnings *[profit]* ganancias (fpl) *o* beneficios (mpl)

earnings per share *or* **earnings yield** dividendo (m) por acción

easy fácil

easy terms facilidades (fpl) de pago

economic económico, -ca

economic cycle ciclo (m) económico

economic development desarrollo (m) económico

economic growth crecimiento (m) económico

economic indicators indicadores (mpl) económicos

economic model modelo (m) económico

economic planning planificación (f) económica

economic system sistema (m) económico

economic trends tendencias (fpl) económicas

economical económico, -ca

economics economía (f)

economies of scale economías (fpl) de escala

economist economista (mf)

economize economizar

economy economía (f)

economy *[system]* sistema (m) económico

economy class clase económica *o* clase turista

ecu *or* **ECU (= European currency unit)** ecu *o* ECU (m)

effect (n) efecto (m)

effect (v) efectuar

effective efectivo, -va

effective date fecha (f) de entrada en vigor

effective demand demanda (f) efectiva

effective yield rendimiento (m) efectivo

effectiveness eficiencia (f) *o* eficacia (f)

efficiency eficiencia (f) *o* eficacia (f)

efficient eficaz *o* eficiente

effort esfuerzo (m)

elasticity elasticidad (f)

elect elegir

election elección (f)

electronic mail correo (m) electrónico

electronic point of sale (EPOS) puntos (mpl) de venta electrónicos

elevator *[goods]* montacargas (m)

elevator *[grain]* elevador (m) de granos

email (= electronic mail) correo (m) electrónico

embargo (n) embargo (m) *o* prohibición (f)

embargo (v) embargar *o* prohibir

embark embarcar

embark on embarcarse en

embarkation embarque (m)

embarkation card tarjeta (f) de embarque

embezzle malversar *o* desfalcar

embezzlement malversación (f) *o* desfalco (m)

embezzler malversador, -ra *o* desfalcador, -ra

emergency emergencia (f) *o* urgencia (f)

emergency reserves reservas (fpl) para imprevistos

employ (v) emplear *o* dar empleo

employed *[in job]* empleado, -da

employed *[used]* en uso *o* utilizado, -da

employee empleado, -da

employer empresario, -ria

employment empleo (m) *o* ocupación (f)

employment agency *or* **employment bureau** oficina (f) de colocación

empty (adj) vacío, -cía

empty (v) vaciar

EMS (= European Monetary System) SME (Sistema Monetario Europeo)

encash hacer efectivo *o* cobrar

encashment cobro (m) en metálico

enclose adjuntar *o* remitir adjunto

enclosure documento (m) adjunto

end (n) fin (m) *o* final (m)

end (v) terminar *o* finalizar

end of season sale rebajas (fpl) de fin de temporada

end product producto (m) final

end user usuario (m) final

endorse a cheque endosar un cheque

endorsee endosatario, -ria

endorsement *[action]* endoso (m)

endorsement *[on insurance]* suplemento (m) de póliza

endorser endosante (mf)

energy *[electricity]* energía (f)

energy *[human]* energía (f) *o* vigor (m)

energy-saving (adj) que ahorra energía

enforce hacer cumplir *o* ejecutar

enforcement ejecución (f)

engaged ocupado, -da

engaged *[telephone]* (línea) ocupada

engaged tone señal (f) de comunicar

English inglés, -esa

enquire (= inquire)

enquiry (= inquiry)

enter *[go in]* entrar en

enter *[write in]* inscribir

enter into *[discussion]* entablar

entering entrada (f) *o* inscripción (f)

enterprise empresa (f)

entitle autorizar

entitlement derecho (m)

entrance (n) entrada (f)

entrepot port puerto (m) distribuidor

entrepreneur empresario, -ria

entrepreneurial empresarial

entrust encargar *o* confiar

entry *[going in]* ingreso (m) *o* entrada (f)

entry *[to market]* acceso (m)

entry *[writing]* asiento (m) *o* anotación (f)

entry visa visado (m) de entrada

epos *or* EPOS (= electronic point of sale) puntos (mpl) de venta electrónicos

equal (adj) igual

equal (v) igualar *o* ser igual a

equality igualdad (f)

equalization equiparación (f)

equip equipar

equipment equipo (m)

equities títulos (mpl) *o* acciones (fpl) ordinarias

equity beneficios (mpl) *o* participación (f) de beneficios

equity capital capital (m) en acciones

erode erosionar *o* desgastar

erroneous erróneo, -nea

error error (m) *o* equivocación (f)

error rate coeficiente (m) de errores *o* tasa (f) de errores

errors and omissions excepted (e. & o.e.) salvo error u omisión

escalate escalar

escape clause cláusula (f) de excepción

escrow account cuenta (f) de garantía bloqueada

escudo *[Portuguese currency]* escudo (m)

essential esencial *o* imprescindible

establish establecer *o* consolidar

establishment *[business]* establecimiento (m)

establishment *[staff]* personal (m) *o* plantilla (f)

estimate (n) *[calculation]* estimación (f) *o* cálculo (m) *o* valoración (f)

estimate (n) *[quote]* presupuesto (m)

estimate (v) estimar *o* calcular *o* valorar

estimated estimado, -da

estimated figures cifras (fpl) estimadas

estimated sales ventas (fpl) estimadas

estimation estimación (f) *o* valoración (f)

EU (= European Union) UE (= Unión Europea)

Eurocheque eurocheque (m)

Eurocurrency eurodivisa (f)

Eurodollar eurodólar (m)

Euromarket euromercado (m)

European europeo, -a

European Investment Bank (EIB) Banco Europeo de Inversiones (BEI)

European Monetary System (EMS) Sistema Monetario Europeo (SME)

European Union (EU) Unión Europea (UE)

evade evadir *o* eludir

evade tax evadir impuestos

evaluate evaluar *o* calcular

evaluate costs evaluar los costes

evaluation evaluación (f)

evasion evasión (f) *o* elusión (f)

ex coupon sin cupón de interés

ex dividend sin dividendo

ex-directory que no figura en la guía telefónica

exact exacto, -ta

exactly exactamente

examination *[inspection]* examen (m) *o* registro (m) *o* inspección (f)

examination *[test]* examen (m)

examine examinar

exceed exceder *o* sobrepasar *o* superar

excellent excelente

except excepto *o* salvo

exceptional excepcional

exceptional items partidas (fpl) excepcionales

excess exceso (m) *o* excedente (m)

excess baggage exceso (m) de equipaje

excess capacity exceso (m) de capacidad

excess profits beneficios (mpl) extraordinarios

excessive excesivo, -va

excessive costs costes (mpl) excesivos

exchange (n) cambio (m) *o* intercambio (m)

exchange (v) *[currency]* cambiar divisas *o* moneda extranjera

exchange (v) *[one thing for another]* canjear *o* intercambiar

exchange control control (m) de divisas

exchange rate tipo de cambio *o* tasa de cambio

exchangeable intercambiable *o* cambiable

Exchequer ministerio (m) de Hacienda

excise (v) *[cut out]* extirpar *o* suprimir

excise duty impuesto (m) sobre el consumo

Excise officer recaudador, -ra de impuestos

exclude excluir

excluding excepto *o* con excepción de

exclusion exclusión (f)

exclusion clause cláusula (f) de exclusión

exclusive agreement contrato (m) en exclusiva

exclusive of no incluido

exclusive of tax impuesto (m) no incluido

exclusivity exclusividad (f)

execute ejecutar *o* cumplir

execution ejecución (f) *o* cumplimiento (m)

executive (adj) ejecutivo, -va

executive (n) ejecutivo, -va

executive director director (m) ejecutivo

exempt (adj) exento, -ta

exempt (v) eximir

exempt from tax exento, -ta de impuestos

exemption exención (f)

exemption from tax exención fiscal

exercise (n) ejercicio (m)

exercise (v) ejercer

exercise an option ejercer derecho de opción

exercise of an option ejercicio (m) del derecho de opción

exhibit (v) exponer

exhibition exhibición (f) *o* exposición (f)

exhibition hall salón (m) *o* sala (f) de exposiciones

exhibitor expositor, -ra

expand ampliar *o* expandir

expansion expansión (f) *o* ampliación (f)

expenditure gasto (m) *o* desembolso (m)

expense gasto (m)

expense account cuenta (f) de gastos de representación

expenses gastos (mpl)

expensive caro, -ra *o* costoso, -sa

experienced experto, -ta *o* experimentado, -da

expertise pericia (f) *o* competencia (f)

expiration expiración (f) *o* terminación (f) *o* vencimiento (m)

expire caducar *o* expirar *o* vencer

expiry caducidad (f) *o* expiración (f) *o* vencimiento (m)

expiry date fecha (f) de caducidad

explain explicar

explanation explicación (f) *o* aclaración (f)

exploit explotar *o* aprovechar

explore explorar

export (n) exportación (f) *o* mercancía (f) exportada

export (v) exportar

export department departamento (m) de exportación

export duty derechos (mpl) de exportación

export licence *or* export permit licencia (f) *o* permiso (m) de exportación

export manager director, -ra de exportación

export trade comercio (m) de exportación

exporter exportador, -ra

exporting (adj) de exportación *o* exportador, -ra

exports exportaciones (fpl)

exposure exposición (f) *o* riesgo (m)

express (adj) *[fast]* rápido, -da *o* urgente

express (adj) *[stated clearly]* expreso, -sa

express (v) *[send fast]* enviar por correo *o* transporte urgente

express (v) *[state]* expresar

express delivery entrega (f) urgente

express letter carta (f) urgente

extend (v) extender *o* ampliar

extend *[grant]* conceder

extend *[make longer]* prolongar *o* prorrogar

extended credit crédito (m) a largo plazo

extension ampliación (f) *o* prolongación (f) *o* prórroga (f)

extension *[telephone]* extensión (f)

external *[foreign]* exterior

external *[outside a company]* externo, -na

external account cuenta (f) de no residente

external audit auditoría (f) externa

external auditor auditor (m) externo

external trade comercio (m) exterior

extra extra *o* no incluido

extra charges gastos (mpl) adicionales y complementarios

extraordinary extraordinario, -ria

extraordinary items partidas (fpl) extraordinarias

extras gastos (mpl) aparte *o* extras (mpl)

Ff

face value valor (m) nominal

facilities instalaciones (fpl) *o* medios (mpl)

facility facilidad (f)

facility *[building]* edificio (m)

factor (n) *[influence]* factor (m) *o* elemento (m)

factor (n) *[person, company]* comisionista (mf) al por mayor

factor (v) gestionar deudas con descuento

factoring gestión (f) de deudas con descuento

factoring charges coste (m) de la gestión de deudas

factors of production factores (mpl) de producción

factory fábrica (f)

factory inspector inspector de fábrica

factory outlet tienda (f) de fábrica

factory price precio (m) de fábrica

fail *[go bust]* quebrar

fail *[to do something]* dejar de hacer algo

fail *[not to succeed]* fallar *o* fracasar

failing that en su defecto

failure fracaso (m)

fair (adj) justo, -ta *o* equitativo, -va

fair (n) feria (f)

fair dealing prácticas (fpl) comerciales justas

fair price precio (m) justo

fair trade política (f) comercial de reciprocidad arancelaria

fair trading prácticas (fpl) comerciales justas

fair wear and tear desgaste (m) natural

fake (n) falsificación (f) *o* imitación (f)

fake (v) falsificar *o* fingir

faked documents documentos (mpl) falsos

fall (n) caída (f) *o* baja (f)

fall (v) *[go lower]* bajar *o* caer

fall (v) *[on a date]* caer

fall behind *[be in a worse position]* quedarse atrás

fall behind *[be late]* retrasarse

fall due vencer

fall off disminuir *o* bajar

fall through venirse abajo

falling decreciente *o* con tendencia a la baja

false falso, -sa *o* falseado, -da

false pretences medios (mpl) fraudulentos

false weight peso (m) escaso

falsification falsificación (f)

falsify falsificar

fame fama (f)

family company empresa (f) familiar

FAO (for the attention of) a la atención de

fare billete (m) *o* pasaje (m)

farm out work mandar trabajo fuera

fast (adj) rápido, -da

fast (adv) rápidamente

fast-selling items artículos (mpl) de fácil venta

fault *[blame]* culpa (f) *o* falta (f)

fault *[mechanical]* defecto (m) *o* fallo (m) *o* tara (f)

faulty equipment equipo (m) defectuoso

favourable favorable *o* propicio, -cia

favourable balance of trade balanza (f) comercial favorable

fax (n) telefax (m) *o* fax (m)

fax (v) enviar por fax

feasibility factibilidad (f) *o* viabilidad (f)

feasibility report informe (m) de viabilidad (de un proyecto)

fee *[admission]* cuota (f) *o* derechos (mpl)

fee *[for services]* honorarios (mpl) *o* emolumentos (mpl)

feedback reacción (f) *o* respuesta (f)

ferry transbordador (m) *o* 'ferry' (m)

fiddle (n) trampa (f) *o* timo (m)

fiddle (v) embaucar *o* falsificar *o* falsear

field campo (m)

field sales manager jefe, -fa de equipo de ventas

field work trabajo (m) de campo *o* estudios (mpl) sobre el terreno

FIFO (= first in first out) primeras entradas, primeras salidas

figure cifra (f)

file (n) archivo (m) *o* fichero (m)

file (n) *[computer]* ficha (f) de ordenador

file (n) *[documents]* expediente (m)

file (v) archivar

file (v) *[register]* presentar

file a patent application solicitar una patente

file documents archivar documentos

filing cabinet archivador (m)

filing card ficha (de registro)

fill a gap llenar *o* ocupar un vacío

final último, -ma *o* final

final demand último requerimiento (m) de pago

final discharge descargo (m) final

final dividend dividendo (m) final

finalize finalizar

finance (n) finanzas (fpl)

finance (v) financiar

finance an operation financiar una operación

finance company sociedad (f) financiera

finance director director, -ra de finanzas

finances finanzas (fpl)

financial financiero, -ra

financial asset activo (m) financiero

financial crisis crisis (f) financiera

financial institution institución (f) financiera

financial position situación (f) financiera

financial resources recursos (mpl) financieros

financial risk riesgo (m) financiero

financial settlement ajuste (m) financiero

financial year ejercicio (m) económico *o* año (m) fiscal

financially financieramente

financing financiación (f) *o* financiamiento (m)

find (v) encontrar

fine (adv) *[very good]* muy bien

fine (adv) *[very small]* en trozos pequeños

fine (n) multa (f)

fine (v) multar

fine tuning ajuste (m) fino

finished acabado, -da *o* terminado, -da

finished goods productos (mpl) acabados

fire (n) fuego (m) *o* incendio (m)

fire damage daños (mpl) causados por incendio

fire insurance seguro (m) contra incendios

fire regulations reglamento (m) sobre incendios

fire risk peligro (m) de incendio

fire-damaged goods mercancías (fpl) dañadas por un incendio

firm (adj) firme

firm (n) empresa (f) *o* firma (f)

firm (v) afirmar

firm price precio (m) en firme

first primero, -ra

first in first out (FIFO) primeras entradas, primeras salidas

first option primera opción

first quarter primer trimestre

first-class de primera clase *o* excelente

fiscal fiscal

fiscal measures medidas (fpl) fiscales

fittings accesorios (mpl)

fix *[arrange]* fijar

fix *[mend]* arreglar

fix a meeting for 3 p.m. fijar una reunión para las 3 de la tarde

fixed fijo, -ja

fixed assets activo (m) fijo

fixed costs costes (mpl) fijos

fixed deposit depósito (m) a plazo fijo

fixed exchange rate cambio (m) fijo

fixed income renta (f) fija

fixed interest interés (m) fijo

fixed scale of charges lista (f) de precios fija

fixed-interest investments inversiones (fpl) de interés fijo

fixed-price agreement acuerdo (m) a tanto alzado

fixing fijación (f)

flat (adj) *[dull]* átono, -na

flat (adj) *[fixed]* fijo, -ja *o* uniforme

flat (n) piso (m) *o* apartamento (m)

flat rate tanto (m) alzado *o* porcentaje (m) fijo

flexibility flexibilidad (f)

flexible flexible

flexible prices precios (mpl) flexibles

flexible pricing policy política (f) de precios flexibles

flight vuelo (m)

flight *[of money]* fuga (f)

flight information información (f) de vuelos

flight of capital evasión (f) *o* fuga (f) de capital(es)

flip chart tablero (m) de hojas sueltas

float (n) *[money]* fondo (m) de caja

float (n) *[of company]* lanzamiento (m) *o* flotación (f)

float (v) *[a currency]* (hacer) flotar una divisa

float a company fundar una compañía

floating flotante

floating exchange rates tipos (mpl) de cambio flotantes

floating of a company lanzamiento (m) de una sociedad

flood (n) inundación (f)

flood (v) inundar *o* desbordar

floor suelo (m)

floor *[level]* piso (m)

floor manager director, -ra de planta

floor plan planta (f)

floor space superficie (f) útil

flop (n) fracaso (m)

flop (v) fracasar

flotation lanzamiento (m) de una nueva compañía

flourish florecer *o* prosperar

flourishing floreciente *o* próspero, -ra

flourishing trade comercio (m) floreciente *o* próspero

flow (n) flujo (m)

flow (v) fluir *o* discurrir

flow chart organigrama (m) *o* diagrama (m) de flujo

flow diagram diagrama (m) de flujos *o* organigrama (m)

fluctuate fluctuar *o* oscilar

fluctuating fluctuante

fluctuation fluctuación (f) *o* oscilación (f)

FOB *or* **f.o.b. (free on board)** franco a bordo

follow seguir

follow up perseguir *o* investigar

follow-up letter carta (f) de reiteración

for sale en venta

forbid prohibir

force majeure fuerza (f) mayor

force prices down hacer bajar los precios

force prices up hacer subir los precios

forced a la fuerza

forced sale venta (f) forzosa

forecast (n) previsión (f) *o* pronóstico (m)

forecast (v) pronosticar *o* prever *o* predecir

forecasting previsión (f)

foreign extranjero, -ra

foreign currency moneda (f) extranjera

foreign exchange *[changing money]* cambio (m) de moneda extranjera

foreign exchange *[currency]* divisas (fpl)

foreign exchange broker *or* **dealer** operador, -ra de cambios

foreign exchange market mercado (m) de divisas

foreign investments inversiones (fpl) exteriores

foreign money order giro (m) postal internacional

foreign trade comercio (m) exterior

foresee prever

forfeit (n) decomiso (m) *o* confiscación (f)

forfeit (v) decomisar *o* perder el derecho a

forfeit a deposit perder un depósito

forfeiture decomiso (m) *o* confiscación (f)

forge falsificar

forgery *[action]* falsificación (f)

forgery *[copy]* documento falso *o* copia falsa

fork-lift truck carretilla (f) elevadora de horquilla

form (n) impreso (m) *o* formulario (m)

form (v) formar

form of words fórmulas (fpl) judiciales

formal formal

formality formalidad (f) *o* trámite (m)

forward a plazo *o* en fecha futura

forward buying compra (f) de futuros

forward contract contrato (m) a plazo fijo

forward market mercado (m) a futuros

forward rate tipo (m) de cambio para operaciones a plazo

forward sales ventas (fpl) a plazo

forwarding expedición (f) *o* envío (m)

forwarding address dirección (f) de reenvío

forwarding agent agente (mf) expedidor, -ra

forwarding instructions instrucciones (fpl) de envío

fourth quarter cuarto trimestre

fragile frágil

frame marco (m)

franc franco (m)

franchise (n) franquicia (f) *o* concesión (f)

franchise (v) franquiciar

franchisee concesionario, -ria

franchiser franquiciador, -ra

franchising franquicia (f) *o* concesión (f)

franco franco *o* libre

frank (v) franquear

franking machine máquina (f) franqueadora

fraud fraude (m) *o* defraudación (f) *o* estafa (f)

fraudulent fraudulento, -ta

fraudulent transaction operación (f) fraudulenta

fraudulently fraudulentamente

free (adj) libre

free (adj) *[no payment]* gratuito, -ta *o* gratis *o* franco

free (adj) *[not occupied]* vacante

free (adv) *[no payment]* gratuitamente *o* gratis

free (v) poner en libertad *o* liberar

free delivery entrega gratuita

free gift regalo (m) *o* obsequio (m)

free market economy economía (f) de libre mercado

free of charge gratis

free of duty libre de derechos de aduana

free of tax libre de impuestos

free on board (f.o.b.) franco a bordo

free on rail franco sobre vagón *o* franco vagón FF.CC.

free port puerto (m) franco

free sample muestra (f) gratuita

free trade libre cambio *o* libre comercio

free trade area zona (f) de libre cambio

free trade zone zona (f) franca

free trial prueba (f) gratuita

free zone zona (f) franca

freelance (adj) de libre dedicación

freelance (n) *or* **freelancer (n)** trabajador, -ra por libre

freeze (n) congelación (f)

freeze (v) *[prices]* congelar

freeze credits bloquear los créditos

freeze wages and prices congelar salarios y precios

freight *[carriage]* flete (m) *o* transporte (m) *o* porte (m)

freight costs gastos (mpl) de transporte

freight depot estación (f) de mercancías

freight forward porte (m) debido

freight plane avión (m) de carga

freight rates precio (m) de transporte *o* tarifas (fpl) de flete

freight train tren (m) de mercancías

freightage flete (m) *o* fletamento (m)

freighter *[plane]* avión (m) de carga

freighter *[ship]* buque (m) de carga

freightliner tren (m) de mercancías de contenedores

frequent frecuente *o* corriente

frozen bloqueado, -da *o* congelado, -da

frozen account cuenta (f) bloqueada

frozen assets activo (m) congelado

frozen credits crédito (m) congelado

fulfil *[carry out]* cumplir

fulfil an order despachar un pedido

fulfilment cumplimiento (m) *o* realización (f)

full lleno, -na

full discharge of a debt pago (m) total de una deuda

full payment pago (m) íntegro

full price precio (m) sin descuento

full refund reembolso (m) total

full-scale (adj) completo, -ta *o* general

full-time a tiempo completo *o* en plena dedicación

full-time employment trabajo (m) a tiempo completo

fund (n) fondo (m)

fund (v) financiar *o* asignar fondos

fundamental fundamental

funding (financing) financiación (f) *o* asignación (f) de fondos

funding *[of debt]* consolidación (f) de fondos

further to con relación a

future delivery entrega (f) futura

futures futuros (mpl)

Gg

gain (n) *[becoming bigger]* aumento (m)

gain (n) *[increase in value]* ganancia (f) *o* beneficio (m)

gain (v) *[become bigger]* aumentar

gain (v) *[get]* ganar

game fuego (m)

gap hueco (m) *o* vacío (m)

gap in the market hueco (m) en el mercado

GDP (= gross domestic product) PIB (Producto Interior Bruto)

gear ajustar

gearing apalancamiento (m)

general general

general audit auditoría (f) general

general average avería (f) gruesa

general insurance seguro (m) general

general manager director, -ra general *o* director, -ra gerente (mf)

general meeting junta (f) general

general office oficina (f) general

general post offfice oficina (f) central de correos

general strike huelga (f) general

gentleman's agreement acuerdo (m) entre caballeros

genuine genuino, -na

genuine purchaser comprador genuino
o compradora genuina

get recibir *o* obtener *o* conseguir

get along ir haciendo

get back *[something lost]* recuperar

get into debt endeudarse

get rid of something deshacerse de
algo

get round *[a problem]* soslayar

get the sack ser despedido

gift regalo (m) *o* obsequio (m)

gift coupon cupón (m) de regalo

gift shop tienda (f) de regalos

gift voucher vale (m) para un regalo

gilt-edged securities títulos (mpl) del
Estado

gilts bonos (mpl) del Tesoro

giro account cuenta (f) del Girobank

giro account number número (m) de
cuenta del Girobank

giro system giro (m) bancario

give (v) dar

give *[as gift]* regalar

give away regalar

glut (n) abundancia (f)

glut (v) inundar el mercado

GNP (= gross national product) PNB
(Producto Nacional Bruto)

go ir

go into business emprender un negocio

go-ahead (adj) emprendedor, -ra *o*
activo, -va

go-slow huelga (f) de celo

going en marcha

going rate precio (m) vigente

gold card tarjeta (f) oro

good bueno, -na

good buy buena compra

good management buena gestión

good quality buena calidad

good value (for money) buen precio

goods mercancías (fpl) *o* bienes (mpl)

goods depot depósito (m) *o* almacén
(m) de mercancías

goods in transit mercancías (fpl) en
tránsito

goods train tren (m) de mercancías

goodwill fondo (m) de comercio

government (adj) estatal *o* del gobierno

government (n) gobierno (m)

government bonds títulos (mpl) del
Estado

government contractor contratista
(mf) del Estado

government stock títulos (mpl) del
Estado

government-backed con apoyo estatal

government-controlled controlado,
-da por el Estado

government-regulated regulado, -da
por el Estado

government-sponsored patrocinado,
-da por el Estado

graded advertising rates tarifas (fpl)
publicitarias regresivas

graded hotel hotel (m) homologado

graded tax impuesto (m) progresivo

gradual gradual *o* progresivo, -va

graduate trainee licenciado, -da en
prácticas

graduated graduado, -da *o* progresivo,
-va

graduated income tax impuesto (m)
progresivo sobre la renta

gram *or* **gramme** gramo (m)

grand total suma (f) total

grant (n) subvención (f) *o* beca (f)

grant (v) conceder *o* otorgar

graph (n) gráfico (m) *o* gráfica (f)

gratis gratis

grid cuadrícula (f)

grid structure estructura (f) cuadricular

gross (adj) bruto, -ta

gross (n) (= 144) gruesa (f)

gross (v) obtener beneficios brutos

gross domestic product (GDP)
Producto Interior Bruto (PIB)

gross earnings ingresos (mpl) brutos

gross income renta (f) bruta

gross margin margen (m) de beneficio
bruto

gross national product (GNP)
Producto Nacional Bruto (PNB)

gross profit beneficio (m) bruto

gross salary sueldo (m) bruto

gross tonnage tonelaje (m) bruto

gross weight peso (m) bruto

gross yield rendimiento (m) bruto

group *[of businesses]* grupo (m)

group *[of people]* grupo (m) *o* agrupación (f)

growth crecimiento (m) *o* desarrollo (m)

growth index índice (m) de crecimiento

growth rate tasa (f) de crecimiento

guarantee (n) garantía (f) *o* aval (m)

guarantee (v) avalar *o* garantizar *o* afianzar

guarantee a debt avalar una deuda

guaranteed minimum wage salario (m) mínimo interprofesional

guarantor fiador, -ra *o* garante (mf)

guideline directriz (f)

guild gremio (m) *o* corporación (f)

guilder *[Dutch currency]* florín (m)

Hh

haggle regatear

half (adj) medio, -dia

half (n) mitad (f)

half a dozen *or* **a half-dozen** media docena (f)

half-price sale rebajas a mitad de precio

half-year semestre (m)

half-yearly accounts cuentas (fpl) semestrales

half-yearly payment pagos (mpl) semestrales

half-yearly statement estado de cuentas semestral

hand in presentar *o* entregar

hand luggage equipaje (m) de mano

hand over entregar

handle (v) *[deal]* manejar *o* tratar

handle (v) *[sell]* comerciar en

handling manejo (m) *o* manipulación (f)

handling charge gasto (m) de tramitación

handwriting letra (f) *o* escritura (f)

handwritten escrito, -ta a mano

handy útil *o* práctico, -ca

harbour puerto (m)

harbour dues derechos (mpl) portuarios

harbour facilities instalaciones (fpl) portuarias

hard (adj) duro (-ra)

hard bargain negocio (m) duro

hard bargaining negocio (m) duro *o* trato (m) difícil

hard copy copia (f) impresa

hard currency moneda (f) convertible

hard disk disco (m) duro

hard selling venta (f) agresiva

harmonization armonización (f) *o* concertación (f)

haulage acarreo (m)

haulage contractor contratista (mf) de transporte por carretera

haulage costs *or* **haulage rates** gastos (mpl) de acarreo

have tener

head jefe, -fa

head of department jefe, -fa de departamento

head office oficina (f) central

headquarters (HQ) sede (f) *o* domicilio (m) social

heads of agreement epígafres (mpl) de un acuerdo

health salud (f)

health insurance seguro (m) de enfermedad

healthy profit beneficio (m) considerable

heavy *[important]* grande *o* importante

heavy *[weight]* pesado, -da

heavy costs *or* **heavy expenditure** grandes costes (mpl) *o* gran gasto (m)

heavy equipment equipo (m) pesado

heavy goods vehicle (HGV) camión (m) de carga pesada

heavy industry industria (f) pesada

heavy machinery maquinaria (f) pesada

hectare hectárea (f)

hedge (n) or **hedging (n)** cobertura (f) o protección (f)

help (n) ayuda (f)

help (v) ayudar

HGV (= heavy goods vehicle) camión (m) de carga pesada

hidden asset bien (m) encubierto

hidden reserves reservas (fpl) ocultas

high alto, -ta

high interest interés (m) elevado

high quality calidad superior o alta calidad

high-quality goods productos (mpl) de primera calidad

high rent alquiler (m) elevado

high taxation imposición (f) alta

highest bidder mejor postor

highly motivated sales staff personal (m) de ventas muy motivado

highly qualified muy cualificado o muy capacitado

highly-geared company sociedad con un gran coeficiente de endeudamiento

highly-paid muy bien pagado

highly-priced muy caro, -ra

hire (n) alquiler (m)

hire a car or **a crane** alquilar un coche o alquilar una grúa

hire car coche (m) de alquiler

hire purchase (HP) compra (f) a plazos

hire staff contratar personal

hire-purchase company compañía (f) que financia la compra a plazos

historic(al) cost coste (m) inicial

historical figures cifras (fpl) históricas

hive off descentralizar

hoard (v) acaparar o acumular

hoarding [for posters] valla (f) publicitaria o cartelera (f)

hoarding [of goods] acaparamiento (m)

hold (n) [ship] bodega (f)

hold (v) [contain] contener o caber

hold (v) [keep] tener o guardar

hold a meeting or **a discussion** celebrar una reunión o tener una discusión

hold out for insistir en

hold over aplazar o posponer

hold the line please or **please hold** no cuelgue

hold up (v) [delay] retrasar

hold-up (n) [delay] retraso (m)

holder [person] poseedor, -ra o tenedor, -ra

holder [thing] soporte (m)

holding company sociedad (f) de cartera o 'holding'

holiday pay paga (f) de vacaciones

home address domicilio (m) particular

home consumption consumo (m) doméstico o consumo interior

home market mercado (m) interior o mercado nacional

home sales ventas (fpl) nacionales

homeward freight flete (m) de vuelta

homeward journey viaje (m) de regreso

homeworker trabajador, -ra a domicilio

honorarium honorarios (mpl)

honour a bill pagar una factura

honour a signature aceptar o reconocer una firma

horizontal communication comunicación (f) horizontal

horizontal integration integración (f) horizontal

hotel hotel (m)

hotel accommodation habitaciones (fpl) de hotel o capacidad (f) hotelera

hotel bill factura (f) de hotel

hotel manager director, -ra de hotel

hotel staff personal (m) del hotel

hour hora (f)

hourly por hora

hourly rate tarifa (f) horaria

hourly wage sueldo (m) por hora

hourly-paid workers trabajadores (mpl) pagados por horas

house casa (f)

house [company] casa (f) comercial

house insurance seguro (m) de la vivienda

house magazine boletín (m) interno de una empresa

house-to-house a domicilio

house-to-house selling venta (f) a domicilio

HP (= hire purchase) compra (f) a plazos

HQ (= headquarters) sede (f) o domicilio (m) social

hurry up darse prisa

hype (n) bombo (m) publicitario

hype (v) hacer publicidad con mucho bombo

hypermarket hipermercado (m)

Ii

illegal ilegal

illegality ilegalidad (f)

illegally ilegalmente

illicit ilícito, -ta

ILO (= International Labour Organization) OIT (Organización Internacional del Trabajo)

IMF (= International Monetary Fund) FMI (Fondo Monetario Internacional)

imitation imitación (f)

immediate inmediato, -ta

immediately inmediatamente

imperfect imperfecto, -ta

imperfection defecto (m) *o* imperfección (f) *o* tara (f)

implement (n) herramienta (f) *o* instrumento (m)

implement (v) ejecutar *o* realizar

implement an agreement poner en práctica un acuerdo

implementation ejecución (f) *o* puesta (f) en práctica

import (n) importación (f)

import (v) importar

import ban prohibición (f) de importar

import duty derechos (mpl) de importación

import levy gravamen (m) sobre las importaciones

import licence *or* **import permit** licencia (f) de importación

import quota cuota (f) de importación *o* cupo (m) de importación

import restrictions restricción (f) a las importaciones

import surcharge sobretasa (f) *o* recargo (m) de importación

import-export (adj) importación-exportación

importance importancia (f)

important importante

importation importación (f)

importer importador, -ra

importing (adj) importador, -ra

importing (n) importación (f)

imports importaciones (fpl)

impose imponer *o* gravar

improvement mejora (f)

impulse impulso (m)

impulse buyer comprador (-ra) impulsivo (-va)

impulse purchase compra (f) impulsiva

in-house interno, -na *o* de la casa

in-house training formación (f) en el puesto de trabajo

incapable incapaz

incentive incentivo (m) *o* estímulo (m)

incentive bonus *or* **incentive payment** prima (f) de incentivo

incidental expenses gastos (mpl) menores

include incluir

inclusive inclusive *o* inclusivo, -va *o* incluido, -da

inclusive charge precio (m) todo incluido

inclusive of tax impuestos (mpl) incluidos

income ingresos (mpl) *o* renta (f)

income tax impuesto (m) sobre la renta

incoming call llamada (f) de fuera

incoming mail correspondencia (f) recibida *o* correo (m) entrante

incompetence incompetencia (f)

incompetent incompetente

incorporate incorporar *o* incluir

incorporate *[a company]* constituir en sociedad

incorporation constitución (f) de una sociedad

incorrect incorrecto, -ta

incorrectly incorrectamente

increase (n) aumento (m) *o* incremento (m)

increase (n) *[higher salary]* aumento (m) de sueldo

increase (v) aumentar *o* subir *o* incrementar

increase (v) in price aumentar *o* subir de precio

increasing creciente *o* en aumento

increasing profits beneficios (mpl) crecientes

increment incremento (m) *o* aumento (m)

incremental incremental

incremental cost coste.(m) incremental

incremental scale escala (f) móvil de salarios

incur incurrir en

incur debts contraer deudas

indebted endeudado, -da

indebtedness deuda (f)

indemnification indemnización (f)

indemnify indemnizar *o* resarcir

indemnify someone for a loss indemnizar a alguien por una pérdida

indemnity indemnidad (f) *o* indemnización (f)

independent independiente

independent company compañía (f) independiente

index (n) *[alphabetical]* índice (m) *o* repertorio (m)

index (n) *[of prices]* índice (m)

index (v) catalogar *o* clasificar

index card ficha (f)

index number índice (m) *o* indicador (m)

index-linked ajustado, -da al coste de la vida

indexation indexación (f) *o* indiciación (f)

indicator indicador (m)

indirect indirecto, -ta

indirect labour costs costes (mpl) laborales indirectos

indirect tax impuesto (m) indirecto

indirect taxation imposición (f) indirecta

induction iniciación (f)

induction courses *or* induction training cursos (mpl) de iniciación

industrial industrial

industrial accident accidente (m) industrial

industrial arbitration tribunal tribunal (m) de arbitraje laboral

industrial capacity capacidad (f) industrial

industrial centre centro (m) industrial

industrial design diseño (m) industrial

industrial disputes conflictos (mpl) colectivos

industrial espionage espionaje (m) industrial

industrial estate zona (f) industrial

industrial expansion expansión (f) industrial

industrial processes procesos (mpl) industriales

industrial relations relaciones (fpl) laborales

industrial tribunal magistratura (f) del trabajo

industrialist industrial (mf)

industrialization industrialización (f)

industrialize industrializar

industrialized societies sociedades (fpl) industriales

industry industria (f)

inefficiency ineficacia (f) *o* incompetencia (f)

inefficient ineficaz *o* incompetente

inflated currency moneda (f) inflacionada

inflated prices precios (mpl) exagerados

inflation inflación (f)

inflationary inflacionario, -ria *o* inflacionista

influence (n) influencia (f)

influence (v) influir *o* influenciar

inform informar

information información (f)

information bureau oficina (f) de información

information officer empleado, -da del servicio de información

infrastructure infraestructura (f)

infringe infringir *o* violar

infringe a patent violar una patente

infringement of customs regulations infracción (f) aduanera

infringement of patent violación (f) de patente

inhabitant habitante (mf)

initial (adj) inicial *o* primero, -ra

initial (v) poner las iniciales a *o* rubricar

initial capital capital (m) inicial

initiate iniciar

initiate discussions iniciar conversaciones

initiative iniciativa (f)

inland interior

innovate innovar

innovation innovación (f)

innovative innovador, -ra

innovator (n) innovador, -ra

input information introducir datos

input tax IVA (sobre los bienes y servicios adquiridos por una empresa)

inquire preguntar *o* pedir información

inquiry petición (f) de informes *o* investigación (f)

insider iniciado (m)

insider dealing información (f) privilegiada

insolvency insolvencia (f)

insolvent insolvente

inspect inspeccionar *o* revisar

inspection inspección (f) *o* control (m)

inspector inspector, -ra

instalment plazo (m)

instant (adj) *[current]* del presente mes *o* de los corrientes

instant (adj) *[immediate]* inmediato, -ta *o* instantáneo, -nea

instant credit crédito (m) instantáneo

institute (n) instituto (m)

institute (v) instituir

institution institución (f)

institutional institucional

institutional investors inversores (mpl) institucionales

instruction instrucción (f)

instrument *[device]* instrumento (m) *o* aparato (m)

instrument *[document]* efecto (m) *o* documento (m) escrito

insufficiency insuficiencia (f)

insufficient funds (US) saldo (m) insuficiente

insurable asegurable

insurance seguro (m)

insurance agent agente (mf) de seguros

insurance broker corredor (m) de seguros

insurance claim declaración (f) de siniestro

insurance company compañía (f) de seguros

insurance contract contrato (m) de seguros

insurance cover cobertura (f) del seguro

insurance policy póliza (f) de seguros

insurance premium prima (f) de seguros

insurance rates tarifas (fpl) de seguros

insurance salesman vendedor, -ra de seguros

insure asegurar

insurer asegurador, -ra

intangible intangible

intangible assets activo (m) intangible

interest (n) interés (m) *o* rédito (m)

interest (v) interesar

interest charges cargos (mpl) en concepto de interés

interest rate tipo (m) de interés *o* tasa (f) de interés

interest-bearing deposits depósitos (mpl) con interés

interest-free credit crédito (m) sin interés

interface (n) interfaz (m)

interface (v) conectar

interim dividend dividendo (m) provisional

interim payment pago (m) a cuenta

interim report informe (m) provisional

intermediary intermediario, -ria

internal *[inside a company]* interno, -na

internal *[inside a country]* interior

internal audit auditoría (f) interna

internal auditor auditor (m) interno

internal telephone teléfono (m) interno

international internacional

international call llamada (f) internacional

international direct dialling llamadas internacionales directas

International Labour Organization (ILO) Organización Internacional del Trabajo (OIT)

international law derecho (m) internacional

International Monetary Fund (IMF) Fondo Monetario Internacional (FMI)

international trade comercio (m) internacional

interpret interpretar

interpreter intérprete (mf)

interruption interrupción (f)

intervention price precio (m) de intervención

interview (n) entrevista (f)

interview (v) entrevistar

interviewee entrevistado, -da

interviewer entrevistador, -ra

introduce presentar o introducir

introduction *[bringing into use]* presentación (f) o introducción (f)

introduction *[letter]* carta (f) de presentación

introductory offer oferta (f) de lanzamiento

invalid inválido, -da

invalidate invalidar

invalidation invalidación (f)

invalidity invalidez (f)

inventory (n) *[list of contents]* inventario (m)

inventory (n) *[stock]* existencias (fpl)

inventory (v) inventariar o hacer un inventario

inventory control control (m) de existencias

invest invertir

investigate investigar

investigation investigación (f)

investment inversión (f)

investment income renta (f) de inversiones

investor inversor, -ra o inversionista (mf)

invisible assets activo (m) invisible

invisible earnings ingresos (mpl) invisibles

invisible trade comercio (m) invisible

invitation invitación (f)

invite invitar

invoice (n) factura (f)

invoice (v) facturar

invoice number número (m) de factura

invoice value precio (m) facturado

invoicing facturación (f)

invoicing department departamento (m) de facturación

IOU (= I owe you) pagaré (m)

irrecoverable debt deuda (f) incobrable

irredeemable bond obligación (f) perpetua

irregular irregular

irregularities irregularidades (fpl)

irrevocable irrevocable

irrevocable acceptance aceptación (f) irrevocable

irrevocable letter of credit carta (f) de crédito irrevocable

issue (n) *[magazine]* número (m)

issue (n) *[of shares]* emisión (f)

issue (v) *[shares]* emitir

issue a letter of credit abrir una carta de crédito

issue instructions dar instrucciones

issuing bank banco (m) emisor

item *[for sale]* artículo (m)

item *[news]* noticia (f)

item *[on agenda]* punto (m)

item *[on balance sheet]* partida (f)

itemize detallar o especificar

itemized account cuenta (f) detallada

itemized invoice factura (f) detallada

itinerary itinerario (m)

Jj

job *[employment]* empleo (m) *o* puesto (m) de trabajo

job *[piece of work]* trabajo (m) *o* tarea (f)

job analysis análisis (m) de un puesto de trabajo

job application solicitud (f) de empleo

job cuts reducción (f) de empleos

job description descripción (f) del puesto de trabajo

job satisfaction satisfacción (f) laboral

job security seguridad (f) en el empleo

job specification descripción (f) del puesto de trabajo

job title cargo (m)

join (v) juntar *o* unir

join (v) *[become part of]* ingresar en

joint común *o* conjunto, -ta *o* colectivo, -va

joint account cuenta (f) conjunta *o* cuenta en participación

joint discussions negociaciones (fpl) conjuntas

joint management dirección (f) conjunta *o* codirección (f)

joint managing director codirector, -ra gerente

joint owner co-propietario, -ria

joint ownership co-propiedad (f) *o* condominio (m)

joint signatory signatario (m) colectivo

joint venture empresa (f) conjunta

jointly conjuntamente *o* en común

journal *[accounts book]* libro (m) diario

journal *[magazine]* revista (f) *o* boletín (m)

journey order pedido (m) cursado al representante (comercial)

judge (n) juez (mf)

judge (v) juzgar

judgement *or* **judgment** juicio (m) *o* sentencia (f)

judgment debtor deudor, -ra judicial

judicial processes procedimientos (mpl) judiciales

jump the queue saltarse la cola

junior (adj) menor *o* más joven *o* subalterno, -na

junior clerk pasante (mf) *o* auxiliar (mf) administrativo, -va

junior executive *or* **junior manager** ejecutivo, -va auxiliar

junior partner socio subalterno *o* de menor antigüedad

junk bonds bonos-basura (mpl)

junk mail publicidad (f) sin interés (por correo)

jurisdiction jurisdicción (f)

justify justificar

Kk

keen competition fuerte competencia (f)

keen demand gran demanda (f)

keen prices precios (mpl) competitivos

keep a promise cumplir una promesa

keep back retener

keep up sostener *o* mantener

keep up with the demand satisfacer la demanda

key (adj) *[important]* clave (f)

key (n) *[on keyboard]* tecla (f)

key (n) *[solution]* clave (f)

key (n) *[to door]* llave (f)

key industry industria (f) clave

key money traspaso (m)

key personnel *or* **key staff** personal (m) clave

key post puesto (m) clave

keyboard (n) teclado (m)

keyboard (v) teclear

keyboarder operador, -ra de teclado

keyboarding tecleo (m) *o* tecleado (m)

kilo *or* **kilogram** kilo (m) *o* kilogramo (m)

knock down (v) *[price]* rematar

knock off *[reduce price]* descontar

knock off *[stop work]* terminar de trabajar

knock-on effect repercusión (f) *o* efecto (m) secundario

knockdown prices precios (mpl) mínimos *o* de saldo

krona *[currency used in Sweden and Iceland]* corona (f)

krone *[currency used in Denmark and Norway]* corona (f)

Ll

label (n) etiqueta (f)

label (v) etiquetar

labelling etiquetado (m)

labour trabajo (m)

labour costs costes (mpl) laborales

labour disputes conflictos (mpl) laborales

labour force mano (f) de obra

lack of funds falta (f) de fondos

land (n) tierra (f)

land (v) *[of plane]* aterrizar

land (v) *[passengers]* desembarcar

land goods at a port descargar mercancías en un puerto

landed costs coste (m) descargado

landing card tarjeta (f) de desembarque

landing charges gastos (mpl) de descarga

landlady propietaria (f) *o* dueña (f)

landlord propietario (m) *o* dueño (m)

lapse (v) caducar

large (adj) grande

laser printer impresora (f) láser

last (adj) último, -ma

last in first out (LIFO) últimos en entrar, primeros en salir

last quarter último trimestre

late (adj) atrasado, -da

late (adv) tarde *o* con retraso

late: to be late retrasarse

late-night opening abierto por la noche

latest último, -ma

launch (n) lanzamiento (m)

launch (v) lanzar

launching lanzamiento (m)

launching costs costes (mpl) de lanzamiento

launching date fecha (f) de lanzamiento

launder (money) blanquear (dinero negro)

law ley (f)

law *[rule]* regla (f) *o* norma (f)

law *[study]* derecho (m)

law courts tribunales (mpl) de justicia

law of diminishing returns ley (f) de rendimientos decrecientes

law of supply and demand ley (f) de la oferta y la demanda

lawful legal *o* lícito, -ta

lawful trade comercio (m) legal

lawsuit pleito (m) *o* juicio (m) *o* proceso (m)

lawyer abogado, -da

lay off workers despedir por falta de trabajo

LBO (= leveraged buyout) compra (f) *o* adquisición (f) apalancada

L/C (= letter of credit) carta (f) de crédito

lead time plazo (m) de espera

leaflet folleto (m) *o* prospecto (m)

leakage pérdidas (fpl) *o* mermas (fpl)

lease (n) arrendamiento (m) *o* arriendo (m)

lease (v) *[of landlord]* arrendar (ceder en arriendo)

lease (v) *[of tenant]* arrendar (tomar en arriendo)

lease back realizar una operación de cesión-arrendamiento

lease-back cesión-arrendamiento (f)

lease equipment arrendar equipo

leasing arrendamiento (m) financiero *o* 'leasing' (m)

leave (n) permiso (m)

leave (v) *[go away]* irse *o* marcharse

leave (v) *[resign]* abandonar *o* dejar

leave of absence excedencia (f)

ledger libro (m) mayor

left *[not right]* izquierdo, -da

left: be left quedar

left luggage office consigna (f)

legal *[according to law]* legal *o* lícito, -ta

legal *[referring to law]* jurídico, -ca *o* judicial

legal action acción (f) legal

legal advice asesoramiento (m) jurídico

legal adviser asesor (m) jurídico

legal costs *or* **legal charges** costas (fpl) judiciales

legal currency moneda (f) de curso legal

legal department asesoría (f) jurídica

legal expenses costas (fpl) judiciales

legal proceedings proceso (m) judicial

legal status condición (f) jurídica *o* personalidad (f) jurídica

legal tender moneda (f) de curso legal

legislation legislación (f)

lend prestar

lender prestamista (mf)

lending concesión (f) de un préstamo

lending limit límite (m) de crédito

less menos

lessee arrendatario, -ria *o* inquilino, -na

lessor arrendador, -ra

let (v) alquilar *o* arrendar

let an office alquilar una oficina

letter carta (f)

letter of application carta (f) de solicitud

letter of appointment carta (f) de nombramiento

letter of complaint carta (f) de reclamación

letter of credit (L/C) carta (f) de crédito

letter of intent carta (f) de intención

letter of reference carta (f) de recomendación

letters of administration nombramiento (m) de administrador judicial

letters patent patente (f) de invención

letting agency agencia (f) de alquiler de viviendas

level nivel (m)

level off *or* **level out** nivelarse *o* estabilizarse

leverage apalancamiento (m) financiero

leveraged buyout (LBO) compra (f) *o* adquisición (f) apalancada

levy (n) recaudación (f) de impuestos

levy (v) recaudar *o* gravar

liabilities deudas (fpl) *o* pasivo (m)

liability responsabilidad (f)

liable for responsable de

liable to sujeto, -ta a

licence licencia (f)

license conceder una licencia *o* autorizar

licensee persona (f) autorizada *o* concesionario, -ria

licensing licencia (f)

lien gravamen (m) *o* derecho (m) de retención

life assurance *or* **life insurance** seguro (m) de vida

life interest renta (f) vitalicia *o* usufructo (m) vitalicio

LIFO (= last in first out) últimos en entrar, primeros en salir

lift (n) ascensor (m)

lift (v) levantar *o* suprimir

lift an embargo levantar un embargo

limit (n) límite (m) *o* acotación (f)

limit (v) limitar

limitation limitación (f)

limited limitado, -da

limited (liability) company (Ltd) sociedad (f) de responsabilidad limitada (S.R.L.)

limited liability responsabilidad (f) limitada

limited market mercado (m) limitado

limited partnership sociedad (f) en comandita

line (n) línea (f) *o* raya (f)

line management gestión (f) lineal

line organization organización (f) lineal

line printer impresora (f) de líneas

link (n) vínculo (m)

liquid assets activo (m) líquido

liquidate a company liquidar una compañía

liquidate stock liquidar existencias

liquidation liquidación (f)

liquidator síndico (m)

liquidity liquidez (f)

liquidity crisis crisis (f) de liquidez

lira *[currency used in Italy and Turkey]* lira (f)

list (n) lista (f) *o* relación (f)

list (n) *[catalogue]* catálogo (m) *o* repertorio (m)

list (v) hacer una lista *o* enumerar

list price precio (m) de catálogo

litre litro (m)

Lloyd's register Registro (m) Marítimo de Lloyd

load (n) cargamento (m)

load (v) cargar

load a lorry *or* **a ship** cargar un camión *o* un barco

load factor coeficiente (m) de ocupación

load line línea (f) de carga *o* línea de flotación

loading bay nave (f) de carga

loading ramp rampa (f) de carga

loan (n) préstamo (m)

loan (v) prestar

loan capital empréstito (m)

loan stock obligaciones (fpl)

local local

local call llamada (f) local

local government administración (f) local

local labour mano (f) de obra local

lock (n) cerradura (f)

lock (v) cerrar con llave

lock up a shop *or* **an office** cerrar una tienda *o* una oficina

lock up capital inmovilizar capital

lock-up premises local (m) sin vivienda incorporada

log (v) anotar *o* apuntar

log calls anotar las llamadas recibidas

logo logotipo (m)

long largo, -ga

long credit crédito (m) a largo plazo

long-dated bill letra (f) a largo plazo

long-distance flight *or* **long-haul flight** vuelo (m) de larga distancia

long-range a largo plazo

long-standing de hace tiempo *o* de muchos años

long-standing agreement acuerdo (m) de muchos años

long-term largo plazo

long-term debts deudas (fpl) a largo plazo

long-term forecast previsión (f) a largo plazo

long-term liabilities pasivo (m) a largo plazo

long-term loan préstamo (m) a largo plazo

long-term objectives objetivos (mpl) a largo plazo

long-term planning planificación (f) a largo plazo

loose (adj) suelto, -ta *o* a granel

loose (adj) *[slack]* flojo, -ja

lorry camión (m)

lorry driver camionero, -ra

lorry-load carga (f) de un camión

lose perder

lose an order perder un pedido

lose money perder dinero

lose value perder valor

loss *[not a profit]* pérdida (f)

loss of an order pérdida (f) de un pedido

loss of customers pérdida (f) de clientela

loss of value pérdida (f) de valor

loss adjustment ajuste (m) de pérdidas

loss-leader artículo (m) de reclamo

lot lote (m)

low (adj) bajo, -ja

low (n) mínimo (m)

low sales ventas (fpl) bajas

low-grade de baja calidad

low-level de bajo nivel *o* de grado inferior

low-quality de poca calidad *o* mediocre

lower (adj) más bajo, -ja *o* inferior

lower (v) bajar

lower prices reducir los precios

lowering disminución (f) *o* reducción (f)

Ltd (= limited company) S.(R.) L. (= sociedad (de responsabilidad) limitada)

luggage equipaje (m) *o* maletas (fpl)

lump sum pago (m) único *o* suma (f) global

luxury goods artículos (mpl) de lujo

Mm

machine máquina (f) *o* aparato (m)

machinery maquinaria (f)

macro-economics macroeconomía (f)

magazine revista (f)

magazine insert encarte (m) publicitario (de una revista)

magazine mailing envío (m) de revistas por correo

magnetic tape *or* **mag tape** cinta (f) magnética

mail (n) correo (m) *o* correspondencia (f)

mail (v) mandar por correo *o* echar al correo

mail shot publicidad (f) por correo

mail-order pedido (m) por correo

mail-order business *or* **mail-order firm** empresa (f) de ventas por correo

mail-order catalogue catálogo (m) de ventas por correo

mailing envío (m) por correo

mailing list lista (f) de destinatarios

mailing piece folleto (m) publicitario enviado por correo

mailing shot envío (m) de publicidad por correo

main principal *o* mayor

main building edificio (m) principal

main office oficina (f) principal

maintain *[keep at same level]* mantener *o* conservar

maintain *[keep going]* mantener *o* sostener

maintenance mantenimiento (m) *o* conservación (f)

maintenance of contacts mantenimiento (m) de relaciones

maintenance of supplies mantenimiento (m) de suministros

major mayor *o* importante

major shareholder accionista (mf) importante

majority mayoría (f)

majority shareholder accionista (mf) mayoritario

make (v) hacer

make good *[a defect or* **loss]** indemnizar *o* compensar

make money ganar dinero

make out *[invoice]* confeccionar *o* extender

make provision for tomar medidas

make up for compensar

make-ready time tiempo (m) de preparación (de una máquina)

maladministration mala administración (f)

man (n) hombre (m)

man (v) asignar personal

man-hour hora-hombre (f)

manage dirigir *o* gestionar *o* administrar

manage to arreglárselas *o* conseguir

manageable manejable

management *[action]* dirección (f) *o* gestión (f)

management *[managers]* junta (f) de directores

management accounts cuentas (fpl) de gestión

management buyout (MBO) compra (f) de una empresa por sus ejecutivos

management consultant asesor, -ra de empresas

management course curso (m) de gestión empresarial

management team equipo (m) directivo

management techniques técnicas (fpl) de dirección de empresas

management trainee ejecutivo, -va en formación

management training formación (f) de mandos

manager *[of branch or shop]* gerente (mf) *o* encargado, -da

manager *[of department]* director, -ra *o* jefe, -fa

managerial directivo, -va

managerial posts órganos (mpl) de gestión

managerial staff personal (m) administrativo

managing director (MD) director, -ra gerente

mandate mandato (m)

manifest manifiesto (m)

manned asistido, -da *o* atendido, -da

manning dotación (f) de personal

manning levels niveles (mpl) de dotación de personal

manpower mano (f) de obra

manpower forecasting previsión (f) de mano de obra

manpower planning planificación (f) de la mano de obra

manpower shortage escasez (f) de mano de obra

manual (adj) manual

manual (n) manual (m)

manual work trabajo (m) manual

manual worker obrero, -ra

manufacture (n) fabricación (f)

manufacture (v) manufacturar *o* fabricar *o* elaborar

manufactured goods productos (mpl) manufacturados

manufacturer fabricante (m)

manufacturer's recommended price (MRP) precio (m) de venta recomendado

manufacturing fabricación (f)

manufacturing capacity capacidad (f) de fabricación

manufacturing costs costes (mpl) de fabricación

manufacturing overheads gastos (mpl) generales de fabricación

margin *[profit]* margen (m)

margin of error margen (m) de error

marginal marginal

marginal cost coste (m) marginal *o* coste incremental

marginal pricing fijación (f) de precios marginal

marine marino, -na

marine insurance seguro (m) marítimo

marine underwriter asegurador, -ra de riesgos marinos

maritime marítimo, -ma

maritime law derecho (m) marítimo

maritime lawyer abogado (m) especializado en derecho marítimo

maritime trade comercio (m) marítimo

mark (n) marca (f) *o* señal (f)

mark (n) *[currency used in Germany]* marco (m)

mark (v) marcar *o* señalar

mark down rebajar

mark up recargar

mark-up *[profit margin]* margen (m) de beneficio

marker pen rotulador (m) *o* marcador (m)

market (n) mercado (m) *o* plaza (f)

market (v) vender

market analysis análisis (m) de mercado

market analyst analista (mf) de mercado

market capitalization capitalización (f) bursátil

market economist economista (mf) de mercado

market forces fuerzas (fpl) del mercado

market forecast previsión (f) de mercado

market leader líder (m) del mercado

market opportunities oportunidades (fpl) de mercado

market penetration penetración (f) en el mercado

market price precio (m) de mercado

market rate precio (m) *o* tarifa (f) de mercado

market research estudio (m) *o* investigación (f) de mercado

market share cuota (f) de mercado

market trends tendencias (fpl) del mercado

market value valor (m) de mercado

marketable vendible *o* comerciable

marketing mercadotecnia (f) *o* 'marketing' (m)

marketing agreement acuerdo (m) de comercialización

marketing department departamento (m) de 'marketing'

marketing division sección (f) de 'marketing'

marketing manager director, -ra de 'marketing'

marketing strategy estrategia (f) de 'marketing'

marketing techniques técnicas (fpl) de 'marketing'

marketplace mercado (m) *o* plaza (f) del mercado

mass masa (f)

mass market product producto destinado a un mercado de masas

mass marketing comercialización (f) a gran escala

mass media medios (mpl) de comunicación

mass production producción (f) en serie

mass-produce fabricar en serie

mass-produce cars fabricar coches en serie

Master's degree in Business Administration (MBA) master (m) en administración de empresas

materials control control (m) de materiales

materials handling manejo (m) de materiales

maternity leave licencia (f) por maternidad

matter (n) cuestión (f) *o* asunto (m)

matter (v) importar

mature (v) vencer

mature economy economía (f) madura

maturity date fecha (f) de vencimiento

maximization maximización (f)

maximize maximizar

maximum (adj) máximo, -ma

maximum (n) máximo (m)

maximum price precio (m) máximo

MBA (= Master in Business Administration) master (m) en administración de empresas

MBO (= management buyout) compra (f) de una empresa por sus ejecutivos

MD (= managing director) director, -ra gerente

mean (adj) medio, -dia

mean (n) promedio (m) *o* media (f)

mean annual increase aumento (m) anual medio

means *[money]* recursos (mpl) *o* medios (mpl)

means *[ways]* medio (m) *o* manera (f)

means test comprobación (f) de los recursos económicos

measurement of profitability evaluación (f) *o* medición (f) de la rentabilidad

measurements medidas (fpl) *o* dimensiones (fpl)

media coverage cobertura (f) periodística

median mediana (f)

mediate mediar

mediation mediación (f)

mediator mediador, -ra *o* intermediario, -ria

mediocre mediocre

medium (adj) medio, -dia *o* mediano, -na

medium (n) medio (m) *o* instrumento (m)

medium-sized mediano, -na

medium-term plazo (m) medio

meet *[be satisfactory]* cumplir *o* satisfacer

meet *[someone]* encontrar *o* encontrarse (con) *o* reunirse

meet a deadline cumplir un plazo establecido

meet a demand satisfacer *o* atender una demanda

meet a target cumplir un objetivo

meet expenses cubrir gastos

meeting reunión (f) *o* asamblea (f)

meeting place lugar (m) de reunión

member *[of a group]* miembro (m) *o* socio, -cia

membership afiliación (f) *o* ingreso (m)

membership *[all members]* los socios *o* los miembros

memo *or* **memorandum** memorandum (m)

memory *[computer]* memoria (f)

mend (v) arreglar

mention (v) mencionar

merchandise (n) mercancías (fpl) *o* género (m)

merchandize (v) comercializar

merchandize a product comercializar un producto

merchandizer comerciante (mf)

merchandizing comercialización (f) *o* mercadeo (m)

merchant comerciante (mf) *o* mercader (m)

merchant bank banco (m) mercantil

merchant navy marina (f) mercante

merchant ship *or* **merchant vessel** buque (m) mercante

merge fusionar

merger fusión (f)

merit mérito (m)

merit award *or* **merit bonus** gratificación (f) por méritos

message mensaje (m) *o* recado (m)

messenger mensajero, -ra

micro-economics microeconomía (f)

microcomputer microordenador (m)

mid-month accounts cuentas (fpl) de mediados de mes

mid-week a mediados de semana

middle management mandos (mpl) intermedios

middle-sized company empresa mediana

middleman intermediario, -ria

mileage allowance kilometraje (m)

million millón (m)

millionaire millonario, -ria

minimum (adj) mínimo, -ma

minimum (n) mínimo (m)

minimum dividend dividendo (m) mínimo

minimum payment pago (m) mínimo

minimum wage salario (m) mínimo

minor shareholders pequeños accionistas (mpl)

minority minoría (f)

minority shareholder accionista (m) minoritario

minus menos

minus factor factor (m) negativo

minute (n) *[time]* minuto (m)

minute (v) tomar nota *o* levantar acta

minutes (n) *[of meeting]* acta (f) de la reunión

misappropriate malversar

misappropriation malversación (f)

miscalculate calcular mal

miscalculation error (m) de cálculo

miscellaneous misceláneo, -nea *o* diverso, -sa

miscellaneous items artículos (mpl) varios

mismanage administrar mal

mismanagement mala administración

miss *[not to hit]* errar *o* fallar

miss *[not to meet]* no encontrar

miss *[train, plane]* perder (el tren *o* avión)

miss a target no cumplir un objetivo

miss an instalment saltarse un plazo

missing (adj) desaparecido, -da

mistake equivocación (f) *o* error (m)

misunderstanding malentendido (m)

mixed mixto, -ta *o* mezclado, -da

mixed economy economía (f) mixta

mobile phone teléfono móvil

mobility movilidad (f)

mobilize movilizar

mobilize capital movilizar capital

mock-up maqueta (f) *o* modelo (m) a escala

mode modo (m)

mode of payment modo (m) de pago

model (n) modelo (mf)

model (n) *[small copy]* maqueta (f) *o* modelo (m) a escala

model (v) *[clothes]* pasar modelos

model agreement prototipo (m) de contrato

modem modem (m)

moderate (adj) moderado, -da

moderate (v) moderar

moderate price precio módico

modern moderno, -na

monetary monetario, -ria

monetary base base (f) monetaria

monetary unit unidad (f) monetaria

money dinero (m)

money changer cambista (mf)

money markets mercados (mpl) monetarios

money order giro (m) postal

money rates tipos (mpl) de interés

money supply oferta (f) monetaria

money up front pago (m) por adelantado

money-making lucrativo, -va o remunerativo, -va

money-making plan plan (m) remunerativo

moneylender prestamista (mf)

monitor (n) *[screen]* pantalla (f)

monitor (v) controlar o comprobar

monopolization monopolización (f)

monopolize monopolizar

monopoly monopolio (m)

month mes (m)

month end fin (m) de mes

month-end accounts cuentas (fpl) de fin de mes

monthly (adj) mensual

monthly (adv) mensualmente

monthly payments pagos (mpl) mensuales

monthly statement estado (m) de cuenta mensual

moonlighter pluriempleado, -da

moonlighting pluriempleo (m)

moratorium moratoria (f)

more más

mortgage (n) hipoteca (f)

mortgage (v) hipotecar

mortgage payments pagos (mpl) de la hipoteca

mortgagee acreedor (-ra) hipotecario (-ria)

mortgager *or* **mortgagor** deudor (-ra) hipotecario (-ria)

most-favoured nation nación (f) más favorecida

motivated motivado, -da

motivation motivación (f)

motor insurance seguro (m) de automóviles

mount up aumentar o subir

mounting creciente

move (v) trasladar(se) o mudar(se)

movement movimiento (m)

movements of capital movimientos (mpl) de capital

MRP (= manufacturer's recommended price) precio (m) de venta recomendado

multicurrency operation operación (f) en multiples divisas

multilateral multilateral

multilateral agreement acuerdo (m) multilateral

multilateral trade comercio (m) multilateral

multinational (n) multinacional (f)

multiple (adj) múltiple

multiple entry visa visado (m) de entradas múltiples

multiple ownership propiedad (f) conjunta

multiple store cadena (f) de grandes almacenes

multiplication multiplicación (f)

multiply multiplicar

multitude multitud (f)

mutual (adj) mutuo, -tua

mutual (insurance) company mutua (f) de seguros

Nn

national (adj) nacional

national advertising publicidad (f) a escala nacional

nationalization nacionalización (f)

nationalized industry industria (f) nacionalizada

nationwide de ámbito nacional

natural resources recursos (mpl) naturales

natural wastage pérdida (f) de trabajadores por jubilación

near letter-quality (NLQ) calidad (f) de semicorrespondencia

necessary necesario, -ria

need (n) necesidad (f)

need (v) necesitar

negative cash flow flujo (m) de caja negativo

neglected business negocio (m) descuidado

neglected shares acciones (fpl) poco buscadas en la bolsa

negligence negligencia (f)

negligent descuidado, -da

negligible insignificante

negotiable negociable

negotiable instrument instrumento (m) negociable

negotiate negociar *o* gestionar

negotiation negociación (f)

negotiator negociador, -ra

net (adj) neto, -ta

net (v) obtener beneficios netos

net assets *or* net worth activo (m) neto *o* patrimonio (m)

net earnings *or* net income ganancias (fpl) netas *o* ingresos (mpl) netos

net income *or* net salary salario (m) neto *o* sueldo (m) neto

net loss pérdida (f) neta

net margin margen (m) neto

net price precio (m) neto

net profit beneficio (m) neto

net receipts ingresos (mpl) netos

net sales ventas (fpl) netas

net weight peso (m) neto

net worth valor (m) neto

net yield rendimiento (m) neto

network (n) red (f)

network (v) difundir a través de la red de emisoras

news (n) noticia (f)

news agency agencia (f) de prensa

newspaper periódico (m)

niche hueco (m) de un mercado

night noche (f)

night rate tarifa (f) nocturna

night shift turno (m) de noche

nil nada (f) *o* cero (m)

nil return declaración (f) de ingresos nulos

NLQ (= near letter-quality) calidad de semicorrespondencia

no-claims bonus prima (f) por ausencia de siniestralidad

no-strike agreement *or* no-strike clause cláusula (f) que prohibe la huelga

nominal capital capital (m) nominal

nominal ledger libro (m) mayor de resultados

nominal rent renta (f) nominal

nominal value valor (m) nominal

nominee candidato (-ta) propuesto (-ta)

nominee account cuenta (f) administrada por un apoderado

non profit-making sin fines lucrativos

non-delivery falta (f) de entrega

non-executive director director (m) no ejecutivo

non-negotiable instrument documento (m) no negociable

non-payment *[of a debt]* impago (m) de una deuda

non-recurring items partidas (fpl) extraordinarias

non-refundable deposit depósito (m) no reembolsable

non-returnable packing envase (m) no retornable

non-stop sin parar *o* sin escalas

non-taxable income ingresos (mpl) libres de impuestos

nonfeasance delito (m) por omisión

norm norma (f)

normal normal

notary public notario (m)

note (n) nota (f)

note (v) *[details]* apuntar *o* anotar

note of hand pagaré (m) *o* letra (f) al propio cargo

nothing nada

notice *[piece of information]* letrero (m) *o* anuncio (m) *o* aviso (m)

notice *[leaving a job]* notificación (f) de despido *o* de dimisión

notice *[period of time]* plazo (m)

notice *[legal document]* aviso (m) *o* notificación (f)

notification notificación (f)

notify notificar *o* avisar

null nulo, -la

number (n) número (m)

number (v) numerar

numbered account cuenta (f) numerada

numeric *or* **numerical** numérico, -ca

numeric keypad teclado (m) numérico

Oo

obey (v) obedecer *o* acatar

objective (adj) objetivo, -va

objective (n) objetivo (m)

obligation *[debt]* deuda (f)

obligation *[duty]* obligación (f) *o* compromiso (m)

obsolescence obsolescencia (f)

obsolescent obsolescente

obsolete obsoleto, -ta

obtain obtener *o* conseguir

obtainable asequible

occupancy ocupación (f)

occupancy rate índice (m) de ocupación

occupant ocupante (mf) *o* habitante (mf) *o* inquilino, -na

occupation ocupación (f)

occupational laboral

occupational accident accidente (m) laboral

odd *[not a pair]* suelto, -ta *o* desparejado, -da

odd *[number]* impar

odd numbers números (mpl) impares

off *[away from work]* ausente del trabajo

off *[cancelled]* cancelado, -da *o* suspendido, -da

off *[reduced by]* con descuento

off the record extraoficialmente *o* fuera de actas

off-peak fuera de horas punta

off-season temporada (f) baja

off-the-job training formación (f) profesional fuera del trabajo

offer (n) oferta (f)

offer (v) ofrecer

offer for sale oferta (f) de venta

offer price precio (m) de oferta

office oficina (f) *o* despacho (m)

office equipment equipo (m) de oficina

office furniture muebles (mpl) de oficina

office hours horario (m) de oficina

office security medidas (fpl) de seguridad (en una oficina)

office space espacio (m) para oficinas

office staff personal (m) administrativo

office stationery artículos (mpl) de papelería para oficina

offices to let oficinas (fpl) de alquiler

official (adj) oficial

official (n) funcionario, -ria

official receiver administrador, -ra judicial *o* síndico (m)

official return declaración (f) oficial

officialese lenguaje (m) burocrático

offload descargar *o* deshacerse de

offshore en aguas territoriales

oil aceite (m)

oil *[petroleum]* petróleo (m)

oil price precio (m) del crudo *o* del
petróleo

oil-exporting countries países (mpl)
exportadores de petróleo

oil-producing countries países (mpl)
productores de petróleo

old viejo, -ja *o* antiguo, -gua

old-established antiguo, -gua

old-fashioned anticuado, -da *o* pasado,
-da de moda

ombudsman defensor (m) del pueblo

omission omisión (f)

omit omitir

on a short-term basis a corto plazo

on account a cuenta

on agreed terms en las condiciones
acordadas

on an annual basis anualmente

on an average por término medio

on approval a prueba

on behalf of en nombre de

on board a bordo

on business por asuntos de negocios

on condition that a condición de que

on credit a crédito

on favourable terms en condiciones
favorables

on line *or* **online** en línea

on order pedido, -da

on request a petición

on sale a la venta

on the increase en aumento

on time a tiempo

on-the-job training formación (f)
profesional en el trabajo

one-off único, -ca

one-off item artículo (m) único

one-sided unilateral

one-sided agreement acuerdo (m)
unilateral

one-way fare billete (m) de ida *o* pasaje
(m) sencillo

one-way trade comercio (m) unilateral

**OPEC (= Organization of Petroleum
Exporting Countries)** OPEP
(Organización de los Países
Exportadores de Petróleo)

open (adj) abierto, -ta

open (v) abrir

open an account abrir una cuenta

open a bank account abrir una cuenta
bancaria

open a line of credit abrir una línea de
crédito

open a meeting abrir la sesión

open a new business abrir un negocio

open account cuenta (f) abierta

open cheque cheque (m) abierto *o*
cheque sin cruzar

open credit crédito (m) abierto

open market mercado (m) libre

open negotiations entablar
negociaciones

open ticket billete (m) abierto

open to offers se admiten ofertas

open-ended agreement acuerdo (m)
modificable

open-plan office oficina (f) de
distribución modificable

opening (adj) inaugural *o* inicial

opening (n) apertura (f) *o* inauguración (f)

opening balance saldo (m) inicial

opening bid oferta (f) inicial

opening hours horario (m) comercial

opening price precio (m) *o* cotización
(f) de apertura

opening stock existencias (fpl) iniciales

opening time hora (f) de apertura

operate (v) operar *o* manejar

operate (v) *[work]* entrar en vigor

operating (n) funcionamiento (m) *o*
operación (f)

operating budget presupuesto (m) de
explotación

operating costs *or* **operating expenses**
gastos (mpl) de explotación

operating manual manual (m) de
funcionamiento

operating profit beneficio (m) de
explotación

operating system sistema (m) operativo

operation operación (f)

operational operacional

operational budget presupuesto (m) de explotación

operational costs gastos (mpl) de explotación

operative (adj) operativo, -va

operative (n) or **operator (n)** operario, -ria o maquinista (mf)

opinion poll encuesta (f) o sondeo (m) de opinión

opportunity oportunidad (f)

option to purchase opción (f) de compra

optional opcional o optativo, -va

optional extras extras (mpl) opcionales

order (n) orden (m)

order (n) *[for goods]* pedido (m)

order (n) *[money]* libramiento (m) o orden (f) de pago

order (v) ordenar

order (v) *[goods]* hacer un pedido o encargar

order book libro (m) de pedidos

order fulfilment despacho (m) de pedidos

order number número (m) de pedido

order picking selección (f) de artículos para un pedido

order processing preparación (f) de pedidos

order: on order pedido, -da

ordinary ordinario, -ria o corriente

ordinary shares acciones (fpl) ordinarias

organization organización (f)

organization *[institution]* organismo (m) o asociación (f)

organization and methods organización y métodos

organization chart organigrama (m)

Organization of Petroleum Exporting Countries (OPEC) Organización de los Países Exportadores de Petróleo (OPEP)

organizational organizativo, -va

organize organizar

origin origen (m)

original (adj) original

original (n) original (m)

OS (= outsize) talla (f) muy grande

out of control fuera de control

out of date anticuado, -da o caducado, -da

out of stock agotado, -da

out of work sin empleo o sin trabajo

out-of-pocket expenses gastos (mpl) reemborsables

outbid pujar más alto o sobrepujar

outgoing saliente

outgoing mail correspondencia (f) de salida

outgoings desembolsos (mpl)

outlay desembolso (m) o gasto (m)

outlet mercado (m)

outline (n) bosquejo (m)

output (n) producción (f) o rendimiento (m)

output (n) *[computer]* datos (mpl) de salida

output (v) producir

output tax impuesto (m) sobre las ventas de bienes o servicios

outright en su totalidad

outside exterior o externo, -na

outside director director externo, directora externa

outside line línea (f) exterior

outside office hours fuera de horas de oficina

outsize (OS) talla (f) muy grande

outstanding *[exceptional]* notable o destacado, -da o sobresaliente

outstanding *[unpaid]* pendiente

outstanding debts deudas (fpl) pendientes

outstanding orders pedidos (mpl) pendientes

overall global o en conjunto o general

overall plan plan (m) general

overbook reservar con exceso

overbooking sobrecontratación (m)

overcapacity sobrecapacidad (f)

overcharge (n) precio (m) excesivo o recargo (m)

overcharge (v) cargar en exceso o cobrar de más

overdraft sobregiro (m) o descubierto (m)

overdraft facility límite (m) de descubierto bancario

overdraw girar en descubierto

overdrawn account cuenta (f) en descubierto

overdue vencido, -da o atrasado, -da

overestimate (v) sobrevalorar *o* sobrestimar

overhead budget presupuesto (m) de gastos generales

overhead costs *or* **expenses** gastos (mpl) generales *o* de producción

overheads gastos (mpl) generales *o* de producción

overmanning exceso (m) de personal *o* excedente (m) laboral

overpayment pago (m) en exceso

overproduce producir en exceso

overproduction sobreproducción (f)

overseas (adj) extranjero, -ra

overseas (adv) en el extranjero

overseas (n) extranjero (m)

overseas markets mercados (mpl) extranjeros

overseas trade comercio (m) exterior

overspend gastar excesivamente

overspend one's budget gastar más de lo presupuestado

overstock (v) acumular en exceso *o* abarrotar

overstocks exceso (m) de existencias

overtime horas (fpl) extraordinarias

overtime ban prohibición (f) de hacer horas extras

overtime pay tarifa (f) de horas extras

overvalue sobrevalorar *o* sobrestimar

overweight: to be overweight pesar en exceso

owe deber

owing debido, -da

owing to debido a *o* a causa de

own (v) poseer *o* tener

own brand goods productos (mpl) de marca propia

own label goods productos (mpl) de marca propia

owner amo (m) *o* propietario, -ria *o* dueño, -ña

ownership propiedad (f) *o* posesión (f)

Pp

p & p (= **postage and packing**) franqueo y embalaje

PA (= **personal assistant**) ayudante (mf) personal

pack (n) paquete (m) *o* envase (m)

pack (v) embalar *o* envasar *o* empaquetar

pack goods into cartons embalar mercancías en cajas de cartón

pack of envelopes paquete (m) de sobres

package *[of goods]* paquete (m) *o* embalaje (m) *o* envase (m)

package *[of economic measures]* conjunto (m) de medidas económicas

package deal acuerdo (m) *o* transacción (f) global

packaging embalaje (m) *o* envase (m)

packaging material material (m) de embalaje

packer embalador, -ra *o* empaquetador, -ra

packet paquete (m) *o* cajetilla (f) *o* bulto (m)

packet of cigarettes paquete (m) *o* cajetilla (f) de cigarrillos

packing embalaje (m) *o* envase (m)

packing case caja (f) de embalar

packing charges gastos (mpl) de embalaje

packing list *or* **packing slip** lista (f) de bultos *o* de contenidos

paid pagado, -da

pallet paleta (f)

palletize empaletar

panel panel (m) *o* tablero (m)

panic buying compra (f) febril

paper bag bolsa (f) de papel

paper feed alimentador (m) del papel

paper loss pérdida (f) sobre el papel

paper profit beneficio (m) ficticio *o* beneficio sobre el papel

paperclip sujetapapeles (m) *o* clip (m)

papers papeles (mpl) *o* documentos (mpl)

paperwork papeleo (m)

par par

par value valor (m) a la par

parcel (n) paquete (m)

parcel (v) empaquetar *o* envolver

parcel post servicio (m) de paquetes postales

parent company sociedad (f) matriz *o* casa (f) matriz

parity paridad (f) *o* igualdad (f)

part (n) parte (m)

part exchange canje (m) parcial

part-owner copropietario, -ria

part-ownership copropiedad (f)

part-time a tiempo parcial

part-time work *or* **part-time employment** trabajo por horas *o* empleo a tiempo parcial

part-timer trabajador, -ra a tiempo parcial

partial loss pérdida (f) parcial

partial payment pago (m) parcial

particulars detalles (mpl) *o* pormenores (mpl)

partner socio, -cia

partnership sociedad (f) *o* asociación (f)

party parte (f)

patent patente (f)

patent agent agente (mf) de patentes y marcas

patent an invention patentar un invento

patent applied for *or* **patent pending** patente (f) solicitada *o* patente en tramitación

patented patentado, -da

pay (n) paga (f)

pay (v) pagar *o* abonar

pay a bill pagar una cuenta

pay a dividend distribuir un dividendo

pay an invoice pagar una factura

pay back devolver *o* reembolsar

pay by cheque pagar con cheque

pay by credit card pagar con tarjeta de crédito

pay cash pagar al contado *o* en efectivo

pay cheque cheque (m) de sueldo *o* cheque de salario

pay desk caja (f)

pay in advance pagar por adelantado

pay in instalments pagar a plazos

pay interest pagar intereses

pay money down hacer un depósito *o* dar una entrada

pay off *[debt]* redimir *o* reembolsar

pay off *[worker]* despedir

pay out pagar *o* desembolsar *o* abonar

pay phone teléfono (m) público

pay rise aumento (m) de sueldo

pay slip hoja (f) de sueldo *o* de salario

pay up pagar una deuda

payable pagadero, -ra

payable at sixty days pagadero a sesenta días

payable in advance pagadero por adelantado

payable on delivery pagadero a la entrega

payable on demand pagadero a la vista

payback clause cláusula (f) de reembolso

payback period periodo (m) de reembolso

payee portador, -ra

payer pagador, -ra

paying (adj) rentable

paying-in slip recibo (m) (de depósito)

payload carga (f) útil

payment pago (m) *o* remuneración (f)

payment by cheque pago (m) mediante cheque

payment by results pago (m) a destajo

payment in cash pago (m) en metálico *o* en efectivo

payment in kind pago (m) en especie

payment on account pago (m) a cuenta

PC (= personal computer) ordenador (m) personal

P/E ratio (= price/earnings ratio) relación (f) precio-beneficios

peak (n) cumbre (f) *o* punto (m) máximo *o* cima (f)

peak (v) llegar al máximo *o* alcanzar el punto más alto

peak output rendimiento (m) máximo

peak period horas (fpl) punta

peg prices estabilizar los precios

penalize penalizar *o* sancionar

penalty pena (f) *o* multa (f)

penalty clause cláusula (f) penal

pending pendiente

penetrate a market penetrar un mercado

pension pensión (f) *o* retiro (m)

pension fund fondo (m) de pensiones

pension scheme plan (m) de pensiones

per per *o* a *o* por

per annum al año

per capita per cápita

per cent por ciento

per day al día

per head por persona

per hour por hora

per week por semana

per year al año

percentage porcentaje (m) *o* tanto (m) por ciento

percentage discount porcentaje (m) de descuento

percentage increase porcentaje (m) de aumento

percentage point punto (m) porcentual

perform (v) actuar *o* ejercer

performance actuación (f) *o* funcionamiento (m) *o* rendimiento (m)

performance rating valoración (f) de resultados

period periodo (m) *o* plazo (m)

period of notice periodo (m) de preaviso

period of validity periodo (m) de validez

periodic *or* **periodical (adj)** periódico, -ca

periodical (n) publicación (f) periódica *o* revista (f)

peripherals periféricos (mpl)

perishable perecedero, -ra

perishable goods artículos (mpl) perecederos

perishables productos (mpl) perecederos

permission permiso (m) *o* licencia (f)

permit (n) permiso (m)

permit (v) permitir

personal personal

personal allowances deducciones (fpl) personales

personal assets bienes (mpl) personales

personal assistant (PA) ayudante (mf) personal

personal computer (PC) ordenador (m) personal

personal income renta (f) personal

personalized con las iniciales

personalized briefcase cartera con las iniciales

personalized cheques cheques con el nombre impreso

personnel personal (m)

personnel department departamento (m) de personal

personnel management dirección (f) de personal

personnel manager jefe, -fa de personal

peseta *[Spanish currency]* peseta (f)

peso *[South American currency]* peso (m)

petty insignificante

petty cash fondos (mpl) *o* dinero (m) para gastos menores

petty cash box caja (f) para gastos menores

petty expenses gastos (mpl) menores

phase (n) fase (f)

phase in introducir gradualmente

phase out reducir *o* retirar gradualmente

phoenix syndrome síndrome del fénix

phone (n) teléfono (m)

phone (v) telefonear *o* llamar (por teléfono)

phone back volver a telefonear *o* llamar

phone call llamada (f) telefónica

phone card teletarjeta (f)

phone number número (m) de teléfono

photocopier fotocopiadora (f)

photocopy (n) fotocopia (f)

photocopy (v) fotocopiar

photocopying fotocopiaje (m) *o* fotocopia (f)

photocopying bureau servicio (m) de fotocopias

picking list inventario (m) de posición (en almacén)

pie chart gráfico (m) circular *o* gráfico sectorial

piece pieza (f)

piece rate precio (m) a destajo

piecework trabajo (m) a destajo

pilferage *or* **pilfering** (pequeño) hurto (m)

pilot (adj) piloto

pilot (n) *[person]* piloto (mf)

pilot scheme programa (m) piloto

pioneer (n) pionero, -ra

pioneer (v) iniciar *o* abrir camino

place (n) lugar (m) *o* posición (f) *o* sitio (m)

place (n) *[job]* puesto (m)

place (v) colocar *o* poner *o* situar

place an order cursar un pedido

place of work lugar (m) de trabajo

plaintiff demandante (mf) *o* querellante (mf)

plan (n) *[drawing]* plano (m)

plan (n) *[project]* plan (m) *o* proyecto (m)

plan (v) planear *o* planificar *o* proyectar

plan investments planificar las inversiones

plane avión (m)

planner planificador, -ra

planning planificación (f)

plant (n) *[factory]* planta (f) *o* fábrica (f)

plant (n) *[machinery]* maquinaria (f)

plant-hire firm empresa (f) de alquiler de maquinaria

platform *[railway station]* andén (m)

PLC *or* **plc** (= **Public Limited Company**) Sociedad Anónima (S.A.)

plug (n) enchufe (m)

plug (v) *[block]* detener *o* frenar

plug (v) *[publicize]* dar publicidad

plummet caer

plus más

plus factor factor (m) positivo

pocket (n) bolsillo (m) *o* bolsa (f)

pocket (v) embolsar

pocket calculator *or* **pocket diary** calculadora (f) de bolsillo *o* diario (m) de bolsillo

point punto (m)

point of sale (p.o.s. *or* **POS)** punto (m) de venta

point of sale material (POS material) publicidad (f) en el punto de venta

policy política (f)

pool resources reunir recursos

poor quality mala calidad (f)

poor service servicio (m) deficiente

popular popular

popular prices precios (mpl) populares

port puerto (m)

port *[computer]* conexión (f)

port authority autoridades (fpl) portuarias

port charges *or* **port dues** derechos (mpl) de dársena *o* portuarios

port of call puerto (m) de escala

port of embarkation puerto (m) de embarque

port of registry puerto (m) de registro

portable portátil

portfolio cartera (f) (de valores)

portfolio management gestión (f) *o* administración (f) de cartera

POS *or* **p.o.s.** (= **point of sale**) punto (m) de venta

POS material (point of sale material) publicidad (f) en el punto de venta

position *[job]* puesto (m) *o* cargo (m) *o* plaza (f)

position *[state of affairs]* posición (f) *o* situación (f) *o* postura (f)

positive positivo, -va

positive cash flow flujo (m) de caja positivo

possess (v) poseer

possession (n) posesión (f)

possibility posibilidad (f)

possible posible

post (n) *[job]* puesto (m)

post (n) *[letters]* correo (m)

post (n) *[system]* correos (mpl)

post (v) enviar *o* mandar por correo *o* echar al correo

post an entry hacer un asiento

post free sin gastos de franqueo

postage franqueo (m) *o* tarifa (f) postal

postage and packing (p & p) (gastos de) franqueo y embalaje

postage paid franqueo (m) concertado *o* porte pagado

postal postal

postal charges *or* **postal rates** gastos (mpl) de franqueo *o* tarifas (fpl) postales

postal order giro (m) postal

postcard (tarjeta) postal

postcode código (m) postal

postdate posfechar

poste restante lista (f) de correos

postpaid porte (m) pagado *o* franqueo (m) concertado

postpone aplazar *o* posponer

postponed aplazado, -da

postponement aplazamiento (m)

potential (adj) potencial

potential (n) potencial (m)

potential customers clientes (mpl) eventuales

potential market mercado (m) potencial

pound libra (f)

pound sterling libra (f) esterlina

power (n) poder (m)

power of attorney poder (m) notarial *o* poderes (mpl)

PR (= public relations) relaciones (fpl) públicas

pre-empt prevenir

pre-financing prefinanciación (f)

prefer preferir

preference preferencia (f)

preference shares acciones (fpl) preferentes

preferential preferente *o* preferencial

preferential creditor acreedor, -ra preferente

preferential duty *or* **preferential tariff** tarifa (f) preferente *o* tarifa preferencial

preferred creditor acreedor, -ra preferente

premises local (m) *o* edificio (m)

premium *[extra charge]* agio (m)

premium *[insurance]* prima (f) de seguros

premium *[on lease]* traspaso (m)

premium offer obsequio (m) publicitario

premium quality alta calidad

prepack *or* **prepackage** preempaquetar

prepaid pagado, -da por adelantado

prepay pagar por adelantado

prepayment pago (m) por adelantado

prescribe prescribir

present (adj) *[being there]* presente

present (adj) *[now]* actual

present (n) *[gift]* regalo (m) *o* obsequio (m)

present (v) *[give]* regalar *o* obsequiar

present (v) *[show a document]* presentar

present a bill for acceptance presentar una letra a la aceptación

present a bill for payment presentar una letra al pago

present value valor (m) actual

presentation presentación (f)

press prensa (f)

press conference conferencia (f) de prensa

press release comunicado (m) de prensa

prestige prestigio (m)

prestige product producto (m) prestigioso

pretax profit beneficio (m) antes de deducir los impuestos

prevent impedir *o* evitar *o* prevenir

prevention prevención (f)

preventive preventivo, -va

previous previo, -via *o* anterior

price (n) precio (m)

price (v) poner precio a

price ceiling límite (m) de precios

price control control (m) de precios

price controls control (m) de precios

price differential coeficiente (m) de ajuste de precios

price ex quay franco en muelle

price ex warehouse franco en almacén

price ex works precio (m) en fábrica *o* franco en fábrica

price label etiqueta (f) de precio

price list lista (f) de precios

price range gama (f) de precios

price reductions rebajas (fpl) de precios

price stability estabilidad (f) de los precios

price tag *or* **price ticket** etiqueta (f) de precio

price(-cutting) war guerra (f) de precios

price-sensitive product producto (m) sensible a los cambios de precio

price/earnings ratio (P/E ratio) relación (f) precio-ganancias

pricing fijación (f) de los precios

pricing policy política (f) de precios

primary primario, -ria

primary industry sector (m) primario

prime principal o primero, -ra

prime cost coste (m) de producción

prime rate tipo (m) preferencial de interés bancario

principal (adj) principal

principal (n) [money] principal (m)

principal (n) [person] mandante (m)

principle principio (m)

print out imprimir

printer [company] imprenta (f)

printer [machine] impresora (f)

printout impresión (f)

prior anterior o previo, -via

private privado, -da o particular

private enterprise empresa (f) privada

private limited company sociedad (f) limitada (S.L.)

private ownership propiedad (f) privada

private property propiedad (f) privada

private sector sector (m) privado

privatization privatización (f)

privatize privatizar

pro forma (invoice) factura (f) pro forma

pro rata prorrata

probation periodo (m) de prueba

probationary de prueba o probatorio, -ria

problem problema (m)

problem area asunto (m) problemático

problem solver mediador (m) de conflictos

problem solving investigación (f) de conflictos

procedure procedimiento (m) o tramitación (f) o trámite (m)

proceed proceder o seguir o continuar

process (n) procedimiento (m)

process (v) preparar o elaborar o tramitar

process (v) [raw materials] elaborar

process figures elaborar cifras

produce (n) productos (mpl)

produce (v) producir o fabricar

produce (v) [bring out] presentar

produce (v) [yield] producir o dar

producer productor, -ra o fabricante (m)

product producto (m)

product advertising anuncio (m) del producto

product cycle ciclo (m) del producto

product design diseño (m) de productos

product development desarrollo (m) de productos

product engineer ingeniero , -ra de producto

product line gama (f) de productos o línea (f) de productos

product mix gama (f) de productos de una compañía

production producción (f)

production [showing] presentación (f)

production cost coste (m) de producción

production department departamento (m) de producción

production line cadena (f) de montaje

production manager director, -ra de producción

production standards normas (fpl) de producción

production target objetivo (m) de producción

production unit unidad (f) de producción

productive productivo, -va

productive discussions conversaciones (fpl) fructíferas

productivity productividad (f)

productivity agreement acuerdo (m) de productividad

productivity bonus prima (f) de productividad

professional (adj) [expert] profesional

professional (n) [expert] profesional (mf)

professional qualifications títulos (mpl) profesionales

profit ganancia (f) o beneficio (m)

profit after tax beneficio (m) neto de impuestos

profit and loss account cuenta (f) de pérdidas y ganancias

profit before tax beneficio (m) antes de deducir los impuestos

profit centre centro (m) de beneficios

profit margin margen (m) de beneficio

profit-making rentable *o* lucrativo, -va

profit-oriented company empresa (f) con fines de lucro

profit-sharing participación (f) en los beneficios

profitability *[making a profit]* rentabilidad (f)

profitability *[ratio of profit to cost]* coeficiente (m) de rentabilidad

profitable rentable *o* productivo, -va *o* lucrativo, -va

program a computer programar un ordenador

programme *or* **program** programa (m)

programming language lenguaje (m) de programación

progress (n) progreso (m) *o* marcha (f) *o* avance (m)

progress (v) progresar *o* avanzar

progress chaser responsable (mf) del progreso de un trabajo

progress payments pagos (mpl) a cuenta

progress report informe (m) sobre la marcha de un trabajo

progressive progresivo, -va

progressive taxation tributación (f) progresiva

prohibitive prohibitivo, -va

project (n) proyecto (m) *o* plan (m)

project (v) proyectar

project analysis análisis (m) de proyectos

project manager director, -ra de proyecto

projected proyectado, -da *o* previsto, -ta

projected sales ventas (fpl) previstas

promise (n) promesa (f)

promise (v) prometer

promissory note pagaré (m) *o* letra (f) al propio cargo

promote *[advertise]* promocionar

promote *[give better job]* ascender

promote a corporate image promocionar la imagen pública de una empresa

promote a new product promocionar un nuevo producto

promotion *[publicity]* promoción (f)

promotion *[to better job]* ascenso (m)

promotion(al) budget presupuesto (m) de promoción

promotion of a product promoción (f) de un producto

promotional de promoción *o* en promoción

prompt pronto, -ta *o* rápido, -da *o* inmediato, -ta

prompt payment pronto pago (m)

prompt service servicio (m) rápido

proof (n) prueba (f)

property (n) propiedad (f)

proportion (n) parte (f) *o* proporción (f)

proportional proporcional

proposal proposición (f) *o* propuesta (f)

propose *[a motion]* proponer

propose to *[do something]* proponer(se)

proposition propuesta (f) *o* proposición (f)

proprietary company (US) sociedad (f) de cartera

proprietor propietario (m) *o* dueño (m)

proprietress propietaria (f) *o* dueña (f)

prosecute procesar *o* enjuiciar

prosecution *[legal action]* procesamiento (m)

prosecution *[party in legal action]* parte (f) acusadora *o* acusación (f)

prosecution counsel fiscal (m)

prospective eventual

prospective buyer posible comprador, -ra

prospects perspectivas (fpl)

prospectus prospecto (m) *o* folleto (m)

protect proteger

protection protección (f)

protectionist proteccionista

protective protector, -ra *o* proteccionista

protective tariff arancel (m) proteccionista

protest (n) protesta (f)

protest (n) *[official document]* protesto (m)

protest (v) protestar contra algo

protest a bill protestar una letra

protest strike huelga (f) de protesta

provide proveer

provide for prever

provided that *or* **providing** a condición de que

provision *[condition]* disposición (f) *o* estipulación (f)

provision *[money put aside]* provisión (f) de fondos *o* reserva (f)

provisional provisional

provisional budget presupuesto (m) provisional

provisional forecast of sales previsión (f) provisional de ventas

proviso condición (f) *o* salvedad (f)

proxy *[deed]* procuración (f) *o* poder (m)

proxy *[person]* poderhabiente (mf) *o* apoderado, -da

proxy vote voto (m) por poderes

public (adj) público, -ca

public finance finanzas (fpl) públicas

public funds fondos (mpl) públicos

public holiday fiesta (f) nacional

public image imagen (f) pública

Public Limited Company (Plc) sociedad (f) anónima (S.A.)

public opinion opinión (f) pública

public relations (PR) relaciones (fpl) públicas

public relations department departamento (m) de relaciones públicas

public relations man persona dedicada a las relaciones públicas

public relations officer responsable (mf) de relaciones públicas

public sector sector (m) público

public transport transporte (m) público

publicity publicidad (f)

publicity budget presupuesto (m) publicitario

publicity campaign campaña (f) publicitaria

publicity department departamento (m) de publicidad

publicity expenditure gastos (mpl) de publicidad

publicity manager director, -ra de publicidad

publicize dar publicidad *o* divulgar

purchase (n) compra (f)

purchase (v) comprar

purchase ledger libro (m) mayor de compras

purchase order orden (f) de compra

purchase price precio (m) de compra

purchase tax impuesto (m) de venta

purchaser comprador, -ra

purchasing compra (f)

purchasing department departamento (m) *o* sección (f) de compras

purchasing manager jefe, -fa de compras

purchasing power poder (m) adquisitivo

put (v) *[place]* poner

put back *[later]* aplazar

put in order ordenar

put in writing poner por escrito

put money down dar una entrada

Qq

qty (= quantity) cantidad (f)

qualified cualificado, -da *o* capacitado, -da

qualified *[with reservations]* con reservas *o* condicionado, -da

qualify capacitar

qualify as obtener *o* sacar el título de

quality calidad (f)

quality control control (m) de calidad

quality controller inspector, -ra de calidad

quality label signo (m) de calidad

quango organismo (m) paraestatal

quantity cantidad (f)

quantity discount descuento (m) por cantidad

quarter *[25%]* cuarto (m) *o* cuarta parte (f)

quarter *[three months]* trimestre (m)

quarter day día (m) de ajuste

quarterly (adj) trimestral

quarterly (adv) trimestralmente *o* cada tres meses

quay muelle (m)

question (n) pregunta (f) *o* cuestión (f)

question (v) preguntar *o* cuestionar

questionnaire cuestionario (m) *o* encuesta (f)

quorum quórum (m)

quota cupo (m) *o* cuota (f)

quotation (n) *or* **quote (n)** cotización (f) *o* presupuesto (m)

quote (v) *[estimate costs]* cotizar *o* ofrecer un precio

quote (v) *[reference]* citar *o* indicar

quoted company sociedad (f) cotizada en bolsa

quoted shares acciones (fpl) que se cotizan en bolsa

Rr

R&D (= research and development) investigación y desarrollo (I+D)

racketeer estafador, -ra *o* timador, -ra

racketeering negocio (m) ilícito

rail ferrocarril (m)

rail transport transporte (m) por ferrocarril

railroad (US) ferrocarril (m)

railway (GB) ferrocarril (m)

railway station estación (f) de ferrocarril

raise (v) aumentar *o* subir

raise (v) *[a question]* plantear

raise (v) *[obtain money]* conseguir

raise an invoice preparar una factura

rally (n) recuperación (f)

rally (v) recuperarse

random al azar *o* aleatorio, -ria

random check chequeo (m) al azar

random error error aleatorio

random sample muestra (f) aleatoria

random sampling muestreo (m) aleatorio

range (n) *[series of items]* gama (f) *o* surtido (m)

range (n) *[variation]* escala (f)

range (v) oscilar

rapid rápido, -da

rate (n) *[amount]* tasa (f) *o* coeficiente (m)

rate (n) *[price]* precio (m) *o* tarifa (f)

rate of exchange tipo (m) de cambio

rate of inflation tasa (f) de inflación

rate of interest rédito (m) *o* tipo (m) de interés

rate of production ritmo (m) de producción

rate of return tasa (f) de rendimiento

ratification ratificación (f)

ratify ratificar

rating clasificación (f)

ratio razón (f) *o* relación (f)

rationalization racionalización (f)

rationalize racionalizar

raw materials materias (fpl) primas

reach llegar *o* alcanzar

reach a decision tomar una decisión

reach an agreement llegar a un acuerdo

readjust reajustar

readjustment reajuste (m)

ready listo, -ta *o* preparado, -da

ready cash efectivo (m)

real real *o* verdadero, -ra

real estate bienes (mpl) raíces *o* propiedad (f) inmobiliaria

real income or **real wages** renta (f) real

real-time system sistema (m) de ordenador a tiempo real

realizable assets activo (m) realizable

realization (n) realización (f)

realization of assets liquidación (f) de activo

realize realizar

realize *[understand]* darse cuenta

realize a project or **a plan** realizar un proyecto o un plan

realize property or **assets** liquidar propiedades o realizar activos

reapplication segunda solicitud (f)

reapply volver a presentarse

reappoint volver a nombrar

reappointment nuevo nombramiento (m)

reason razón (f)

reassess revaluar

reassessment revaluación (f)

rebate *[money back]* reembolso (m)

rebate *[price reduction]* rebaja (f) o descuento (m)

receipt *[paper]* recibo (m) o resguardo (m)

receipt *[receiving]* recepción (f)

receipt book talonario (m) de recibos

receipts ingresos (mpl) o entradas (fpl)

receivable a cobrar o por cobrar

receivables efectos (mpl) a cobrar

receive recibir

receiver (who receives) destinatario, -ria o receptor (m)

receiver *[liquidator]* síndico (m)

reception recepción (f) o acogida (f)

reception clerk recepcionista (mf)

reception desk recepción (f)

receptionist recepcionista (mf)

recession recesión (f)

reciprocal recíproco, -ca o bilateral

reciprocal agreement acuerdo (m) recíproco o acuerdo bilateral

reciprocal trade comercio (m) recíproco

reciprocity reciprocidad (f)

recognition reconocimiento (m)

recognize a union reconocer a un sindicato

recommend recomendar o aconsejar

recommendation recomendación (f)

reconcile cuadrar o ajustar

reconciliation reconciliación (f) o concertación (f)

reconciliation of accounts conciliación (f) de cuentas

record (n) récord (m)

record (n) *[for personnel]* historial (m) o expediente (m)

record (n) *[of what has happened]* acta (f) o registro (m) o informe (m)

record (v) registrar o anotar

record-breaking récord

recorded delivery entrega (f) con acuse de recibo

records archivos (mpl)

recoup one's losses resarcirse de las pérdidas

recover *[get better]* recuperarse o mejorar

recover *[get something back]* recuperar o recobrar

recoverable recuperable

recovery *[getting better]* reactivación (f)

recovery *[getting something back]* recuperación (f) o rescate (m)

rectification rectificación (f)

rectify corregir o rectificar

recurrent que se repite o constante

recycle reciclar

recycled paper papel (m) reciclado

red tape burocracia (f) o papeleo (m)

redeem amortizar o redimir

redeem a bond vender un bono o amortizar una obligación

redeem a debt pagar una deuda

redeem a pledge rescatar una prenda

redeemable rescatable o amortizable

redemption *[of a loan]* amortización (f) o rescate (m)

redemption date fecha (f) de amortización o fecha de rescate

redevelop renovar

redevelopment renovación (f) urbana

redistribute redistribuir

reduce (a price) rebajar o reducir (un precio)

reduce expenditure reducir gastos

reduced rate precio (m) reducido o tarifa (f) reducida

reduction reducción (f) o rebaja (f)

redundancy excedente (m) de plantilla o despido (m)

redundant redundante

re-elect reelegir

re-election reelección (f)

re-employ emplear de nuevo

re-employment reempleo (m)

re-export (n) reexportación (f)

re-export (v) reexportar

refer *[pass to someone]* remitir

refer *[to item]* referirse o mencionar

reference referencia (f)

reference number número (m) de referencia

refinancing of a loan refinanciación (f) de un préstamo

refresher course curso (m) de reciclaje o curso de actualización

refund (n) devolución (f) o reembolso (m)

refund (v) reembolsar o devolver

refundable reembolsable

refundable deposit depósito (m) reembolsable

refunding of a loan conversión (f) de un préstamo

refusal negativa (f) o rechazo (m)

refuse (v) rehusar o negar(se) o rechazar

regarding relativo a o en cuanto a

regardless of sin tener en cuenta

region región (f)

regional regional

register (n) *[large book]* libro (m) de registro

register (n) *[official list]* registro (m)

register (v) *[at hotel]* registrarse o inscribirse

register (v) *[in official list]* registrar o inscribir (en un registro)

register (v) *[letter]* certificar

register a company inscribir una compañía en un registro

register a property registrar una propiedad

register a trademark registrar una marca comercial

register of directors relación (f) de directivos de una empresa

register of shareholders libro (m) registro de accionistas

registered (adj) registrado, -da o certificado, -da

registered design diseño (m) registrado

registered letter carta (f) certificada

registered office domicilio (m) social

registered trademark marca (f) registrada

registrar registrador, -ra o secretario, -ria (general)

Registrar of Companies Registro (m) Mercantil

registration registro (m) o inscripción (f) o matrícula (f)

registration fee cuota (f) de inscripción o matrícula (f)

registration form boletín (m) de inscripción

registration number número (m) de registro o número de matrícula

registry registro (m)

registry office oficina (f) del registro civil

regular *[always at same time]* regular

regular *[ordinary]* normal o ordinario, -ria o corriente

regular customer cliente (mf) habitual

regular income ingreso (m) fijo

regular route ruta (f) habitual

regular size tamaño (m) normal

regular staff personal (m) fijo

regulate *[adjust]* regular

regulate *[by law]* reglamentar

regulation regulación (f) o reglamentación (f)

regulations normas (fpl) o reglamento (m)

reimbursement reembolso (m) o reintegro (m)

reimbursement of expenses reembolso (m) de gastos

reimport (n) reimportación (f)

reimport (v) reimportar

reimportation reimportación (f)

reinsurance reaseguro (m)

reinsure reasegurar

reinsurer reasegurador, -ra

reinvest reinvertir

reinvestment reinversión (f)

reject (n) producto (m) defectuoso

reject (v) rechazar

rejection rechazo (m)

relating to referente o relativo a

relation relación (f)

relations relaciones (fpl)

release (n) liberación (f)

release (v) *[free]* liberar

release (v) *[make public]* divulgar o publicar

release (v) *[put on the market]* poner a la venta o lanzar al mercado

release dues despachar pedidos atrasados

relevant apropiado, -da o pertinente

reliability fiabilidad (f)

reliable fiable o de confianza o cumplidor, -ra

remain *[be left]* quedar o sobrar

remain *[stay]* quedarse

remainder *[things left]* resto (m)

remember recordar o acordarse (de)

remind recordar

reminder recordatorio (m) o advertencia (f)

remit (v) remitir

remit by cheque remitir por cheque

remittance envío (m) o giro (m)

remote control mando (m) a distancia

removal mudanza (f) o traslado (m)

removal *[sacking someone]* destitución (f) o despido (m)

remove (v) quitar o destituir o suprimir

remove *[to new house]* trasladar o mudar

remunerate remunerar

remuneration remuneración (f)

render an account presentar una cuenta o una factura

renew renovar o prorrogar

renew a lease prorrogar un arrendiamiento

renew a subscription renovar una suscripción o un abono

renewal renovación (f) o prórroga (f)

renewal notice notificación (f) de renovación

renewal premium prima (f) de renovación

rent (n) alquiler (m) o renta (f)

rent (v) *[pay money for]* alquilar o arrendar

rent collector cobrador (m) de alquileres

rent control control (m) de rentas o control de alquileres

rent tribunal tribunal (m) de rentas

rent-free exento de alquiler

rental alquiler (m)

rental income ingresos (mpl) o renta (f) por alquiler

renunciation renuncia (f)

reorder (n) nuevo pedido (m)

reorder (v) renovar un pedido

reorganization reorganización (f)

reorganize reorganizar

rep (= representative) representante (mf)

repair (n) reparación (f)

repair (v) reparar o componer

repay pagar o reembolsar o resarcir

repayable reembolsable

repayment reembolso (m) o pago (m)

repeat repetir

repeat an order renovar un pedido

repeat order pedido (m) suplementario

replace reemplazar o sustituir o reponer

replacement *[item]* reemplazo (m) o repuesto (m)

replacement *[person]* sustituto, -ta

replacement value valor (m) de reposición

reply (n) respuesta (f) o contestación (f)

reply (v) responder o contestar

reply coupon boletín (m) de respuesta

report (n) informe (m) o memoria (f)

report (v) informar

report (v) *[go to a place]* presentarse

report a loss anunciar un déficit

report for an interview presentarse a una entrevista

report (v) on progress informar sobre la marcha

report to someone rendir cuentas a alguien

repossess recuperar o recobrar

represent representar

representative (adj) representativo, -va

representative (n) representante (mf)

repudiate repudiar

repudiate an agreement negarse a cumplir un acuerdo

reputation reputación (f)

request (n) ruego (m) *o* petición (f) *o* solicitud (f)

request (v) pedir *o* solicitar

request: on request a petición

require requerir

require *[demand]* exigir

requirements requisitos (mpl)

resale reventa (f)

resale price precio (m) de reventa

rescind rescindir *o* anular

research (n) investigación (f)

research (v) investigar

research and development (R & D) investigación y desarrollo (I+D)

research programme programa (m) de investigación

research worker *or* **researcher** investigador, -ra

reservation reserva (f)

reserve (n) reserva (f)

reserve (n) *[supplies]* reservas (fpl)

reserve (v) reservar

reserve currency divisas (fpl) de reserva

reserve price precio (m) mínimo aceptable

reserves reservas (fpl)

residence residencia (f)

residence permit permiso (m) de residencia

resident (adj) residente

resident (n) residente (mf) *o* habitante (mf)

resign resignar *o* dimitir

resignation dimisión (f) *o* renuncia (f)

resolution resolución (f)

resolve resolver *o* decidir

resources recursos (mpl)

respect (v) respetar *o* acatar

respond responder

response respuesta (f) *o* reacción (f)

responsibilities responsabilidades (fpl) *o* obligaciones (fpl)

responsibility responsabilidad (f)

responsible (for) responsable

responsible to someone ser responsable ante alguien

rest (n) descanso (m)

rest (n) *[remainder]* resto (m)

restock renovar existencias *o* repostar

restocking renovación (f) de existencias

restraint restricción (f)

restraint of trade restricción (f) comercial

restrict restringir *o* limitar

restrict credit limitar el crédito

restriction restricción (f) *o* limitación (f)

restrictive restrictivo, -va

restrictive practices prácticas (fpl) restrictivas

restructure reestructurar

restructuring reestructuración (f)

restructuring of a loan consolidación (f) de un préstamo

restructuring of the company reestructuración (f) de la compañía

result *[general]* resultado (m)

result from resultar de *o* derivar de

result in resultar *o* dar por resultado

results *[company's profit or loss]* resultados (mpl)

resume reanudar

resume negotiations reanudar las negociaciones

retail (n) venta (f) al por menor *o* venta al detalle

retail (v) vender *o* venderse al por menor

retail dealer comerciante (mf) al por menor *o* minorista (mf)

retail goods vender al por menor

retail outlets tiendas (fpl) al detall

retail price precio (m) al por menor

retail price index índice (m) de precios al comsumo

retailer detallista (mf) *o* minorista (mf)

retailing comercio (m) al por menor

retire *[from one's job]* jubilarse *o* retirarse

retirement jubilación (f) *o* retiro (m)

retirement age edad (f) de jubilación

retiring saliente

retrain reciclar

retraining reciclaje (m) profesional

retrenchment reducción (f) de gastos

retrieval recuperación (f) *o* rescate (m)

retrieval system sistema (m) de recuperación

retrieve recuperar *o* rescatar

retroactive retroactivo, -va

retroactive pay rise aumento (m) retroactivo de salarios

return (n) vuelta (f) *o* regreso (m)

return (n) *[profit]* ganancia (f) *o* rendimiento (m)

return (n) *[sending back]* devolución (f)

return (v) *[send back]* devolver

return a letter to sender devolver una carta al remitente

return address remite (m)

return on investment (ROI) rendimiento (m) de la inversión

returnable retornable

returned empties envases (mpl) devueltos

returns *[profits]* beneficios (mpl)

returns *[unsold goods]* productos (mpl) devueltos sin vender

revaluation revaluación (f)

revalue revaluar

revenue ingreso (m)

revenue accounts contabilidad (f) de ingresos

revenue from advertising ingresos (mpl) por publicidad

reversal inversión (f) *o* revocación (f)

reverse (adj) revertido, -da

reverse (v) revocar

reverse charge call llamada (f) a cobro revertido

reverse takeover contra OPA (f)

reverse the charges llamar a cobro revertido

revise revisar *o* corregir

revoke revocar

revolving credit crédito (m) renovable

rider cláusula (f) adicional

right (adj) *[not left]* derecho, -a

right (adj) *[not wrong]* correcto, -ta

right (n) *[legal title]* derecho (m)

right of veto derecho (m) de veto

right of way derecho (m) de paso

right-hand man brazo (m) derecho *o* hombre (m) de confianza

rightful legítimo, -ma

rightful claimant derechohabiente (m)

rightful owner propietario legítimo, propietaria legítima

rights issue emisión (f) de derechos

rise (n) *[increase]* alza (f) *o* subida (f) *o* aumento (m)

rise (n) *[salary]* aumento (m) de salario

rise (v) subir

risk (n) riesgo (m)

risk (v) *[money]* arriesgar

risk capital capital-riesgo (m)

risk premium prima (f) de riesgo

risk-free investment inversión (f) sin riesgo

risky arriesgado, -da

rival company empresa (f) competidora

road carretera (f)

road haulage transporte (m) por carretera

road haulier transportista (mf)

road tax impuesto (m) de circulación

road transport transporte (m) por carretera

rock-bottom prices precios (mpl) reventados

ROI (= return on investment) rendimiento (m) de la inversión

roll on/roll off ferry ferry roll-on roll-off

roll over credit *or* **a debt** refinanciar un crédito *o* una deuda

rolling plan plan (m) periódicamente actualizado

room *[general]* sala (f)

room *[hotel]* habitación (f)

room *[space]* espacio (m)

room reservations departamento (m) de reservas

room service servicio (m) de habitaciones de un hotel

rough *[estimate]* aproximado, -da

rough calculation cálculo (m) aproximado

rough draft borrador (m) *o* bosquejo (m)

rough estimate cálculo (m) aproximado

round down redondear por defecto

round up redondear por exceso

routine (adj) rutinario, -ria *o* habitual

routine (n) rutina (f) *o* costumbre (f)

routine call llamada (f) rutinaria

routine work trabajo (m) rutinario

royalty canon (m) *o* derechos (mpl) de autor

rubber check (US) cheque (m) sin fondos

rule (n) norma (f) *o* regla (f)

rule (v) *[be in force]* regir

rule (v) *[give decision]* decretar

ruling (adj) vigente

ruling (n) decisión (f) *o* fallo (m)

run (n) *[regular route]* ruta (f) habitual

run (n) *[rush to buy]* demanda (f) excesiva

run (n) *[work routine]* ciclo (m) de trabajo

run (v) *[be in force]* ser válido *o* regir

run (v) *[buses, trains]* circular (v)

run (v) *[manage]* dirigir *o* llevar

run (v) *[work machine]* utilizar *o* hacer funcionar

run a risk correr un riesgo

run into debt endeudarse *o* adeudarse

run out agotar las existencias

run to ascender

running (n) *[of machine]* funcionamiento (m)

running costs *or* **running expenses** gastos (mpl) corrientes *o* gastos de mantenimiento

running total total (m) acumulado

rush (n) prisa (f)

rush (v) precipitarse

rush hour horas punta

rush job trabajo (m) urgente

rush order pedido (m) urgente

Ss

sack (v) someone despedir a alguien

safe (adj) seguro, -ra

safe (n) caja (f) fuerte *o* caja de caudales

safe deposit caja (f) de seguridad

safe investment inversión (f) segura

safeguard proteger

safety seguridad (f)

safety measures medidas (fpl) de seguridad

safety precautions precauciones (fpl) *o* medidas (fpl) de precaución

safety regulations normas (fpl) de seguridad

salaried asalariado, -da

salary salario (m) *o* sueldo (m)

salary cheque cheque (m) de sueldo

salary review revisión (f) de sueldos

sale (n) *[at a low price]* liquidación (f) *o* saldo (m) *o* rebajas (fpl)

sale (n) *[selling]* venta (f)

sale by auction venta (f) en subasta

sale or return venta (f) a prueba *o* venta en depósito

saleability facilidad (f) de venta

saleable vendible

sales ventas (fpl)

sales analysis análisis (m) de ventas

sales book libro (m) de ventas

sales budget presupuesto (m) de ventas

sales campaign campaña (f) de ventas

sales chart gráfico (m) de ventas

sales clerk vendedor, -ra

sales conference reunión (f) de ventas

sales curve curva (f) de ventas

sales department sección (f) de ventas

sales drive campaña (f) *o* promoción (f) de ventas

sales executive ejecutivo (m) de ventas

sales figures cifras (fpl) de ventas

sales force personal (m) de ventas

sales forecast previsión (f) de ventas

sales ledger libro (m) mayor de ventas

sales ledger clerk encargado, -da del libro de ventas

sales literature información (f) publicitaria

sales manager director, -ra comercial

sales people personal (m) de ventas

sales pitch rollo (m) publicitario

sales promotion promoción (f) de ventas

sales receipt comprobante (m) de caja

sales representative representante (mf)

sales revenue ingresos (mpl) de ventas *o* facturación (f)

sales target objetivo (m) de ventas

sales tax impuesto (m) sobre la venta

sales team equipo (m) de ventas

sales volume volumen (m) de ventas

salesman *[in shop]* dependiente (m) *o* vendedor (m)

salesman *[representative]* representante (mf)

salvage (n) *[action]* salvamento (m) *o* rescate (m)

salvage (n) *[things saved]* objetos (mpl) salvados

salvage (v) salvar

salvage vessel buque (m) de salvamento

sample (n) *[group]* muestra (f) *o* muestreo (m)

sample (v) *[ask questions]* hacer un muestreo

sample (v) *[test]* probar

sampling *[statistics]* muestreo (m) por áreas

satisfaction satisfacción (f)

satisfy *[customer]* satisfacer

satisfy a demand satisfacer una demanda

saturate saturar

saturate the market saturar el mercado

saturation saturación (f)

save (v) ahorrar *o* economizar

save (v) *[on computer]* archivar *o* guardar

save on ahorrar *o* economizar

save up ahorrar

savings ahorros (mpl)

savings account cuenta (f) de ahorro

scale *[system]* escala (f)

scale down *or* **scale up** reducir *o* aumentar a escala

scale of charges lista (f) de precios

scarcity value valor (m) de escasez

scheduled flight vuelo (m) regular

scheduling programación (f)

screen (n) pantalla (f)

screen candidates seleccionar candidatos, -tas *o* pasar por la criba

scrip certificado (m) provisional de acciones

scrip issue emisión (f) de acciones gratuitas

seal (n) precinto (m)

seal (v) *[attach a seal]* sellar *o* precintar

seal (v) *[envelope]* cerrar

sealed envelope sobre (m) cerrado

sealed tenders ofertas (fpl) lacradas

season *[time for something]* temporada (f)

season *[time of year]* estación (f)

season ticket abono (m) *o* billete (m) de abono

seasonal estacional

seasonal adjustments ajustes (mpl) estacionales

seasonal demand demanda (f) estacional

seasonal variations variaciones (fpl) estacionales

seasonally adjusted figures cifras (fpl) ajustadas estacionalmente

second (adj) segundo, -da

second (v) *[member of staff]* trasladar temporalmente

second quarter segundo trimestre

second-class de segunda clase *o* de segunda categoría

secondary secundario, -ria

secondary industry industria (f) secundaria

secondhand usado, -da *o* de segunda mano

seconds artículos (mpl) con desperfectos

secret (adj) secreto, -ta

secret (n) secreto (m)

secretarial college escuela (f) de secretariado

secretary secretario, -ria

secretary *[government minister]* ministro (m) del gobierno

section (n) sección (f) *o* departamento (m)

sector sector (m)

secure funds conseguir fondos

secure investment inversión (f) segura

secure job empleo (m) seguro

secured creditor acreedor, -ora con garantía

secured debts deudas (fpl) garantizadas

secured loan préstamo (m) garantizado

securities títulos (mpl) *o* valores (mpl)

security *[being safe]* seguridad (f)

security *[guarantee]* fianza (f) *o* garantía (f)

security guard guardia (m) de seguridad *o* vigilante (m)

security of employment seguridad (f) de empleo

security of tenure derecho (m) de ocupación

see-safe venta (f) a prueba *o* venta en depósito

seize embargar *o* confiscar *o* incautar *o* secuestrar

seizure embargo (m) *o* incautación (f) *o* secuestro (m)

selection selección (f) *o* surtido (m)

selection procedure procedimiento (m) de selección

self-employed (trabajador, -ra) autónomo, -ma

self-financing (adj) autofinanciado, -da

self-financing (n) autofinanciación (f)

self-regulation autoregulación (f)

self-regulatory autoregulado, -da

sell vender

sell forward vender con entrega aplazada *o* vender a futuros

sell off liquidar

sell out *[all stock]* agotar las existencias

sell out *[sell one's business]* vender un negocio

sell-by date fecha (f) de caducidad

seller vendedor, -ra

seller's market mercado (m) de vendedores

selling (n) venta (f)

selling price precio (m) de venta

semi-finished products productos (mpl) semiacabados

semi-skilled workers obreros (mpl) semicualificados

send enviar

send a package by airmail enviar un paquete por correo aéreo

send a package by surface mail enviar un paquete por vía terrestre o marítima

send a shipment by sea enviar una carga por vía marítima

send an invoice by post enviar una factura por correo

sender remitente (mf)

senior mayor *o* más antiguo *o* superior

senior manager *or* **senior executive** director, -ra principal

senior partner socio, -cia principal

sentence sentencia (f)

separate (adj) separado, -da

separate (v) separar *o* dividir

separate: under separate cover por separado

sequester *or* **sequestrate** secuestrar *o* embargar

sequestration embargo (m)

sequestrator embargador, -ra

serial number número (m) de serie

serve servir *o* atender

serve a customer atender a un cliente

service (n) servicio (m)

service (n) *[of machine]* revisión (f)

service (v) *[a machine]* revisar

service a debt pagar los intereses de una deuda

service centre centro (m) de reparaciones

service charge suplemento (m) por el servicio

service department servicio (m) de mantenimiento

service industry industria (f) de servicios

service manual manual (m) de mantenimiento

set (adj) fijo, -ja

set (n) juego (m)

set (v) establecer *o* fijar

set against compensar *o* deducir

set price precio (m) fijo

set targets fijar objetivos

set up a company crear *o* fundar una compañía

set up in business poner un negocio *o* establecerse

setback revés (m)

settle *[an invoice]* saldar *o* pagar una factura

settle *[arrange things]* establecerse

settle a claim pagar una reclamación

settle an account liquidar *o* saldar una cuenta

settlement *[agreement]* acuerdo (m) (después de un conflicto)

settlement *[payment]* finiquito (m) *o* pago (m)

setup *[company]* empresa (f)

setup *[organization]* sistema (m)

share (n) participación (f)

share (n) *[in a company]* acción (f)

share (v) *[divide among]* dividir *o* repartir

share (v) *[use with someone]* compartir

share an office compartir una oficina

share capital capital (m) en acciones

share certificate título (m) *o* certificado (m) de una acción

share issue emisión (f) de acciones

shareholder accionista (mf)

shareholding tenencia (f) de acciones

sharp practice negocio (m) deshonesto (pero no ilegal)

sheet of paper hoja (f) de papel

shelf estantería (f) *o* anaquel (m)

shelf filler empleado, -da para mantener llenos los estantes

shelf life of a product periodo (m) de conservación de un producto

shell company sociedad (f) ficticia (para la compra de acciones)

shelter refugio (m)

shelve dar carpetazo *o* arrinconar

shelving *[shelves]* estantería (f)

shift (n) *[change]* cambio (m)

shift (n) *[team of workers]* turno (m)

shift key tecla (f) de mayúsculas

shift work trabajo (m) por turnos

ship (n) barco (m) *o* buque (m)

ship (v) expedir

ship broker agente (m) marítimo

shipment envío (m) *o* carga (f)

shipper expedidor, -ra *o* transportista (mf)

shipping envío (m) *o* expedición (f)

shipping agent agente (m) marítimo *o* agencia (f) de transportes

shipping charges *or* **shipping costs** costes (mpl) de envío

shipping clerk agente (mf) expedidor, -ra

shipping company compañía (f) naviera *o* compañía marítima

shipping instructions instrucciones (fpl) de envío

shipping line compañía (f) naviera

shipping note nota (f) de envío

shop tienda (f)

shop around comparar precios

shop assistant dependiente, -ta

shop window escaparate (m)

shop-soiled deteriorado, -da

shopkeeper tendero, -ra *o* comerciante (mf)

shoplifter ratero, -ra de tiendas *o* mechera (f)

shoplifting hurto (m) en las tiendas

shopper comprador, -ra

shopping *[action]* ir de compras *o* ir de tiendas

shopping *[goods bought]* compras (fpl)

shopping arcade galería (f) comercial

shopping centre centro (m) comercial

shopping mall galería (f) comercial

shopping precinct zona (f) comercial peatonal

short credit crédito (m) a corto plazo

short of menos de lo necesario *o* escaso, -sa

short-dated bills letras (fpl) a corto vencimiento

short-term (adj) a corto plazo

short-term contract contrato (m) de corta duración

short-term credit crédito (m) a corto plazo

short-term debts deudas (fpl) a corto plazo

short-term loan préstamo (m) a corto plazo

shortage escasez (f) *o* falta (f)

shortfall déficit (m) *o* insuficiencia (f)

shortlist (n) preselección (f) *o* terna (f)

shortlist (v) preseleccionar

show (n) *[exhibition]* exposición (f) *o* feria (f)

show (v) mostrar *o* indicar *o* enseñar

show a profit mostrar un beneficio

showcase vitrina (f)

showroom sala (f) de exposición

shrink-wrapped envasado, -da al vacío

shrink-wrapping envase (m) al vacío

shrinkage contracción (f) *o* encogimiento (m) *o* reducción (f)

shut (adj) cerrado, -da

shut (v) cerrar

side lado (m)

sideline negocio (m) suplementario

sight vista (f)

sight draft giro (m) a la vista

sign (n) señal (f) *o* letrero (m) *o* rótulo (m)

sign (v) firmar

sign a cheque firmar un cheque

sign a contract firmar un contrato

signatory signatario, -ria *o* firmante (mf)

signature firma (f)

simple interest interés (m) simple

single único, -ca *o* sencillo, -lla

Single European Market Mercado Único Europeo

sink (v) hundirse

sister company compañía (f) asociada

sister ship buque (m) gemelo (de la misma flota)

sit-down protest sentada (f)

sit-down strike huelga (f) de brazos caídos

site sitio (m) *o* lugar (m) *o* solar (m)

site engineer ingeniero, -ra de obra

sitting tenant inquilino, -na en posesión

situated situado, -da

situation situación (f)

situations vacant ofertas (fpl) de trabajo

size tamaño (m) *o* dimensiones (fpl)

skeleton staff personal (m) reducido al mínimo

skill habilidad (f) *o* técnica (f) *o* destreza (f)

skilled cualificado, -da *o* especializado, -da

skilled labour mano (f) de obra cualificada

skilled workers obreros (mpl) cualificados

slack flojo, -ja *o* débil

slash prices *or* **credit terms** reducir drásticamente (los precios o las condiciones)

sleeping partner socio (m) comanditario *o* socio en comandita

slip (n) *[mistake]* error (m)

slip (n) *[piece of paper]* resguardo (m)

slow lento, -ta *o* atrasado, -da

slow down desacelerar *o* reducir

slow payer moroso, -sa

slowdown desaceleración (f) *o* reducción (f)

slump (n) *[depression]* depresión (f) *o* crisis (f) económica

slump (n) *[rapid fall]* baja (f) *o* caída (f) repentina

slump (v) caer en picado *o* hundirse

slump in sales caída (f) de las ventas

small pequeño, -ña

small ads anuncios (mpl) breves

small businesses pequeñas (fpl) empresas

small businessman pequeño (m) empresario

small change moneda (f) suelta

small-scale a pequeña escala

small-scale enterprise empresa (f) a pequeña escala

smart card tarjeta (f) inteligente

soar dispararse *o* remontarse

social social

social costs costes (mpl) sociales

social security seguridad (f) social

society sociedad (f) *o* club (m)

socio-economic groups grupos (mpl) socioeconómicos

soft currency moneda (f) débil

soft loan préstamo (m) sin interés *o* crédito (m) blando

soft sell venta (f) sin presionar al cliente

software programa (m) informático *o* 'software' (m)

sole único, -ca *o* exclusivo, -va

sole agency representación (f) exclusiva

sole agent representante (m) exclusivo

sole owner propietario único, propietaria única

sole right exclusiva (f)

sole trader comerciante (m) exclusivo

solicit orders solicitar pedidos

solicitor abogado, -da

solution solución (f)

solve a problem resolver *o* solucionar un problema

solvency solvencia (f)

solvent (adj) solvente

soon pronto

source of income fuente (f) de ingresos

space espacio (m)

spare part pieza (f) de recambio *o* de repuesto

spare time tiempo (m) libre

special especial

special drawing rights (SDRs) derechos (mpl) especiales de giro (DEG)

special offer oferta (f) especial

specialist especialista (mf)

specialization especialización (f)

specialize especializar

specification especificación (f)

specify especificar *o* precisar *o* indicar

speech of thanks palabras (fpl) de agradecimiento

spend *[money]* gastar

spend *[time]* pasar

spending money dinero (m) para gastos personales

spending power poder (m) adquisitivo

spinoff efecto (m) indirecto

spoil estropear

sponsor (n) patrocinador, -ra *o* padrino (m)

sponsor (v) patrocinar

sponsorship patrocinio (m)

spot *[place]* lugar (m)

spot cash pago (m) al contado *o* dinero (m) en mano

spot price precio (m) de entrega inmediata

spot purchase compra (f) al contado

spread a risk repartir un riesgo

spreadsheet hoja (f) de cálculo

square (n) plaza (f)

stability estabilidad (f)

stabilization estabilización (f)

stabilize estabilizar(se)

stable estable

stable currency moneda (f) estable

stable economy economía (f) estable

stable exchange rate tipo (m) de cambio estable

stable prices precios (mpl) estables

staff (n) personal (m) *o* plantilla (f)

staff (v) contratar personal

staff appointment empleo (m) fijo

staff meeting reunión (f) *o* asamblea (f) de personal

stage (n) fase (m) *o* etapa (f)

stage (v) *[organize]* presentar

stage a recovery experimentar una recuperación

staged payments pagos (mpl) por etapas

stagger escalonar

stagnant estancado, -da

stagnation estancamiento (m)

stamp (n) sello (m)

stamp (n) *[on document]* estampilla (f) *o* timbre (m)

stamp (v) *[letter]* franquear *o* poner el sello

stamp (v) *[mark]* sellar *o* timbrar

stamp duty impuesto (m) del timbre

stand (n) local (m) de exposición *o* 'stand' (m)

stand down retirarse (de una elección)

stand security for avalar a

stand surety for someone avalar *o* afianzar

standard (adj) normal *o* estándar

standard (n) norma (f) *o* modelo (m) *o* patrón (m)

standard letter carta (f) tipo *o* carta estándar

standard rate (of tax) tasa (f) de impuestos normal

standardization normalización (f) *o* estandarización (f)

standardize normalizar *o* estandarizar

standby arrangements planes (mpl) de contingencia

standby credit crédito (m) de apoyo *o* crédito 'stand by'

standby ticket billete (m) en lista de espera

standing reputación (f)

standing order domiciliación (f) bancaria

staple (n) grapa (f)

staple (v) grapar

staple industry industria (f) principal

staple papers together grapar papeles

staple product producto (m) principal

stapler grapadora (f)

start (n) comienzo (m) o principio (m) o inicio (m)

start (v) comenzar o empezar

start-up puesta (f) en marcha (de un negocio)

start-up costs costes (mpl) o gastos (mpl) iniciales

starting (adj) inicial

starting date fecha (f) inicial

starting point punto (m) de partida

starting salary salario (m) inicial

state (n) estado (m)

state (v) declarar o afirmar

state-of-the-art muy moderno

statement declaración (f) o informe (m)

statement of account estado (m) de cuentas

statement of expenses relación (f) de gastos

station *[train]* estación (f)

statistical estadístico, -ca

statistical analysis análisis (m) estadístico

statistician estadístico, -ca

statistics estadísticas (fpl)

status status (m) o posición (f)

status inquiry petición (f) de informes sobre crédito

status symbol símbolo (m) de prestigio

statute of limitations ley (f) de prescripción

statutory statutario, -ria o reglamentario, -ria o legal

statutory holiday fiesta (f) oficial o vacaciones (fpl) reglamentarias

stay (n) *[time]* estancia (f) o permanencia (f)

stay (v) permanecer o quedarse o alojarse

stay of execution aplazamiento (m) de una sentencia

steadiness estabilidad (f)

sterling libra (f) esterlina

stevedore estibador (m)

stiff competition competencia (f) dura

stimulate the economy estimular la economía

stimulus estímulo (m)

stipulate estipular

stipulation estipulación (f)

stock (n) *[goods]* existencias (fpl)

stock (v) *[goods]* almacenar o tener existencias

stock code código (m) de almacenamiento

stock control control (m) de existencias

stock controller jefe, -fa de almacén

stock exchange bolsa (f)

stock level nivel (m) de existencias

stock list inventario (m) o lista (f) de existencias

stock market mercado (m) de valores o bolsa (f)

stock market valuation tasación (f) de acciones

stock movements movimientos (mpl) de existencias

stock of raw materials reservas (fpl) de materias primas

stock size talla (f) o tamaño (m) corriente

stock turnover rotación (f) de existencias

stock up acumular

stock valuation valoración (f) de existencias

stockbroker corredor, -ra o agente (mf) de bolsa

stockbroking correduría (f) de bolsa

stockist distribuidor, -ra

stockpile (n) reservas (fpl)

stockpile (v) acumular

stockroom almacén (m) o depósito (m)

stocktaking inventario (m)

stocktaking sale liquidación (f) de inventario

stop (n) parada (f) o alto (m)

stop (v) parar o frenar o detener

stop a cheque detener el pago de un cheque

stop an account suspender una cuenta

stop payments suspender pagos

stoppage suspensión (f) o paro (m)

stoppage of payments suspensión (f) de pagos

storage (n) almacenaje (m)

storage (n) [cost] coste (m) de almacenaje

storage (n) [in warehouse] depósito (m) o almacenamiento (m)

storage capacity capacidad (f) de almacenaje

storage facilities instalaciones (fpl) de almacenaje

storage unit unidad (f) de almacenaje

store (n) almacén (m) o depósito (m)

store (n) [items kept] reserva (f)

store (n) [large shop] grandes almacenes (mpl)

store (v) almacenar o guardar

storeroom almacén (m) o depósito (m)

storm damage daños (mpl) por tormenta

straight line depreciation amortización (f) anual uniforme o lineal

strategic estratégico, -ca

strategic planning planificación (f) estratégica

strategy estrategia (f)

street directory guía (f) urbana o callejero (m)

strength fuerza (f) o vitalidad (f)

strike (n) huelga (f)

strike: go on strike ir a la huelga

strike (v) ir a la huelga o declararse en huelga

striker huelguista (mf)

strong fuerte o vigoroso, -sa o firme

strong currency moneda (f) fuerte

structural estructural

structural adjustment ajuste (m) estructural

structural unemployment paro (m) estructural

structure (n) estructura (f)

structure (v) [arrange] estucturar

study (n) estudio (m)

study (v) estudiar

sub judice sub judice o en manos de los tribunales

subcontract (n) subcontrato (m)

subcontract (v) subcontratar

subcontractor subcontratista (mf)

subject (n) asunto (m) o tema (f)

subject to sujeto, -ta a

sublease (n) subarriendo (m)

sublease (v) subarrendar

sublessee subarrendatario, -ria

sublessor subarrendador, -ra

sublet subarrendar

subsidiary (adj) subsidiario, -ria o secundario, -ria

subsidiary (n) filial (f)

subsidiary company compañía (f) filial o compañía subsidiaria

subsidize subvencionar

subsidy subsidio (m) o subvención (f)

subtotal total (m) parcial

subvention subvención (f)

succeed [do well] tener éxito o prosperar

succeed [follow someone] suceder

succeed in conseguir hacer algo

success éxito (m)

successful afortunado, -da o próspero, -ra

successful bidder adjudicatario, -ria

sue demandar

suffer damage sufrir daños

sufficient suficiente

sum suma (f) o total (m)

summons citación (f) judicial o emplazamiento (m)

sundries or **sundry items** artículos (mpl) varios

superior (adj) [better quality] superior

supermarket supermercado (m)

superstore hipermercado (m)

supervise supervisar

supervision supervisión (f)

supervisor supervisor, -ra

supervisory de supervisión o de control

supplement suplemento (m)

supplementary suplementario, -ria

supplier suministrador, -ra o proveedor, -ra o abastecedor, -ra

supply (n) [action] oferta (f) o abastecimiento (m) o suministro (m)

supply (n) [stock of goods] reserva (f) o provisión (f)

supply (v) suministrar *o* abastecer *o* proveer

supply and demand oferta (f) y demanda

supply price precio (m) de oferta

supply side economics economía (f) de oferta

support (v) respaldar *o* apoyar

support price precio (m) de subvención

surcharge sobretasa (f) *o* recargo (m)

surety (n) *[person]* garante (mf) *o* fiador, -ra

surety (n) *[security]* fianza (f) *o* garantía (f)

surface (n) superficie (f)

surface mail correo (m) por vía terrestre o marítima

surface transport transporte (m) por carretera o por vía marítima

surplus excedente (m) *o* exceso (m) *o* superávit (m)

surplus dividend dividendo (m) por superávit

surrender (n) *[insurance policy]* rescate (m)

surrender a policy rescatar una póliza

surrender value valor (m) de rescate

survey (n) *[examination]* inspección (f)

survey (n) *[general report]* estudio (m) *o* informe (m)

survey (v) *[inspect]* inspeccionar

surveyor inspector, -ra de obra

suspend suspender

suspension suspensión (f)

suspension of deliveries suspensión (f) de entregas

suspension of payments suspensión (f) de pagos

swap (n) intercambio (m)

swap (v) cambiar *o* intercambiar

swatch muestra (f) pequeña

switch (v) *[change]* cambiar

switch over to cambiarse a *o* pasarse a

switchboard centralita (f)

swop (= swap) intercambio (m)

symbol (n) símbolo (m)

sympathy strike huelga (f) de solidaridad

synergy sinergia (f)

system sistema (m)

systems analysis análisis (m) de sistemas

systems analyst analista (mf) de sistemas

Tt

tabulate tabular

tabulation tabulación (f)

tabulator tabulador, -ra

tachograph tacógrafo (m)

tacit agreement acuerdo (m) tácito

tacit approval aprobación (f) tácita

take (n) *[money received]* ingresos (mpl) *o* recaudación (f)

take (v) tomar

take (v) *[need]* llevar *o* hacer falta

take (v) *[receive money]* ingresar en caja *o* recibir

take a call recibir una llamada

take a risk arriesgarse

take action tomar medidas

take legal action entablar un pleito

take legal advice consultar a un abogado

take note tomar nota

take off *[deduct]* rebajar *o* quitar

take off *[plane]* despegar

take on freight fletar

take on more staff emplear más personal

take out a policy hacerse un seguro

take over tomar posesión *o* hacerse cargo *o* sustituir

take place tener lugar

take someone to court llevar a alguien ante los tribunales

take stock hacer un inventario

take the initiative tomar la iniciativa

take the soft option decidirse por la opción más fácil

take time off work tomarse tiempo libre (durante el trabajo)

take up an option suscribir una opción

takeover adquisición (f)

takeover bid oferta (f) pública de adquisición (OPA)

takeover target objeto (m) de una OPA

takings ingresos (mpl) o recaudación (f) (de un negocio)

tangible tangible

tangible assets activo (m) tangible

tanker buque (m) cisterna o petrolero (m)

tare tara (f)

target (n) objetivo (m) o meta (f)

target (v) tener como objetivo

target market mercado (m) previsto

tariff *[price]* tarifa (f) o precio (m)

tariff barriers barreras (fpl) arancelarias

task tarea (f)

tax (n) impuesto (m)

tax (v) gravar con un impuesto

tax adjustment ajuste (m) impositivo

tax allowance desgravación (f) fiscal

tax assessment cálculo (m) de la base impositiva

tax avoidance evasión (f) o elusión (f) de impuestos

tax code código (m) impositivo o código fiscal

tax collection recaudación (f) de impuestos

tax collector recaudador, -ra de impuestos

tax concession desgravación (f) fiscal o privilegio (m) fiscal

tax consultant asesor, -ra fiscal

tax credit crédito (m) por impuestos pagados

tax deducted at source impuestos (mpl) retenidos en el origen

tax deductions retención (f) fiscal o deducción (f) de impuestos

tax evasion evasión (f) de impuestos o fraude (m) fiscal

tax exemption exención (f) fiscal

tax form formulario (m) de declaración de la renta

tax haven paraíso (m) fiscal

tax inspector inspector, -ra de Hacienda

tax loophole laguna (f) fiscal

tax offence infracción (f) fiscal

tax paid impuesto (m) pagado

tax rate tipo (m) impositivo o tipo de gravamen

tax reductions reducción (f) de los impuestos

tax relief desgravación (f) fiscal

tax return *or* **tax declaration** declaración (f) de renta

tax shelter amparo (m) fiscal

tax system sistema (m) tributario

tax year año (m) fiscal o ejercicio (m) fiscal

tax-deductible desgravable

tax-exempt exento, -ta de impuestos

tax-free libre de impuestos

taxable sujeto, -ta a impuesto o imponible

taxable income renta (f) imponible

taxation imposición (f) o impuesto (m)

taxpayer contribuyente (mf)

teach (v) enseñar

technique técnica (f)

telephone (n) teléfono (m)

telephone (v) telefonear o llamar

telephone book guía (f) telefónica

telephone call llamada (f) telefónica

telephone directory guía (f) telefónica

telephone exchange central (f) telefónica

telephone line línea (f) telefónica

telephone number número (m) de teléfono

telephone subscriber abonado (m) telefónico

telephone switchboard centralita (f) telefónica

telephonist telefonista (mf)

telesales ventas (fpl) por teléfono

telex (n) télex (m)

telex (v) enviar por télex

teller cajero, -ra de un banco

temp (n) secretario, -ria eventual o interino, -ina

temp (v) hacer trabajo eventual

temp agency agencia (f) de trabajo temporal

temporary employment ocupación (f) temporal *o* empleo (m) eventual

temporary staff personal (m) eventual

tenancy *[agreement]* contrato (m) de arrendamiento (m)

tenancy *[period]* periodo (m) de arrendamiento (m)

tenant inquilino, -na *o* arrendatario, -ria

tender (n) *[offer to work]* oferta (f)

tender for a contract licitar para un contrato

tenderer postor (m) *o* licitador (m)

tendering oferta (f)

tenure *[right]* tenencia (f) *o* ocupación (f) *o* posesión (f)

tenure *[time]* mandato (m)

term *[part of academic year]* trimestre (m)

term *[time of validity]* plazo (m) *o* término (m)

term insurance seguro (m) temporal

term loan préstamo (m) a plazo fijo

terminal (adj) terminal

terminal bonus bonificación (f) recibida al concluir un seguro

terminate terminar

terminate an agreement poner término a un acuerdo

termination terminación (f)

termination clause cláusula (f) resolutoria

terms condiciones (fpl) *o* términos (mpl)

terms of employment condiciones (fpl) de servicio

terms of payment condiciones (fpl) de pago

terms of reference mandato (m) *o* campo (m) de aplicación

terms of sale condiciones (fpl) de venta

territory territorio (m)

tertiary industry industria (f) terciaria *o* industria de los servicios

tertiary sector sector (m) terciario *o* sector de los servicios

test (n) examen (m) *o* ensayo (m) *o* prueba (f)

test (v) probar *o* someter a prueba

text texto (m)

theft robo (m)

third party tercero (m)

third quarter tercer trimestre (m)

third-party insurance seguro (m) contra terceros

threshold umbral (m)

threshold price precio (m) umbral

throughput rendimiento (m)

ticket (n) billete (m) *o* entrada (f)

tie-up *[link]* enlace (m) *o* conexión (f)

tight money dinero (m) escaso

tighten up on intensificar (el control)

till (n) caja (f)

time and motion study estudio (m) de desplazamientos y tiempos

time deposit depósito (m) *o* imposición (f) a plazo

time limit plazo (m) *o* término (m)

time limitation plazo (m) de tiempo límite

time rate tarifa (f) horaria *o* tarifa por horas

time scale calendario (m)

time: on time a tiempo

timetable (n) horario (m) *o* calendario (m)

timetable (v) preparar un horario

timing medida (f) de tiempo

tip (n) *[advice]* confidencia (f)

tip (n) *[money]* propina (f)

tip (v) *[give money]* dar una propina

tip (v) *[say what might happen]* pronosticar *o* prevenir

TIR (= Transports Internationaux Routiers) Transporte Internacional por Carretera

token símbolo (m)

token charge precio (m) simbólico

token payment pago (m) simbólico

toll peaje (m)

toll free (US) a cobro revertido

toll free number (US) número (m) de llamada gratuita

ton tonelada (f)

tonnage tonelaje (m)

tonne tonelada (f) métrica

tool (n) herramienta (f)

tool up instalar la maquinaria en una fábrica

top (adj) superior *o* principal

top (n) *[highest point]* cima (f) *o* cumbre (f)

top (n) *[upper surface]* parte (f) superior

top (v) *[go higher than]* superar

top management alta dirección (f)

top quality alta calidad (f) *o* calidad superior

top-selling más vendido, -da

total (adj) total

total (n) total (m) *o* totalidad (f)

total (v) totalizar *o* sumar

total amount cantidad (f) total

total assets activos (mpl) totales

total cost coste (m) total

total expenditure gastos (mpl) totales

total income renta (f) total

total invoice value valor (m) total de factura

total output producción (f) total

total revenue ingreso (m) total

track record antecedentes (mpl)

trade (n) *[business]* comercio (m)

trade (v) comerciar

trade agreement acuerdo (m) *o* tratado (m) comercial

trade association agrupación (f) sectorial

trade cycle ciclo (m) económico

trade deficit *or* **trade gap** déficit (m) comercial

trade description descripción (f) comercial

trade directory guía (f) comercial

trade discount descuento (m) para comerciantes del sector

trade fair feria (f) comercial

trade in *[buy and sell]* comerciar

trade-in canje (m) parcial

trade-in price precio (m) con entrega de artículo usado

trade journal *or* **trade magazine** revista (f) profesional especializada

trade mission misión (f) comercial

trade price precio (m) al detallista

trade terms descuento (m) para comerciantes del sector

trade union sindicato (m)

trade unionist sindicalista (mf)

trademark *or* **trade name** marca (f) comercial *o* nombre (m) comercial

trader comerciante (mf)

trading comercio (m)

trading company sociedad (f) comercial

trading loss pérdida (f) de ejercicio

trading partner empresa (f) que comercia con otra

trading profit beneficios (mpl) de explotación

train (n) tren (m)

train (v) *[learn]* prepararse *o* formarse *o* aprender

train (v) *[teach]* preparar *o* capacitar *o* formar

trainee aprendiz, -za

traineeship aprendizaje (m)

training aprendizaje (m) *o* capacitación (f) *o* formación (f)

training levy impuesto (m) para financiar la formación profesional

training officer responsable (mf) de la capacitación

transact business hacer negocios

transaction transacción (f) *o* operación (f)

transfer (n) traslado (m) *o* transferencia (f)

transfer (n) *[travel]* transbordo (m)

transfer (v) *[move to new place]* trasladar *o* transferir

transfer fee traspaso (m)

transfer of funds transferencia (f) de fondos

transferable transferible

transferred charge call llamada (f) a cobro revertido

transit tránsito (m)

transit lounge sala (f) de tránsito

transit visa visado (m) de tránsito

translate traducir

translation traducción (f)

translation bureau agencia (f) de traducciones

translator traductor, -ra

transport (n) transporte (m)

transport (v) transportar *o* llevar

transport facilities medios (mpl) de transporte

treasury Tesoro (m) *o* Hacienda (f) Pública

treble triplicar

trend tendencia (f)

trial *[court case]* proceso (m) *o* juicio (m)

trial *[test of product]* prueba (f) *o* ensayo (m)

trial and error tanteo (m)

trial balance balance (m) de comprobación

trial period periodo (m) de prueba

trial sample muestra (f)

triple (adj) triple

triple (v) triplicar

triplicate: in triplicate por triplicado

troubleshooter mediador, -ra

troubleshooting (n) investigación (f) de conflictos

truck *[lorry]* camión (m)

truck *[railway wagon]* vagón (m) (de ferrocarril)

trucker camionero, -ra

trucking acarreo (m) *o* transporte (m) por carretera

true (adj) verdadero, -ra

true copy compulsa (f) *o* copia (f) exacta

trust company compañía (f) fiduciaria

turn down rechazar

turn over (v) *[make sales]* girar (volumen de ventas)

turnkey operation operación (f) llaves en mano

turnkey operator agente (mf) de operaciones llaves en mano

turnover *[of staff]* rotación (f) de personal

turnover *[of stock]* rotación (f) (de mercancías)

turnover *[sales]* volumen (m) de ventas *o* cifra (f) de negocios

turnover tax impuesto (m) sobre el volumen de ventas

turnround *[goods sold]* rotación (f) de existencias

turnround *[making profitable]* reactivación (f)

turnround *[of plane]* descarga (f) y carga de un avión

Uu

unaccounted for inexplicado, -da *o* desaparecido, -da *o* sin figurar

unaudited no verificado, -da

unaudited accounts cuentas (fpl) sin verificar

unauthorized expenditure gastos (mpl) no autorizados

unavailability indisponibilidad (f)

unavailable inasequible

unchanged inalterado, -da *o* invariable

unchecked figures cifras (fpl) sin comprobar

unclaimed baggage equipaje (m) no reclamado

unconditional incondicional *o* sin condiciones

unconfirmed sin confirmar

undated sin fecha

undelivered no entregado, -da

under *[according to]* conforme a *o* según

under *[down]* abajo

under *[less than]* por debajo de *o* menos de

under construction en construcción

under contract bajo contrato

under control bajo control

under new management cambio (m) de dirección

undercharge cobrar de menos

undercut a rival vender a precio más bajo que un rival

underdeveloped countries países (mpl) subdesarrollados

underequipped mal equipado, -da

underpaid mal pagado, -da

undersell vender más barato

undersigned abajo firmante (mf)

underspend gastar menos

understand entender *o* comprender

understanding acuerdo (m)

undertake emprender *o* encargarse de *o* comprometerse

undertaking *[company]* empresa (f)

undertaking *[promise]* compromiso (m) *o* promesa (f)

underwrite *[guarantee]* avalar

underwrite *[pay costs]* garantizar el pago

underwriting syndicate consorcio (m) asegurador *o* emisor

undischarged bankrupt quebrado (m) no rehabilitado

uneconomic rent renta (f) que no llega a cubrir los costes

unemployed parado, -da *o* desempleado, -da

unemployment paro (m) *o* desempleo (m)

unemployment pay subsidio (m) de paro

unexplained inexplicado, -da

unfair injusto, -ta

unfair competition competencia (f) desleal

unfair dismissal despido (m) injusto

unfavourable desfavorable *o* adverso, -sa

unfavourable exchange rate tipo (m) de cambio desfavorable

unfulfilled order pedido (m) no servido *o* pedido por servir

unilateral unilateral

union sindicato (m)

union recognition reconocimiento (m) de un sindicato

unique selling point *or* **proposition (USP)** argumento (m) de venta

unit unidad (f)

unit *[in unit trust]* título (m)

unit cost coste (m) unitario *o* coste por unidad

unit price precio (m) por unidad

unit trust fondos (mpl) mutuos *o* fondos de inversión

unite (v) unir

unlimited liability responsabilidad (f) ilimitada

unload (v) descargar

unload *[get rid of]* deshacerse de

unobtainable inalcanzable *o* imposible de conseguir

unofficial extraoficial *o* no oficial *o* oficioso, -sa

unpaid impagado, -da *o* sin pagar

unpaid invoices facturas (fpl) impagadas

unsealed envelope sobre (m) abierto

unsecured creditor acreedor, -ra común *o* sin garantía

unskilled no cualificado, -da

unsold no vendido, -da *o* sin vender

unsubsidized no subvencionado, -da

unsuccessful fracasado, -da *o* sin éxito

up front por adelantado

up to hasta

up to date actual *o* moderno, -na *o* al día

up-market de primera calidad

update (n) actualización (f)

update (v) actualizar *o* poner al día

updating (n) actualización (f) *o* puesta (f) al día

upset price precio (m) inicial

upturn mejora (f) *o* reactivación (f)

upward trend tendencia (f) alcista

urgent urgente

use (n) uso (m)

use (v) emplear *o* usar *o* utilizar

use up spare capacity utilizar capacidad ociosa

useful útil

user usuario, -ria

user-friendly de fácil uso *o* de fácil manejo

USP (= unique selling point *or* **proposition)** argumento (m) de venta

usual normal *o* usual *o* habitual

utilization utilización (f) *o* uso (m)

Vv

vacancy *[for job]* plaza (f) *o* vacante (f)

vacant vacante *o* libre *o* disponible

vacate desocupar

valid válido, -da *o* valedero, -ra

validity validez (f)

valuation valoración (f) *o* evaluación (f) *o* tasación (f)

value (n) valor (m)

value (v) valorar *o* tasar *o* evaluar

value added tax (VAT) impuesto (m) sobre el valor añadido (IVA)

valuer tasador, -ra

van camioneta (f)

variable costs costes (mpl) variables

variance variación (f) *o* discrepancia (f)

variation variación (f)

VAT (= value added tax) IVA (impuesto sobre el valor añadido)

VAT declaration declaración (f) del IVA

VAT inspector inspector, -ra del IVA

VAT invoice factura (f) con el IVA

vehicle vehículo (m)

vendor vendedor, -ra

venture (n) *[business]* empresa (f)

venture (v) *[risk]* arriesgar

venture capital capital-riesgo (m)

venue lugar (m) *o* punto (m) de reunión

verbal verbal

verbal agreement acuerdo (m) verbal

verification verificación (f)

verify verificar

vertical communication comunicación (f) vertical

vertical integration integración (f) vertical

vested interest interés (m) personal *o* intereses (mpl) creados

veto a decision vetar una decisión

via por *o* vía

viable viable

violate (v) violar

VIP lounge salón (m) VIP (salón de personalidades)

visa visado (m)

visible imports importaciones (fpl) visibles

visible trade comercio (m) de visibles

visit (n) visita (f)

visit (v) visitar

void (adj) *[not valid]* nulo, -la *o* inválido, -da

void (v) invalidar

volume volumen (m)

volume discount descuento (m) por volumen

volume of sales volumen (m) de ventas

volume of trade *or* volume of business volumen (m) comercial *o* volumen de negocios

voluntary liquidation liquidación (f) voluntaria

voluntary redundancy baja (f) incentivada *o* voluntaria

vote of thanks voto (m) de gracias

voucher bono (m) *o* vale (m)

voucher *[document from an auditor]* comprobante (m)

Ww

wage sueldo (m) *o* salario (m)

wage claim reivindicación (f) salarial

wage freeze congelación (f) de salarios

wage levels niveles (mpl) de salarios

wage negotiations negociaciones (fpl) salariales

wage scale escala (f) salarial *o* escala de salarios

waive a payment renunciar a un pago

waiver *[of right]* renuncia (f)

waiver clause cláusula (f) de renuncia

warehouse (n) almacén (m)

warehouse (v) almacenar

warehouseman almacenista (mf)

warehousing almacenaje (m)

warn (v) avisar

warning (n) aviso (m) *o* advertencia (f)

warrant (n) *[document]* autorización (f) *o* orden (f)

warrant (v) *[guarantee]* garantizar

warrant (v) *[justify]* justificar

warranty (n) garantía (f)

wastage pérdida (f) *o* desperdicio (m)

waste (n) desperdicio (m) *o* desecho (m) *o* residuos (mpl)

waste (v) *[use too much]* desperdiciar *o* malgastar

waybill carta (f) de porte

weak (adj) débil *o* flojo, -ja

weak market mercado (m) débil

wear and tear desgaste (m) natural *o* normal

week semana (f)

weekly semanalmente

weigh pesar

weighbridge báscula (f) puente *o* puente-báscula (m)

weight peso (m)

weight limit peso (m) máximo

weighted average promedio (m) ponderado *o* media (f) ponderada

weighted index índice (m) ponderado

weighting ponderación (f)

welcome (n) acogida (f)

welfare (n) bienestar (m)

well-paid job trabajo (m) bien remunerado

wharf muelle (m) *o* embarcadero (m)

white knight rescatador, -ra de empresas

whole-life insurance seguro (m) corriente de vida

wholesale (adv) al por mayor

wholesale dealer mayorista (mf) *o* comerciante (mf) al por mayor

wholesale discount descuento (m) al por mayor

wholesale price precio (m) al por mayor

wholesale price index índice (m) de precios al por mayor

wholesaler mayorista (mf) *o* comerciante (mf) al por mayor

wide (adj) amplio, -plia

wildcat strike huelga (f) salvaje

win a contract conseguir un contrato

wind up *[a company]* liquidar una sociedad

wind up *[a meeting]* terminar *o* concluir

winding up liquidación (f)

window ventana (f)

window display escaparate (m)

withdraw retirar (una oferta) *o* sacar (dinero)

withdraw a takeover bid retirar una oferta de adquisición

withdrawal *[of money]* retirada (f) *o* retiro (m) *o* reintegro (m)

withholding tax retención (f) de impuestos en origen

witness (n) testimonio (m) *o* testigo (mf)

witness (v) *[a document]* firmar como testigo

witness an agreement actuar de testigo

word-processing tratamiento (m) de textos

wording texto (m)

work (n) trabajo (m)

work (v) trabajar

work in progress trabajo (m) en curso

work permit permiso (m) de trabajo

work-to-rule huelga (f) de celo *o* paro (m) técnico

worker trabajador, -ra *o* obrero, -ra *o* operario, -ria

worker director delegado, -da del personal

workforce mano (f) de obra

working capital capital (m) operativo *o* capital circulante

working conditions condiciones (fpl) de trabajo

working party grupo (m) de trabajo

workman obrero (m)

workshop taller (m)

workstation *[at computer]* estación (f) *o* puesto (m) de trabajo

world mundo (m)

world market mercado (m) mundial

worldwide (adj) mundial *o* global

worldwide (adv) mundialmente

worry (n) inquietud (f) *o* preocupación (f)

worth (n) *[value]* valor (m)

worth: be worth valer

worthless sin valor

wrap up *[goods]* envolver

wrapper *or* **wrapping** envoltorio (m)

wrapping paper papel (m) de envolver

wreck (n) *[company]* empresa (f) en ruinas

wreck (n) *[ship]* naufragio (m)

wreck (v) *[ruin]* naufragar *o* fracasar

writ orden (f) *o* mandato (m)

write escribir

write down *[assets]* depreciar el valor de un activo

writedown *[of asset]* depreciación (f) de un activo

write off *[debt]* anular *o* cancelar

write-off *[loss]* deuda (f) incobrable *o* pérdida (f) total

write out copiar *o* escribir sin abreviar

write out a cheque extender un cheque

writing escrito (m) *o* escritura (f) *o* letra (f)

written agreement acuerdo por escrito

wrong erróneo, -nea *o* equivocado, -da

wrongful dismissal despido (m) injusto

Xx Yy Zz

year año (m)

year end cierre (m) del ejercicio

yearly payment pago (m) anual

yellow pages páginas (fpl) amarillas

yield (n) *[on investment]* rendimiento (m) *o* producción (f) *o* renta (f)

yield (v) *[interest]* rendir *o* devengar

young joven

younger más joven *o* menor

zero cero (m)

zero-rated con un IVA del 0%

zip code (US) código (m) postal

Español-Inglés
Spanish-English

Aa

abajo down *or* under *or* below

abajo firmante (mf) undersigned (n)

abandonar leave (v) *or* abandon (v)

abandono (m) de responsabilidad disclaimer (n)

abarrotar overstock (v)

abastecedor (-ra) supplier

abastecer supply (v) *or* cater for (v)

abastecimiento (m) supply (n)

abierto (-ta) open (adj)

abierto por la noche late-night opening

abogado (-da) lawyer (n) *or* solicitor (n) *or* counsel (n)

abogado defensor defence counsel

abogado especializado en derecho marítimo maritime lawyer

abonado (-da) telefónico (-ca) telephone subscriber

abonar pay (v) *or* pay out (v)

abonar *[acreditar]* credit (v)

abono (m) *[billete]* season ticket (n)

abono (m) *[crédito]* credit entry (n)

abordar *[embarcarse]* board (v)

abrir open (v)

abrir la sesión open a meeting

abrir un negocio open (v) *or* start (v) new business

abrir una carta de crédito issue a letter of credit

abrir una cuenta open an account

abrir una cuenta bancaria open a bank account

abrir una línea de crédito open a line of credit

abundancia (f) abundance (n) *or* glut (n)

acabado (-da) finished (adj)

acaparamiento (m) hoarding

acaparar *[acumular]* hoard (v)

acaparar *[capturar]* capture (v)

acaparar el mercado corner (v) the market *or* monopolize (v)

acarreo (m) haulage (n)

acarreo *[transporte]* trucking (n)

acarreo: gastos de acarreo haulage costs *or* haulage rates

acatar respect (v) *or* obey (v)

accesible accessible (adj)

acceso (m) access (n)

acceso *[mercado]* entry (n)

accesorios (mpl) fittings (n)

accidente (m) accident (m)

accidente industrial industrial accident

accidente laboral occupational accident

acción (f) action (n)

acción (f) *[finanzas]* share (n)

acción de primera categoría blue chip (n)

acción legal (legal) action

acción preferente acumulativa cumulative preference share

acciones (fpl) ordinarias ordinary shares *or* equities (n)

acciones poco buscadas en la bolsa neglected shares

acciones preferentes preference shares

acciones que se cotizan en bolsa quoted shares

accionista (mf) shareholder (n)

accionista importante major shareholder

accionista mayoritario majority shareholder

accionista minoritario minority shareholder

aceite (m) oil (n)

aceptable acceptable (adj)

aceptación (f) acceptance (n)

aceptación de una oferta acceptance of an offer

aceptación irrevocable irrevocable acceptance

aceptar accept (v) *or* allow (v) *or* agree (v)

aceptar hacer algo agree to do something

aceptar la entrega de mercancías accept delivery of a shipment

aceptar la responsabilidad de algo accept liability for something

aceptar una letra accept a bill

aclaración (f) explanation (n)

aclarar clear (v) *or* clarify (v)

acogida (f) reception (n) *or* welcome (n)

acomodamiento (m) composition (n) (with creditors)

acomodo (m) *[acuerdo]* arrangement (n)

aconsejar advise (v) *or* recommend (v)

acordado (-da) agreed (adj)

acordar agree (v)

acordarse (de) remember (v)

acotación (f) *[límite]* limit (n)

acreditar credit (v)

acreedor (-ra) creditor (n)

acreedor común *o* sin garantía unsecured creditor

acreedor con garantía secured creditor

acreedor diferido deferred creditor

acreedor hipotecario mortgagee (n)

acreedor preferente preferential creditor *or* preferred creditor

acta (f) *[registro]* record (n)

acta (f) de la reunión minutes (n)

acta (f) notarial affidavit (n)

Acta Unica Europea Single European Act

actividad (f) activity (n)

activo (m) asset (n)

activo (-va) active (adj) *or* go-ahead (adj)

activo circulante current assets

activo congelado frozen assets

activo fijo fixed assets

activo financiero financial asset

activo intangible intangible assets

activo invisible invisible assets

activo líquido liquid assets

activo neto net assets *or* net worth

activo realizable realizable assets

activo tangible tangible assets

activo y pasivo (m) assets and liabilities

activos (mpl) totales total assets

actuación (f) performance (n)

actual present (adj) *or* current (adj)

actual *[moderno]* up to date (adj)

actualización (f) update (n) *or* updating (n)

actualizar update (v)

actuar act (v) *or* perform (v)

actuar de testigo en la firma de un contrato witness an agreement

actuario (-ria) actuary (n)

acuerdo (m) agreement (n) *or* compromise (n)

acuerdo: negarse a cumplir un acuerdo repudiate an agreement

acuerdo *[arreglo]* arrangement (n) *or* understanding (n)

acuerdo *[después de un conflicto]* settlement (n)

acuerdo a tanto alzado fixed-price agreement

acuerdo bilateral *o* reciproco reciprocal agreement

acuerdo comercial trade agreement

acuerdo de doble imposición double taxation agreement

acuerdo (m) de comercialización marketing agreement

acuerdo de muchos años long-standing agreement

acuerdo de productividad productivity agreement

acuerdo entre caballeros gentleman's agreement

acuerdo global package deal (n)

acuerdo modificable open-ended agreement

acuerdo multilateral multilateral agreement

acuerdo por escrito written agreement

acuerdo tácito tacit agreement

acuerdo unilateral one-sided agreement

acuerdo verbal verbal agreement

acumulación (f) accrual (n)

acumulación de interés accrual of interest

acumulación de trabajo atrasado backlog (n)

acumular accumulate (v) *or* hoard (v)

acumular *[existencias]* stockpile (v) *or* stock up (v)

acumular en exceso overstock (v)

acumularse accumulate (v) *or* accrue (v)

acumulativo (-va) cumulative (adj)

acusación (f) accusation (n) *or* charge (n)

acusación *[parte acusadora]* prosecution (n)

acusado (-da) defendant (n)

acusar accuse (v) or charge (v)

acusar recibo de una carta acknowledge (v) receipt of a letter

acuse (m) de recibo acknowledgement (n)

ad valorem ad valorem

adecuado (-da) adequate (adj)

adelantado (-da) advanced (adj)

adelantado: por adelantado up front

adeudar debit (v)

adeudarse run (v) into debt

adeudo (m) debit entry (n)

adicional additional (adj)

adjudicación (f) adjudication (n)

adjudicar award (v)

adjudicar un contrato (a alguien) award a contract (to someone)

adjudicar un derecho (a alguien) assign (v) a right (to someone)

adjudicatario (-ria) successful bidder (n)

adjuntar attach (v) or enclose (v)

adjunto (-ta) deputy (n)

administración (f) administration (n)

administración de cartera portfolio management

administración local local government

administrador (-ra) judicial official receiver (n)

administrar manage (v)

administrar mal mismanage (v)

administrar una propiedad manage property

administrativo (-va) administrative (adj)

admisible acceptable (adj)

admitir admit (v)

adquirir acquire (v) or buy (v)

adquirir una compañía acquire a company

adquisición (f) acquisition (n) or takeover (n)

adquisición apalancada leveraged buyout (LBO)

aduana (f) customs (n)

Aduanas y Arbitrios Customs and Excise

aduanero (-ra) customs officer or customs official

adverso (-sa) unfavourable (adj)

advertencia (f) reminder (n) or warning (n)

aerograma (m) air letter (n)

aeropuerto (m) airport (n)

afianzar guarantee (v) or stand surety (v)

afiliación (f) affiliation (n) or membership (n)

afiliado (-da) affiliated (adj) or associate (adj)

afirmar firm (v)

afirmar [declarar] state (v)

afirmativo (-va) affirmative (adj)

afortunado (-da) successful (adj)

agencia (f) agency (n)

agencia de alquiler de viviendas letting agency

agencia de cambio bureau de change

agencia de cobro de morosos debt collection agency

agencia de informes comerciales credit agency

agencia de prensa news agency

agencia de publicidad advertising agency

agencia de trabajo temporal temp agency

agencia de traducciones translation bureau

agencia de transportes shipping agent

agencia exclusiva concession (n)

agenda (f) appointments book (n) or diary (n)

agenda de mesa desk diary

agente (mf) agent (n) or broker (n)

agente de aduanas customs broker

agente de operaciones llaves en mano turnkey operator

agente de patentes y marcas patent agent

agente de seguros insurance agent

agente del credere del credere agent

agente en exclusiva sole agent

agente expedidor forwarding agent or shipping clerk

agente marítimo shipping agent or ship broker

agio (m) [especulación] premium (n)

agotado (-da) out of stock

agotar las existencias sell out (v) *or* run out (v)

agrario (-ria) agricultural

agregado (-da) comercial commercial attaché

agrícola agricultural

agropecuario (-ria) agricultural

agrupación (f) group (n) *or* consolidation (n)

agrupación sectorial trade association

agrupar batch (v) *or* bracket together *or* consolidate (v)

agua: en aguas territoriales offshore

ahorrar save (v) *or* save up *or* save on

ahorrar: que ahorra energía energy-saving (adj)

ahorros (mpl) savings (n)

aire (m) air (n)

ajustado (-da) al coste de la vida index-linked

ajustar adjust (v) *or* gear (v)

ajustar *[cuadrar]* reconcile (v)

ajuste (m) adjustment (n)

ajuste estructural structural adjustment

ajuste financiero financial settlement

ajuste impositivo tax adjustment

ajuste fino fine tuning

ajustes (mpl) estacionales seasonal adjustments

albarán (m) delivery note (n)

alcanzar reach (v)

alcanzar el punto más alto peak (v)

alcista (mf) *[bolsa]* bull (n)

aleatorio (-ria) random (adj)

alegar claim (v)

alimentación (f) continua continuous feed

alimentador (m) del papel paper feed

almacén (m) warehouse (n) *or* store (n) *or* storeroom (n)

almacén *[depósito]* depository (n) *or* stockroom (n)

almacén central depot (n)

almacén de mercancías goods depot

almacén frigorífico cold store

almacenaje (m) storage (n) *or* warehousing (n)

almacenaje frigorífico cold storage

almacenamiento (m) storage (n)

almacenar store (v) *or* warehouse (v)

almacenar *[tener existencias]* stock (v)

almacenista (m) warehouseman

almuerzo (m) de negocios business lunch

alojarse stay (v)

alquilar rent (v) *or* let (v)

alquilar *[fletar]* charter (v)

alquilar un coche o una grúa hire (v) a car or a crane

alquilar una oficina let an office

alquiler (m) rental (n) *or* hire (n) *or* rent (n)

alquiler (m) *[medio de transporte]* charter (n) *or* chartering (n)

alquiler (m) elevado high rent

alternativa (f) alternative (n)

alternativo (-va) alternative (adj)

alta calidad high quality *or* premium quality *or* top quality

alta dirección top management

alto (-ta) high (adj)

alto (m)*[freno]* stop (n)

alza (f) rise (n)

amarradero (m) berth (n)

ámbito: de ámbito nacional nationwide (adj)

americano (-na) American (n & adj)

amo (m) owner (n)

amo *[jefe]* boss (n)

amortizable redeemable (adj)

amortización (f) amortization (n) *or* depreciation (n)

amortización *[rescate]* redemption (n)

amortización acelerada accelerated depreciation

amortización anual uniforme *o* **lineal** straight line depreciation

amortizar amortize (v) *or* depreciate (v)

amortizar *[redimir]* redeem (v)

amortizar una obligación redeem a bond

amparo (m) fiscal tax shelter (n)

ampliación (f) expansion (n) *or* extension (n)

ampliar expand (v) *or* extend (v)

amplio (-plia) wide (adj)

análisis (m) analysis

análisis coste-beneficio cost-benefit analysis

análisis de costes cost analysis

análisis de mercado market analysis

análisis de proyectos project analysis

análisis de sistemas systems analysis

análisis de un puesto de trabajo job analysis

análisis de ventas sales analysis

análisis estadístico statistical analysis

analista (mf) de mercado market analyst (n)

analista de sistemas systems analyst

analizar analyse (v) or analyze (v)

analizar las posibilidades del mercado analyse the market potential

anaquel (m) shelf (n)

andén (m) platform (n)

anexo (m) annex (n) or appendix (n)

anotación (f) entry (n)

anotar log (v) or note (v)

anotar [registrar] minute (v) or record (v)

anotar las llamadas recibidas log calls

anotar una contrapartida o un contraasiento contra an entry

antecedentes (mpl) track record

antedatar backdate (v) or antedate (v)

anteproyecto (m) draft plan or draft project

anterior prior (adj) or previous (adj)

antes: lo antes posible as soon as possible (a.s.a.p.)

anticipado (-da) advance (adj)

anticipar advance (v)

anticipar [prever] anticipate (v)

anticipo (m) advance (n)

anticipo a cuenta advance on account

anticipo de caja a cuenta cash advance

anticuado (-da) dated (adj) or out of date or old-fashioned

antiguo (-gua) old (adj) or old-established

antiguo: más antiguo senior

anual annual (adj)

anualmente annually (adv) or on an annual basis

anulación (f) cancellation (n)

anular cancel (v)

anular [deuda] write off (v)

anular un acuerdo call off a deal

anular un cheque cancel a cheque

anular un contrato cancel a contract

anunciante (mf) advertiser (n)

anunciar announce (v) or advertise (v)

anunciar un nuevo producto advertise a new product

anunciar una vacante advertise a vacancy

anuncio [aviso] announcement (n) or notice (n)

anuncio (m) [publicitario] advertisement (n) or commercial (n)

anuncio del producto product advertising

anuncios (mpl) breves small ads

anuncios por palabras classified ads or advertisements

añadir add (v)

añadir el 10% por el servicio add on 10% for service

año (m) year (n)

año base base year

año civil calendar year

año fiscal financial year or tax year

año: al año per annum or per year

año: de muchos años long-standing

apalancamiento (m) gearing (n)

apalancamiento financiero leverage (n)

aparato (m) device (n) or instrument (n) or machine (n)

apartamento (m) apartment (n) or flat (n)

apelación (f) appeal (n)

apelar appeal (v)

apéndice (m) appendix (n)

apertura (f) opening (n)

aplazado (-da) deferred (adj) or postponed (adj)

aplazamiento (m) deferment (n) or postponement (n)

aplazamiento de pago deferment of payment

aplazamiento de una sentencia stay of execution

aplazar defer (v) or postpone (v) or put back (v) or hold over (v)

aplazar una reunión adjourn a meeting

aplicación (f) application (n) or enforcement (n)

aplicar apply (v)

apoderado (-da) attorney (n) or proxy (n)

apoyar back up (v) or support (v)

apoyo (m) financiero backing (n)

apoyo: con apoyo estatal government-backed

apreciación (f) appreciation (n)

apreciar appreciate (v)

aprecio (m) appreciation (n)

apremiar chase (v)

aprendiz (-za) apprentice (n) or trainee (n)

aprendizaje (m) training (n) or traineeship (n)

aprobación (f) approval (n)

aprobación tácita tacit approval

aprobar approve (v)

aprobar los términos de un contrato approve the terms of a contract

apropiación (f) indebida de fondos conversion of funds

apropiado (-da) appropriate (adj) or relevant (adj)

aprovechar capitalize on (v) or exploit (v)

aproximadamente approximately (adv)

aproximado (-da) approximate (adj)

aproximado (-da) *[cálculo]* rough (adj)

aptitud (f) capacity (n) or ability (n)

apuntar note (v) or log (v)

arancel (m) duty (n)

arancel aduanero customs tariff

arancel proteccionista protective tariff

arbitraje (m) arbitration (n)

arbitrar arbitrate (v) or moderate (v)

arbitrar un litigio adjudicate or arbitrate in a dispute

árbitro (mf) arbitrator (n) or adjudicator

archivador (m) filing cabinet

archivar save (v) or back up (v) or file (v)

archivar documentos file (v) documents

archivo (m) file (n) or computer file

archivos (mpl) records (n)

área (f) area (n)

argumento (m) argument (n)

argumento (m) de venta unique selling point or proposition (USP)

armonización (f) harmonization (n)

arreglar fix (v) or mend (v)

arreglárselas cope (v) or manage to (v)

arreglo (m) arrangement (n)

arrendador (-ra) lessor (n)

arrendamiento (m) lease (n)

arrendamiento financiero leasing (n)

arrendar lease (v) or let (v)

arrendar equipo lease equipment

arrendatario (-ria) lessee (n) or tenant (n)

arriendo (m) lease (n)

arriesgado (-da) risky

arriesgar risk (v) or venture (v)

arriesgarse take a risk

arrinconar shelve (v)

arruinado (-da) broke (adj)

arruinar bankrupt (v)

artículo (m) article (n) or item (n)

artículo de reclamo loss-leader

artículo único one-off item

artículos (mpl) con desperfectos seconds (n)

artículos de fácil venta fast-selling items

artículos de lujo luxury goods

artículos de papelería para oficina office stationery

artículos varios sundries (n) or sundry items or miscellaneous items

artículos perecederos perishable goods

asalariado (-da) salaried

asamblea (f) assembly (n) or meeting (n)

asamblea (f) de personal) staff meeting

ascender *[promoción]* promote (v)

ascender *[total]* run to (v) or amount to (v)

ascenso (m) promotion (n)

ascensor (m) lift (n)

asegurable insurable (adj)

asegurador (-ra) insurer (n)

asegurador de riesgos marinos marine underwriter

asegurar insure (v)

asegurar la vida de alguien assure someone's life

asequible available (adj) or obtainable (adj)

asesor (-ra) adviser (n) or advisor (n) or consultant (n)

asesor de empresas management consultant

asesor fiscal tax consultant

asesor jurídico legal adviser

asesoramiento (m) jurídico legal advice

asesoría (f) consultancy (firm)

asesoría jurídica legal department

asiento (m) entry (n)

asiento de débito debit entry

asignación (f) assignment (n)

asignación (f) de fondos funding

asignar allocate (v) or assign (v)

asignar *[fondos]* appropriate (v) or fund (v)

asignar fondos a un proyecto commit or earmark funds to a project

asignar personal man (v)

asistencia (f)*[ayuda]* assistance (n)

asistencia (f)*[reunión]* attendance (n)

asistido (-da) *[atendido]* attended (adj) or manned (adj)

asistido por ordenador computer-assisted

asistir *[ayudar]* assist (v)

asistir *[reunión]* attend (v)

asociación (f) association (n) or partnership (n)

asociado (-da) associate (adj)

aspirante (mf) candidate (n)

aspirar a aim (v)

asunto (m) matter (n) or subject (n)

asunto *[de negocios]* business (n)

asunto problemático problem area

atacar attack (v)

atasco (m) bottleneck (n)

atención (f) attention (n)

atención al cliente customer service

atención: a la atención de FAO (for the attention of)

atender serve (v)

atender a un cliente serve a customer

atender una demanda meet a demand

atendido (-da) manned (adj)

aterrizar land (v)

átono (-na) flat (adj) or dull (adj)

atracar berth (v) or dock (v)

atractivo (m) appeal (n) or attraction (n)

atractivo para los clientes customer appeal

atraer attract (v) or appeal to (v)

atrasado (-da) slow (adj)

atrasado *[pago]* late (adj) or overdue (adj)

atrasos (mpl) arrears (n)

auditar audit (v)

auditor (m) externo external auditor

auditor interno internal auditor

auditoría (f) audit (n) or auditing (n)

auditoría externa external audit

auditoría general general audit

auditoría interna internal audit

auge (m) boom (n)

aumentar *[subir]* raise (v) or increase (v) or climb (v) or mount up

aumentar *[ganar]* gain (v)

aumentar *[prosperar]* boom (v)

aumentar a escala scale up (v)

aumentar de precio increase in price

aumento (m) increase (n) or increment (n)

aumento: en aumento on the increase or increasing (adj)

aumento *[valor]* appreciation (n)

aumento anual medio mean annual increase

aumento de salario o **de sueldo** rise (n) or increase (n) or pay rise

aumento de sueldo por coste de vida cost-of-living increase

aumento retroactivo de salarios retroactive pay rise

ausencia (f) absence (n)

ausente absent (adj)

ausente del trabajo off *[away from work]*

autentificar authenticate (v)

autobús (m) bus (n)

autobús del aeropuerto airport bus

autoedición (f) desk-top publishing (DTP)

autofinanciación (f) self-financing (n)

autofinanciado (-da) self-financing (adj)

autónomo (-ma) self-employed

autorregulación (f) self-regulation

autorregulado (-da) self-regulatory

autoridad (f) authority (n)

autoridades (fpl) portuarias port authority

autorización (f) authorization (n) *or* warrant (n)

autorizado (-da) authorized (adj)

autorizar authorize (v) *or* entitle (v)

autorizar *[licencia]* license (v)

autorizar el pago authorize payment

autoservicio (m) mayorista cash and carry

auxiliar (mf) assistant (n)

auxiliar (mf) administrativo (-va) junior clerk

aval (m) guarantee (n)

avalar guarantee (v) *or* underwrite (v)

avalar a stand security or surety for

avalar una deuda guarantee a debt

avance (m) advance (n) *or* progress (n)

avanzar advance (v) *or* progress (v)

avería (f) *[máquina]* breakdown (n)

avería (f) *[seguro]* average (n)

avería gruesa general average

averiarse break down (v)

avión (m) plane (n)

avión charter charter plane

avión de carga freighter (n) *or* freight plane

avisar notify (v) *or* warn (v)

aviso (m) notice (n) *or* warning (n)

ayuda (f) assistance (n) *or* help (n)

ayudante (mf) assistant (n)

ayudante personal personal assistant (PA)

ayudar assist (v) *or* help (v)

azar: al azar random (adj)

Bb

baja (f) decline (n) *or* fall (n) *or* drop (n)

baja: con tendencia a la baja falling

baja incentivada *o* **voluntaria** voluntary redundancy

bajada (f) de precio decrease in price

bajar lower (v) *or* drop (v)

bajar *[disminuir]* decline (v) *or* fall *or* fall off

bajista (mf) bear (n)

bajo contrato under contract

bajo control under control

bajo (-ja) low (adj)

bajo: más bajo lower (adj)

balance (m) de comprobación trial balance

balance general *o* **de situación** balance sheet

balanza (f) comercial balance of trade

balanza comercial favorable favourable balance of trade

balanza de pagos balance of payments

banca (f) banking

bancarrota: en bancarrota bankrupt (adj)

banco (m) bank (n)

banco central central bank

banco comercial clearing bank

banco de crédito credit bank

banco de descuento discount house *or* discounter

banco emisor issuing bank

Banco Europeo de Inversiones (BEI) European Investment Bank (EIB)

banco mercantil merchant bank

banquero (-ra) banker

barato (-ta) cheap

barco (m) ship (n)

barco de carga cargo ship

barrera (f) barrier

barreras (fpl) arancelarias customs barriers *or* tariff barriers

basar base (v)

báscula (f) puente weighbridge

base (f) base (n) *or* basis

base de datos database

base monetaria monetary base

básico (-ca) basic (adj) *or* simple

beca (f) grant (n)

beneficiario (-ria) beneficiary

beneficiarse de benefit from (v)

beneficio (m) benefit (n) *or* profit *or* gain

beneficio antes de deducir los impuestos pretax profit *or* profit before tax

beneficio bruto gross profit

beneficio considerable healthy profit

beneficio de explotación operating profit

beneficio ficticio paper profit

beneficio neto net profit

beneficio neto de impuestos profit after tax

beneficio sobre el papel paper profit

beneficios (mpl) returns *or* profits

beneficios (mpl) *[participación]* equity

beneficios crecientes increasing profits

beneficios de explotación trading profit

beneficios de la empresa corporate profits

beneficios distribuibles distributable profit

beneficios extraordinarios excess profits

beneficios netos de impuestos after-tax profit

bien: muy bien fine (adv) *or* very good

bien (m) encubierto hidden asset

bienes (mpl) goods (n)

bienes (mpl) de capital *[activo fijo]* capital assets

bienes de capital *[equipo]* capital goods

bienes de consumo consumer goods

bienes de consumo duraderos consumer durables

bienes de equipo capital equipment

bienes duraderos durable goods

bienes personales personal assets

bienes raíces real estate

bienestar (m) welfare (n)

bilateral bilateral *or* reciprocal

billete (m) banknote *or* bill (n) (US)

billete (m) *[pasaje]* fare (n) *or* ticket (n)

billete abierto open ticket

billete de abono season ticket

billete de banco banknote *or* currency note *or* (US) bill

billete en lista de espera standby ticket

billete de ida *o* **pasaje sencillo** one-way fare

blanco (m) blank (n)

blanco: en blanco blank (adj)

blanquear (dinero negro) launder (money)

bloqueado (-da) frozen

bloquear block (v)

bloquear los créditos freeze credits

bodega (f) *[buque]* hold (n)

boicot (m) boycott (n)

boicotear boycott (v)

boletín (m) bulletin *or* journal

boletín de inscripción registration form

boletín de respuesta reply coupon

boletín interno de una empresa house magazine

bolsa (f) stock exchange *or* stock market

bolsa (f) *[bolsillo]* pocket (n)

bolsa (f) *[saco]* bag

bolsa de contratación commodity market *or* commodity exchange

bolsa de papel paper bag

bolsillo (m) pocket (n)

bombo (m) publicitario hype (n)

bonificación (f) bonus

bonificación recibida al concluir un seguro terminal bonus

bono (m) bond *or* debenture

bono (m) *[vale]* voucher

bono (m) de interés fijo debenture

bonos (mpl) del Tesoro gilts

bonos-basura (mpl) junk bonds

boom (m) boom (n)

bordo: a bordo on board

borrador (m) (rough) draft

bosquejo (m) rough draft *or* outline

brazo (m) derecho right-hand man

británico (-ca) British

bruto (-ta) gross (adj)

buen precio good value (for money)

buena calidad good quality

buena compra good buy

buena gestión good management

bueno (-na) good

bulto (m) packet (n)

buque (m) ship (n)

buque cisterna tanker

buque de carga freighter

buque de contenedores container ship

buque de salvamento salvage vessel

buque gemelo (de la misma flota)
sister ship

buque mercante merchant ship *or*
merchant vessel

burocracia (f) bureaucracy *or* red tape

búsqueda (f) de clientes canvassing

Cc

caber hold (v) *or* contain (v)

cada tres meses quarterly (adv)

cadena (f) chain

cadena de grandes almacenes
multiple store

cadena de montaje assembly line *or*
production line

caducado (-da) out of date

caducar *[expirar]* expire (v)

caducar *[prescribir]* lapse (v)

caducidad (f) *[expiración]* expiry

caer fall (v) *or* plummet

caer en picado slump (v)

caída (f) drop (n) *or* fall (n)

caída repentina slump (n)

caída de las ventas drop in sales *or*
slump in sales

caja (f) case (n) *or* box

caja (f) *[supermercado]* supermarket
checkout

caja (f) *[taquilla]* till *or* pay desk *or* cash
desk

caja de artículos sueltos para la venta
dump bin

caja de cartón carton *or* cardboard box

caja de embalar packing case

caja de seguridad safe deposit

caja fuerte safe (n)

caja para gastos menores petty cash
(box)

caja registradora cash register *or* cash
till

caja de caudales safe (n)

cajero (-ra) cashier

cajero (-ra) de un banco teller

cajero (m) automático cash dispenser

cajetilla (f) packet

cajetilla de cigarrillos packet of
cigarettes

cajón (m) crate (n)

calculadora (f) calculator

calculadora de bolsillo pocket
calculator

calcular calculate *or* count (v)

calcular *[estimar]* estimate (v)

calcular el promedio average (v)

calcular mal miscalculate (v)

cálculo (m) calculation *or* estimate

cálculo aproximado rough estimate *or*
rough calculation

cálculo de costos costing

cálculo de la base impositiva tax
assessment

calendario (m) time scale *or* timetable
(n)

calidad (f) quality

calidad: de baja calidad *o* de poca
calidad low-quality *or* low-grade

calidad: de calidad superior
high-grade

calidad: de primera calidad up-market

calidad de semicorrespondencia near
letter-quality (NLQ)

calidad superior *o* high quality top
quality

callejero (m) street directory

Cámara (f) de Comercio Chamber of
Commerce

cambiable exchangeable

cambiar change (v) *or* switch (v) *or*
swap (v)

cambiar de dueño change hands

cambiar divisas *o* **moneda extranjera** exchange (v) (currency)

cambiarse a *o* **pasarse a** switch over to

cambio (m) change

cambio (m) *[divisas]* exchange (n)

cambio (m) *[movimiento]* shift (n)

cambio de dirección under new management

cambio de moneda extranjera foreign exchange

cambio en especie bartering

cambio fijo fixed exchange rate

cambista (mf) money changer

camión (m) lorry *or* truck

camión con remolque articulated lorry *or* articulated vehicle

camión de carga pesada heavy goods vehicle (HGV)

camionero (-ra) lorry driver *or* trucker

camioneta (f) van

campaña (f) campaign

campaña de ventas sales campaign *or* sales drive

campaña publicitaria advertising campaign *or* publicity campaign

campo (m) area *or* field

campo (m) *[rural]* country

campo de aplicación *[mandato]* terms of reference

canal (m) channel (n)

canales (mpl) de distribución channels of distribution *or* distribution channels

cancelación (f) cancellation

cancelación de una cita cancellation of an appointment

cancelado (-da) off *or* cancelled

cancelar cancel *or* write off *[debt]*

candidato (-ta) candidate

candidato (-ta) a un puesto de trabajo applicant for a job

candidato (-ta) propuesto (-ta) nominee (n)

canje (m) parcial part exchange *or* trade-in

canjear exchange (v)

canon (m) royalty

cantidad (f) quantity (qty) *or* amount (n)

cantidad total total amount

capacidad (f) capacity

capacidad de almacenamiento *o* **de almacenaje** storage capacity

capacidad de endeudamiento borrowing power

capacidad de fabricación manufacturing capacity

capacidad hotelera hotel accommodation

capacidad industrial industrial capacity

capacitación (f) training

capacitado (-da) qualified

capacitar train (v) *or* qualify

capaz able *or* capable

capaz de capable of

capital (m) capital

capital circulante working capital

capital disponible available capital

capital en acciones equity capital *or* share capital

capital inicial initial capital

capital nominal nominal capital

capital-riesgo (m) risk capital *or* venture capital

capitalista (mf) capitalist

capitalización (f) capitalization

capitalización bursátil market capitalization

capitalización de las reservas capitalization of reserves

capitalizar capitalize

carga (f) cargo *or* shipment

carga aérea air freight

carga de un camión lorry-load

carga en cubierta deck cargo

carga por peso muerto deadweight cargo

carga útil payload

cargamento (m) load (n)

cargar load (v)

cargar en cuenta debit an account

cargar en exceso overcharge (v)

cargar un camión *o* **un barco** load a lorry *or* a ship

cargar una compra en cuenta charge a purchase

cargo (m) charge (n)

cargo: a cargo de chargeable (to)

cargo (m) *[puesto]* job title *or* position

cargos (mpl) adicionales additional charges

cargos en concepto de interés interest charges

carnet (m) *[socio]* membership card

carnet (m) *[documento]* carnet

caro (-ra) dear *or* expensive

caro: muy caro highly-priced

carpeta (f) folder (n)

carpeta: dar carpetazo a shelve (v)

carretera (f) road

carretilla (f) elevadora de horquilla fork-lift truck

carta (f) letter

carta adjunta *o* **explicatoria** covering letter *or* covering note

carta certificada registered letter

carta comercial business letter

carta de crédito letter of credit (L/C)

carta de crédito general circular letter of credit

carta de crédito irrevocable irrevocable letter of credit

carta de intención letter of intent

carta de nombramiento letter of appointment

carta de porte waybill

carta de presentación introduction *[letter]*

carta de reclamación letter of complaint

carta de recomendación letter of reference

carta de reiteración follow-up letter

carta de solicitud letter of application

carta tipo *o* **carta estándar** standard letter

carta urgente express letter

cartel (m) cartel

cartelera (f) hoarding *[for posters]*

cartera (f) *[maletín]* briefcase

cartera (de valores) portfolio

cartera con las iniciales personalized briefcase

cartón (m) cardboard *or* carton

cartulina (f) card *[material]*

casa (f) house *[for family]*

casa comercial business *or* house

casa: de la casa in-house

casa matriz parent company

cash flow (m) cash flow

cash flow actualizado discounted cash flow (DCF)

catalogar index (v)

catálogo (m) catalogue *or* list (n)

catálogo de ventas por correo mail-order catalogue

categoría (f) category

categoría (f) *[clase]* class *or* tax bracket

categoría: de segunda categoría second-class

causa (f) *[proceso]* court case

causa: a causa de owing to

cedente (mf) assignor

ceder en arriendo lease (v)

celebrar una reunión hold a meeting

censor (m) jurado de cuentas certified accountant

censor (-ra) auditor

central central

central (f) telefónica telephone exchange

centralita (f) switchboard

centralita telefónica telephone switchboard

centralización (f) centralization

centralización de las compras central purchasing

centralizar centralize

centro (m) centre

centro comercial business centre *or* shopping centre

centro de beneficios profit centre

centro de costes cost centre

centro de la ciudad city centre *or* downtown (n) (US)

centro de transporte depot

centro industrial industrial centre

centro de reparaciones service centre

cercano (-na) close to

cero (m) zero *or* nil

cerrado (-da) closed *or* shut (adj)

cerradura (f) lock (n)

cerrar close (v) *or* shut (v) *or* close down

cerrar *[sobre]* seal (v)

cerrar con llave lock (v)

cerrar un trato clinch a deal

cerrar una cuenta close an account

cerrar una cuenta bancaria close a bank account

cerrar una tienda *o* **una oficina** lock up a shop *or* an office

certificado (m) certificate

certificado de aduana clearance certificate

certificado de aprobación certificate of approval

certificado de depósito certificate of deposit

certificado de garantía certificate of guarantee

certificado de origen certificate of origin

certificado de registro certificate of registration

certificado (-da) registered (adj)

certificar certify (v) *or* register (v)

cesión (f) cession

cesión-arrendamiento (f) lease-back

cesionario (-ria) assignee

cheque (m) cheque

cheque abierto open cheque

cheque al portador cheque to bearer

cheque conformado certified cheque

cheque cruzado crossed cheque

cheque de administración cashier's check (US)

cheque de sueldo salary cheque *or* pay cheque

cheque en blanco blank cheque

cheque en pago de dividendos dividend warrant

cheque sin cruzar open cheque

cheque sin fondos rubber check (US)

chequeo (m) al azar random check

cheques (mpl) con el nombre impreso personalized cheques

chocar crash (v)

chófer (m) driver

choque (m) crash (n) *or* accident

cíclico (-a) cyclical

ciclo (m) cycle

ciclo de trabajo run (n) *or* work routine

ciclo del producto product cycle

ciclo económico economic cycle *or* trade cyle

ciento: por ciento per cent

cierre (m) closing (n) *or* closure

cierre: al cierre closing (adj)

cierre del ejercicio year end

cif (coste, seguro y flete) c.i.f. (= cost, insurance and freight)

cifra (f) figure

cifra de negocios turnover *or* sales

cifras (fpl) ajustadas estacionalmente seasonally adjusted figures

cifras de ventas sales figures

cifras estimadas estimated figures

cifras históricas historical figures

cifras reales actuals

cifras sin comprobar unchecked figures

cima (f) top (n) *or* peak *or* highest point

cinta (f) magnética magnetic tape *or* mag tape

circuito cerrado closed circuit TV

circulación (f) circulation *[of money]*

circular (f) circular (n) *or* circular letter

circular (v) run (v)

cita (f) appointment *or* meeting

citación (f) judicial summons

citar quote (v)

clarificar clear (v) * clarify (v)

claro (-ra) clear (adj) *or* easy to understand

clase (f) *[categoría]* class *or* tax bracket

clase: de primera clase first-class

clase económica *o* **turista** economy class

clase preferente (en aviones) business class

clasificación (f) classification *or* rating

clasificación crediticia credit rating

clasificar classify *or* index (v)

cláusula (f) clause *or* article

cláusula adicional rider

cláusula de excepción escape clause

cláusula de exclusión exclusion clause

cláusula de reembolso payback clause

cláusula de renuncia waiver clause

cláusula de rescisión cancellation clause

cláusula penal penalty clause

cláusula que prohibe la huelga no-strike agreement *or* no-strike clause

cláusula resolutoria termination clause

clausura (f) closure

clausurar una sesión close a meeting

clave (f) key

cliente (mf) client *or* customer

cliente habitual regular customer

clientela (f) clientele *or* custom

clientes (mpl) eventuales potential customers

clip (m) paperclip

club (m) club *or* society

co-propiedad (f) joint ownership

co-propietario (-ria) joint owner

coacreedor (-ra) co-creditor

coaseguro (m) co-insurance

cobertura (f) cover *or* hedge (n) *or* hedging

cobertura del dividendo dividend cover

cobertura del seguro insurance cover

cobertura periodística media coverage

cobrable cashable

cobrador (-ra) collector

cobrador (m) de alquileres rent collector

cobrar charge (v) *or* collect (v) *or* encash

cobrar: por cobrar receivable

cobrar a la entrega charges forward

cobrar de más overcharge (v)

cobrar de menos undercharge (v)

cobrar un cheque cash a cheque

cobrar una deuda collect a debt

cobro (m) collection

cobro a la entrega cash on delivery (c.o.d.)

cobro de morosos debt collection

cobro en metálico encashment

cobro por recogida collection charges *or* collection rates

cobro: a cobro revertido reversed charge *or* toll free (US)

coche (m) de alquiler hire car

coche en gran demanda best-selling car

codificación (f) coding

código (m) code

código de almacenamiento stock code

código de barras bar code

código fiscal *o* **código impositivo** tax code

código postal postcode *or* zip code (US) *or* area code

códigos (mpl) legibles por ordenador computer-readable codes

codirección (f) joint management

codirector (-ra) co-director

codirector (-ra) gerente joint managing director

coeficiente (m) rate (n)

coeficiente de amortización depreciation rate

coeficiente de ajuste de precios price differential

coeficiente de errores error rate

coeficiente de ocupación load factor

coeficiente de rentabilidad profitability

coincidir (con) agree with

colaboración (f) collaboration *or* contribution

colaborar collaborate

colateral collateral (adj)

colectivo (-va) collective

colgar: no cuelgue hold the line please

colocar place (v)

columna (f) del debe debit column

columna del haber credit column

comenzar begin *or* start (v)

comerciable marketable

comercial commercial (adj)

comercialización (f) commercialization *or* merchandizing

comercialización a gran escala mass marketing

comercializar commercialize (v) *or* merchandize (v)

comercializar un producto merchandize a product

comerciante (mf) dealer *or* merchant *or* trader *or* merchandizer

comerciante al por mayor wholesaler *or* wholesale dealer

comerciante al por menor retail dealer

comerciante exclusivo sole trader

comerciar handle (v) *or* sell

comerciar (en) deal in *or* trade in

comerciar con alguien deal with someone *or* do business with someone

comercio (m) commerce *or* trade (n) *or* trading

comercio al por menor retailing

comercio de exportación export trade

comercio de visibles visible trade

comercio exterior external trade *or* export trade *or* foreign trade

comercio floreciente flourishing trade

comercio interior domestic trade

comercio internacional international trade

comercio invisible invisible trade

comercio legal lawful trade

comercio marítimo maritime trade

comercio multilateral multilateral trade

comercio recíproco reciprocal trade

comercio unilateral one-way trade

cometer commit (v)

comienzo (m) beginning *or* start (n)

comisión (f) commission

comisión (f) *[corretaje]* brokerage *or* broker's commission

comisión de arbitraje arbitration board *or* arbitration tribunal

comisionista (mf) commission agent

comisionista al por mayor factor (n)

comité (m) commission *or* committee

cómodo (-da) convenient

compañía (f) company

compañía asociada *o* **afiliada** associate company *or* sister company

compañía de seguros insurance company

compañía fiduciaria trust company

compañía filial *o* **compañía subsidiaria** subsidiary company

compañía independiente independent company

compañía naviera *o* **compañía marítima** shipping company *or* shipping line

compañía que financia la compra a plazos hire-purchase company

comparable comparable

comparación (f) comparison

comparar compare

comparar con compare with

comparar precios shop around

compartir share (v)

compartir una oficina share an office

compensación (f) compensation

compensar *[deducir]* set against

compensar *[indemnizar]* compensate *or* make up for

competencia (f) competition

competencia (f) *[pericia]* expertise

competencia desleal unfair competition

competencia dura stiff competition

competencia encarnizada cut-throat competition

competente competent *or* capable

competidor (-ra) competitor

competir (con) compete (with)

competitividad (f) competitiveness

competitivo (-va) competitive *or* competing (adj)

con precio competitivo competitively priced

complementario (-ria) complementary

completamente nuevo (-va) brand new

completar complete (v)

completo (-ta) complete (adj) *or* comprehensive *or* full-scale

componer repair (v)

compra (f) purchase *or* purchasing *or* buying

compra a granel bulk buying

compra a plazos hire purchase (HP)

compra al contado cash purchase *or* spot purchase

compra apalancada leveraged buyout (LBO)

compra de futuros forward buying

compra de una empresa por sus ejecutivos management buyout (MBO)

compra febril panic buying

compra impulsiva impulse purchase

comprador (-ra) buyer *or* purchaser *or* shopper

comprador impulsivo impulse buyer

comprador genuino genuine purchaser

comprar buy *or* purchase (v)

comprar a futuros buy forward

comprar en efectivo buy for cash

compras (fpl) shopping

comprender understand

comprobación (f) check (n) *or* examination

comprobación de los recursos económicos means test

comprobante (m) voucher

comprobante de caja sales receipt

comprobar check (v) *or* monitor

comprometerse undertake (v)

compromiso (m) compromise (n)

compromiso (m) *[promesa]* undertaking *or* promise

compromiso (m) *[cita]* appointment *or* meeting

compromiso (m) *[obligación]* obligation *or* duty

compromisos (mpl) commitments

compulsa (f) certified copy *or* true copy

común common

común: en común jointly

comunicación (f) communication

comunicación horizontal horizontal communication

comunicación vertical vertical communication

comunicaciones (fpl) communications

comunicado (m) communication *or* message

comunicado de prensa press release

comunicar communicate *or* announce

comunidad (f) community

con cum

conceder grant (v) *or* extend (v)

conceder *[adjudicar]* award (v)

conceder *[dar]* allow *or* give

conceder una licencia license

concertación (f) harmonization *or* reconciliation

concesión (f) concession *or* right *or* franchise (n)

concesión de un préstamo lending

concesionario (-ria) concessionaire *or* dealer *or* franchisee *or* licensee

conciliación (f) conciliation

conciliación de cuentas reconciliation of accounts

concluir conclude *or* wind up *or* complete

conclusión (f) conclusion (n) *or* close (n)

condición (f) condition

condición: a condición de que on condition that *or* provided that

condición: sin condiciones unconditional

condición: en las condiciones acordadas on agreed terms

condición (f) *[salvedad]* proviso

condición jurídica legal status

condicionado (-da) qualified *or* with reservations

condicional conditional

condiciones (fpl) terms *or* conditions

condiciones: en condiciones favorables on favourable terms

condiciones de empleo conditions of employment

condiciones de pago terms of payment

condiciones de servicio terms of employment

condiciones de trabajo working conditions

condiciones de venta conditions of sale *or* terms of sale

condominio (m) joint ownership

conducir drive (v)

conductor (m) driver

conectar connect *or* interface (v)

conexión (f) connection *or* tie-up *or* link

conexión (f) *[informática]* computer port

confeccionar make out

conferencia (f) de prensa press conference

confesar confess *or* declare

confianza (f) confidence

confianza: de confianza reliable

confiar entrust

confidencia (f) tip (n)

confidencial confidential

confidencialidad (f) confidentiality

confirmación (f) confirmation

confirmar confirm

confirmar: sin confirmar unconfirmed

confirmar a alguien en su puesto de trabajo confirm someone in a job

confirmar una reserva confirm a booking

confiscación (f) forfeiture

confiscar confiscate *or* seize

conflicto (m) de intereses conflict of interest

conflictos (mpl) colectivos industrial disputes

conflictos laborales labour disputes

conforme a *[según]* according to *or* under

conformidad (f) *[acuerdo]* compliance

congelación (f) freeze (n)

congelación de créditos credit freeze

congelación de salarios wage freeze

congelado (-da) frozen

congelar freeze (v)

congelar salarios y precios freeze wages and prices

conglomerado (m) conglomerate

congreso (m) congress *or* conference

conjuntamente jointly

conjunto (m) de medidas económicas package of economic measures

conjunto (-ta) joint

conjunto: en conjunto overall

conmutar commute *or* exchange

conocimiento (m) de embarque bill of lading

conseguir get *or* manage to

conseguir hacer algo succeed in

conseguir fondos secure funds *or* raise money

conseguir un contrato win a contract

consejero (-ra) consultant *or* adviser

consejero (-ra) *[director]* director

consejo (m) (de administración) board (n) of directors

conservación (f) maintenance

conservar maintain

considerar consider

consigna (f) left luggage office

consignación (f) consignment

consignador (-ra) consignor

consignar consign *or* dispatch (v)

consignar *[asignar]* appropriate (v)

consignatario (-ria) consignee

consolidación (f) de fondos funding (of debt)

consolidación de un préstamo restructuring of a loan

consolidado (-da) consolidated

consolidar consolidate *or* establish

consorcio (m) consortium

consorcio emisor *o* **asegurador** underwriting syndicate

constante constant *or* recurrent

constar de consist of

constitución (f) de una sociedad incorporation

constituir en sociedad incorporate (a company)

constituirse parte civil bring a civil action

construcción: en construcción under construction

construir build *or* develop

consultar consult

consultar a un abogado take legal advice

consultoría (f) consultancy firm

consumidor (-ra) consumer

consumo (m) consumption

consumo doméstico *o* **consumo interior** home consumption

contabilidad (f) accounting *or* bookkeeping

contabilidad de costes cost accounting

contabilidad de costes actuales current cost accounting

contabilidad de ingresos revenue accounts

contable (mf) accountant *or* bookkeeper

contable de costes cost accountant

contable jefe chief accountant *or* controller (US)

contactar contact (v)

contacto (m) contact (n)

contado: al contado cash (adv)

contar count (v)

contenedor (m) container

contener contain *or* hold (v)

contener *[parar]* check (v) *or* stop

contenerización (f) containerization

contenido (m) contents

contestación (f) answer (n) *or* reply (n)

contestador (m) automático answering machine

contestar answer (v) *or* reply (v)

contestar el teléfono answer the telephone

contestar una carta answer a letter

contingencia (f) contingency

continuación (f) continuation

continuamente continually

continuar continue *or* proceed (v)

continuo (-nua) continual *or* continuous

contra OPA (f) reverse takeover

contraasiento (m) contra entry

contracción (f) shrinkage

contractual contractual

contraer deudas incur debts

contraoferta (f) counterbid *or* counter-offer

contrapartida (f) contra entry

contrario (-ria) contrary

contraste (m) contrast (n)

contratar contract (v)

contratar personal hire staff

contratista (mf) contractor

contratista de transporte por carretera haulage contractor

contratista del Estado government contractor

contrato (m) contract (n) *or* agreement (n)

contrato: según contrato contractually *or* according to the contract

contrato a plazo fijo forward contract

contrato de Bolsa contract note

contrato de corta duración short-term contract

contrato de empleo contract of employment

contrato de seguros insurance contract

contrato de venta bill of sale

contrato en exclusiva exclusive agreement

contribución (f) contribution

contribución de capital contribution of capital

contribuir contribute

contribuyente (mf) contributor *or* taxpayer

control (m) control (n) *or* check *or* inspection

control: de control supervisory

control de alquileres *o* **de rentas** rent control

control de calidad quality control

control de crédito credit control

control de divisas exchange control

control de existencias stock control *or* inventory control (US)

control de materiales materials control

control de precios price control

control presupuestario budgetary control

controlado (-da) por el Estado government-controlled

controlar control (v) *or* monitor (v)

controlar un negocio control a business

convenido (-da) agreed

conveniente convenient

convenio (m) agreement *or* covenant (n)

convenio salarial colectivo collective wage agreement

conversaciones fructíferas productive discussions

conversión (f) conversion

conversión de divisas currency conversion

conversión de un préstamo refunding of a loan

convertibilidad (f) convertibility

convertir convert

convocar call *or* convene

cooperación (f) co-operation

cooperar co-operate

cooperativa (f) co-operative (n)

cooperativo (-va) co-operative (adj)

coparticipación (f) copartnership

copia (f) copy (n) *or* duplicate (n)

copia auténtica *o* **certificada** certified copy

copia carbón carbon copy

copia de reserva *o* **de seguridad** backup copy

copia exacta true copy

copia falsa forgery

copia impresa hard copy

copia impresa *[de ordenador]* computer printout

copiar copy (v) *or* duplicate (v)

copiar *[escribir]* write out

copiar una factura duplicate an invoice

copropiedad (f) co-ownership *or* part-ownership

copropietario (-ria) co-owner *or* part-owner

corona (f) krone *or* krona

corporación (f) corporation *or* guild

corrección (f) correction

correcto (-ta) correct (adj) *or* right *or* accurate

corredor (m) de seguros insurance broker

corredor (-ra) de bolsa stockbroker

correduría (f) de bolsa stockbroking

corregir correct (v) *or* rectify *or* revise

correo (m) mail (n) *or* post (n)

correo aéreo airmail (n)

correo electrónico electronic mail (email)

correo entrante incoming mail

correo por vía terrestre o marítima surface mail

correos (mpl) post (n)

correr un riesgo run a risk

correspondencia (f) correspondence *or* mail

correspondencia de salida outgoing mail

correspondencia recibida incoming mail

corresponder agree with

corresponder a algo correspond with something

correspondiente (mf) correspondent

corresponsal (mf) correspondent *or* journalist

corretaje (m) brokerage *or* broker's commission

corriente common *or* frequent

corriente *[actual]* current

corriente *[ordinario]* ordinary *or* regular

corriente: precio corriente average price

corrientes: de los corrientes instant (adj)

corto: a corto plazo short-term (adj) *or* on a short-term basis

costar cost (v)

costas (fpl) costs

costas judiciales legal costs *or* legal charges *or* legal expenses

coste (m) *o* **charge (n)** cost (n)

coste de almacenaje storage (n)

coste de la gestión de deudas factoring charges

coste de producción production cost

coste del transporte haulage costs *or* haulage rates

coste de ventas cost of sales

coste de vida cost of living

coste descargado landed costs

coste directo direct cost

coste incremental incremental cost *or* marginal cost

coste inicial historic(al) cost

coste marginal marginal cost

coste total total cost

coste unitario *o* **coste por unidad** unit cost

coste, seguro y flete (cif) cost, insurance and freight (c.i.f.)

costear los gastos de alguien defray someone's expenses

costes (mpl) de distribución distribution costs

costes de envío shipping charges *or* shipping costs

costes de fabricación manufacturing costs

costes de lanzamiento launching costs

costes de puesta en marcha start-up costs

costes excesivos excessive costs

costes fijos fixed costs

costes laborales labour costs

costes laborales indirectos indirect labour costs

costes sociales social costs

costes variables variable costs

costo (m) cost (n)

costo más honorarios cost plus

costoso (-sa) costly *or* expensive

costumbre (f) routine (n)

cotejar check (v) *or* compare (v)

cotidiano (-na) day-to-day

cotización (f) quote (n) *or* quotation

cotización de apertura opening price

cotizar *[calcular]* quote (v)

cotizar *[contribuir]* contribute (v)

crack (m) financial crash (n)

crear una compañía set up a company

creciente increasing *or* mounting

crecimiento (m) growth

crecimiento económico economic growth

crédito (m) credit (n)

crédito: a crédito on credit

crédito a corto plazo short-term credit

crédito a largo plazo long credit *or* extended credit

crédito abierto open credit

crédito al consumidor consumer credit

crédito bancario bank credit

crédito barato cheap money

crédito blando soft loan

crédito congelado frozen credits

crédito de apoyo standby credit

crédito instantáneo instant credit

crédito por impuestos pagados tax credit

crédito renovable revolving credit

crédito sin interés interest-free credit

crédito 'stand by' standby credit

crisis (f) de liquidez liquidity crisis

crisis del dólar dollar crisis

crisis económica *[depresión]* slump (n) *or* depression

crisis financiera financial crisis

crónico (-ca) chronic

cruzar un cheque cross a cheque

cuadrar *[ajustar]* reconcile

cuadrar *[saldar]* balance (v)

cuadrícula (f) grid

cualificado (-da) skilled *or* qualified

cualificado: no cualificado unskilled

cualificado: muy cualificado highly qualified

cuanto: en cuanto a regarding

cuarta parte (f) *o* cuarto (m) quarter *[25%]*

cuarto trimestre fourth quarter

cúbico (-ca) cubic

cubierta (f) deck

cubierto: precio del cubierto cover charge

cubierta (f) *[funda]* cover (n)

cubrir cover (v)

cubrir gastos break even *or* cover costs *or* meet expenses

cubrir un riesgo cover a risk

cuenta (f) account

cuenta (f) *[restaurante]* bill (n)

cuenta: a cuenta on account

cuenta: anticipo a cuenta advance on account

cuenta: anticipo de caja a cuenta cash advance

cuenta: por cuenta y riesgo del comprador caveat emptor

cuenta a plazo deposit account

cuenta abierta open account *or* charge account

cuenta acreedora account in credit

cuenta administrada por un apoderado nominee account

cuenta bancaria bank account

cuenta bloqueada frozen account *or* account on stop

cuenta compensada contra account

cuenta con saldo positivo account in credit

cuenta conjunta joint account

cuenta corriente current account *or* drawing account *or* cheque account

cuenta de ahorro savings account

cuenta de caja cash account

cuenta de capital capital account

cuenta de crédito credit account

cuenta de depósito deposit account

cuenta de garantía bloqueada escrow account

cuenta de gastos de representación expense account

cuenta de no residente external account

cuenta de pérdidas y ganancias profit and loss account

cuenta detallada itemized account

cuenta en descubierto overdrawn account

cuenta en participación joint account

cuenta inactiva dead account

cuenta numerada numbered account

cuenta presupuestaria budget account

cuentas a cobrar *o* por cobrar accounts receivable

cuentas a pagar *o* por pagar accounts payable

cuentas anuales annual accounts

cuentas de fin de mes month-end accounts

cuentas de gestión management accounts

cuentas de mediados de mes mid-month accounts

cuentas semestrales half-yearly accounts

cuentas sin verificar unaudited accounts

cuestión (f) matter (n) *or* question (n)

cuestionar question (v)

cuestionario (m) questionnaire

culpa (f) blame (n)

culpa (f) *[falta]* fault *or* blame

culpar blame (v)

cumbre (f) peak (n) *or* top (n) *or* highest point

cumplidor (-ra) reliable

cumplimiento (m) *[realización]* fulfilment

cumplimiento (m) *[ejecución]* execution

cumplir carry out *or* fulfil (v)

cumplir *[satisfacer]* meet

cumplir *[ejecutar]* execute

cumplir un plazo establecido meet a deadline

cumplir una promesa keep a promise

cuota (f) quota *or* fee

cuota de depreciación allowance for depreciation

cuota de importación import quota

cuota de inscripción registration fee

cuota de mercado market share

cupo (m) quota

cupo de importación import quota

cupón (m) coupon

cupón: con cupón de interés cum coupon

cupón: sin cupón de interés ex coupon

cupón de anuncio coupon ad

cupón de regalo gift coupon

curriculum (vitae) (m) curriculum vitae (CV)

cursar un pedido place an order

curso (m) comercial commercial course

curso de actualización *o* **curso de reciclaje** refresher course

curso de gestión empresarial management course

cursos (mpl) de iniciación induction courses *or* induction training

curva (f) curve

curva de ventas sales curve

Dd

dañado (-da) damaged

dañar damage (v)

daño (m) damage (n)

daños (mpl) causados por incendio fire damage

daños materiales damage to property

daños por tormenta storm damage

daños y perjuicios damages

dar give

dar *[conceder]* allow

dar *[producir]* produce (v)

dar carpetazo shelve (v)

dar empleo employ (v)

dar instrucciones brief (v) *or* issue instructions

dar por resultado result in

dar publicidad publicize *or* plug (v)

dar una entrada pay *or* put money down

dar una propina tip (v)

darse cuenta realize *or* understand

darse prisa hurry up

datos (mpl) data

datos de salida computer output

debajo: por debajo de under *or* less than

debate (m) debate *or* discussion

debe (m) debit *or* debtor side

debe y haber debits and credits

deber owe

debidamente duly *or* legally

debido a due to *or* owing to

debido (-da) owing

débil slack *or* weak

débito (m) debit (n) *or* charge (n)

decidir decide *or* resolve

decidirse por la opción más fácil take the soft option

decimal (m) decimal (n)

decisión (f) decision

decisión (f) *[fallo]* ruling (n)

decisivo (-va) deciding

declaración (f) declaration *or* statement *or* announcement declaración (f) *[renta]* return (n)

declaración de aduana customs declaration

declaración de ingresos nulos nil return

declaración de quiebra declaration of bankruptcy

declaración de renta tax return *or* tax declaration

declaración de siniestro insurance claim

declaración del IVA VAT declaration

declaración oficial official return

declarado (-da) declared

declarar declare *or* state (v)

declarar *[renta]* return (v)

declarar a alguien en quiebra declare someone bankrupt

declarar mercancías en la aduana declare goods to customs

decomisar forfeit (v)

decomiso (m) forfeiture *or* forefeit (n)

decreciente decreasing (adj) *or* falling

decretar rule (v) *or* give decision

deducción (f) deduction

deducción (f) de impuestos tax deductions

deducciones (fpl) personales personal allowances

deducible deductible

deducir deduct (v)

deducir *[compensar]* set against

deducir *[inferir]* deduce *or* infer (v)

deducir del sueldo dock (v)

defectivo (-va) defective

defecto (m) defect *or* (mechanical) fault *or* imperfection

defecto: en su defecto failing that

defectuoso (-sa) defective *or* faulty

defender defend

defenderse en juicio defend a lawsuit

defensa (f) defence

defensor (m) del pueblo ombudsman

déficit (m) deficit *or* shortfall

déficit comercial trade deficit *or* trade gap

deflación (f) deflation

deflacionista deflationary

defraudación (f) fraud

DEG (derechos especiales de giro) special drawing rights (SDRs)

dejar *[abandonar]* leave (v)

dejar de hacer algo fail to do something

dejar un margen allow for

dejar un margen del 10% para el porte allow 10% for carriage

delegación (f) delegation

delegado (-da) delegate (n) *or* deputy (n)

delegado (-da) del personal worker director

delegar delegate (v)

delito (m) por omisión nonfeasance

demanda (f) demand (n)

demanda (f) *[reclamación]* claim (n)

demanda de pago call (n) for money

demanda de pago de acciones call (n)

demanda efectiva effective demand

demanda estacional seasonal demand

demanda excesiva run (n)

demanda por daños y perjuicios action for damages

demanda: oferta y demanda supply and demand

demandado (-da) defendant

demandante (mf) claimant *or* plaintiff

demandar sue

demora (f) delay (n)

demorar delay (v)

demostración (f) demonstration

demostrar demonstrate

departamental departmental

departamento (m) department *or* division *or* section

departamento de 'marketing' marketing department

departamento de atención al cliente customer service department

departamento de compras buying department *or* purchasing department

departamento de contabilidad accounts department

departamento de diseño design department

Departamento de Estado government department

departamento de exportación export department

departamento de facturación invoicing department

departamento de informática computer department

departamento de personal personnel department

departamento de producción production department

departamento de publicidad publicity department

departamento de reclamaciones claims department

departamento de relaciones públicas public relations department

departamento de reservas room reservations

depender de depend on

dependienta (f) saleswoman *or* shop assistant

dependiente (m) salesman *or* shop assistant

depositante (mf) depositor

depositar *[ingresar]* deposit (v) *or* bank (v)

depósito (m) bank deposit *or* down payment

depósito (m) *[almacén]* store (n) *or* storeroom *or* stockroom

depósito (m) *[almacenamiento]* storage (n)

depósito (m) *[almacén de mercancías]* goods depot

depósito a la vista demand deposit

depósito a plazo time deposit

depósito a plazo fijo fixed deposit

depósito aduanero bonded warehouse

depósito no reembolsable non-refundable deposit

depósito reembolsable refundable deposit

depósitos (mpl) bancarios bank deposits

depósitos con interés interest-bearing deposits

depreciación (f) depreciation

depreciación de un activo writedown (n)

depreciar(se) depreciate *or* amortize

depreciar el valor de un activo write down *[an asset]*

depresión (f) depression *or* slump (n)

derecho (m) law *or* right (n) *or* entitlement

derecho (-cha) right (adj)

derecho civil civil law

derecho de aduana customs duty

derecho de contratos contract law

derecho de ocupación security of tenure

derecho de paso right of way

derecho de retención lien

derecho de veto right of veto

derecho internacional international law

derecho marítimo maritime law

derecho mercantil commercial law

derechohabiente (m) rightful claimant

derechos (mpl) admission fee

derechos de autor royalty

derechos de dársena port charges *or* port dues

derechos de exportación export duty

derechos de importación import duty

derechos especiales de giro (DEG) special drawing rights (SDRs)

derechos portuarios harbour dues

derivar de derive from *or* result from

derrumbamiento (m) collapse (n)

derrumbarse collapse (v)

desaceleración (f) slowdown

desacelerar slow down

desaconsejar advise against

desacreditar discredit (v)

desacuerdo (m) disagreement

desaparecido (-da) missing *or* unaccounted for

desarrollar develop

desarrollo (m) development *or* growth

desarrollo de productos product development

desarrollo económico economic development

desbordar flood (v)

descanso (m) break (n) *or* rest (n)

descarga (f) y carga de un avión turnround

descargar unload

descargar mercancías en un puerto land goods at a port

descargo (m) *[deuda]* discharge (n)

descargo (m) final final discharge

descender fall (v) *or* drop (v)

descenso (m) decline (n) *or* downturn *or* decrease

descentralización (f) decentralization

descentralizar decentralize *or* hive off

descontable discountable

descontar discount (v) *or* knock off *or* deduct (v)

descontar del sueldo dock (v)

describir describe

descripción (f) description

descripción comercial trade description

descripción del puesto de trabajo job description *or* job specification

descubierto (m) *[sobregiro]* overdraft

descuento (m) discount (n) *or* rebate

descuento: con descuento off *or* reduced by

descuento al por mayor wholesale discount

descuento básico basic discount

descuento para comerciantes del sector trade discount *or* trade terms

descuento por cantidad quantity discount

descuento por pago al contado cash discount

descuento por volumen volume discount

descuidado (-da) negligent

desechable disposable

desecho (m) waste (n)

desembarcar land (v)

desembolsar disburse *or* pay out

desembolso (m) disbursement *or* expenditure *or* outlay

desembolsos (mpl) outgoings *or* expenditure

desempleado (-da) unemployed

desempleo (m) unemployment

desfalcador (-ra) embezzler

desfalcar embezzle

desfalco (m) embezzlement

desfavorable unfavourable

desgastar erode

desgaste (m) natural (fair) wear and tear

desglosar break down (v) *or* itemize

desglose (m) breakdown (n)

desgravable tax-deductible

desgravación (f) concession

desgravación fiscal tax allowance *or* tax relief *or* tax concession

deshacerse de unload *or* offload *or* get rid of

deshacerse de las existencias sobrantes dispose of excess stock

deshacerse de algo get rid of something

deshonorar dishonour

desistir de una acción abandon an action

desocupar vacate (v)

despachar dispatch (v)

despachar pedidos atrasados release dues

despachar un pedido fulfil an order

despacho (m) *[envío]* dispatch (n) *or* sending (out)

despacho (m) *[oficina]* office

despacho aduanero *o* **de aduanas** customs clearance

despacho de billetes booking office

despacho de pedidos order fulfilment

desparejado (-da) odd

despedir discharge *or* pay off

despedir a alguien sack someone

despedir a un empleado dismiss an employee

despedir por falta de trabajo lay off workers

despegar take off

desperdiciar waste (v) *or* use too much

desperdicio (m) waste (n) *or* wastage

desperfectos (mpl) breakages

despido (m) dismissal *or* sacking

despido (m) *[excedente de plantilla]* redundancy

despido injusto unfair dismissal *or* wrongful dismissal

desregulación (f) deregulation

destacado (-da) outstanding *or* exceptional

destinatario (-ria) addressee *or* receiver

destino (m) destination

destitución (f) removal *or* sacking

destreza (f) skill

desvalorización (f) devaluation

desvalorizar devalue

detallado (-da) detailed

detallar detail (v) *or* itemize *or* break down

detalle (m) detail (n)

detalles (mpl) particulars

detallista (mf) retailer

detener *[frenar]* plug (v) *or* block (v) *or* stop (v)

detener el pago de un cheque stop a cheque

deteriorado (-da) damaged *or* shop-soiled

determinar determine

deuda (f) debt *or* indebtedness

deuda incobrable irrecoverable debt *or* write-off

deuda morosa bad debt

deudas (fpl) liabilities

deudas a corto plazo short-term debts

deudas a largo plazo long-term debts

deudas a pagar debts due

deudas garantizadas secured debts

deudas pendientes outstanding debts

deudor (-ra) debtor *or* defaulter

deudor (-ra) hipotecario (-ria) mortgager *or* mortgagor

deudor (-ra) judicial judgment debtor

devaluación (f) devaluation

devaluar devalue (v)

devengar earn (v) *or* bear (v) *or* yield (v) *or* accrue (v) (interest)

devolución (f) return (n)

devolución (f) *[reembolso]* refund (n)

devolver return (v) *or* send back

devolver una carta al remitente return a letter to sender

devolver una letra dishonour a bill

día (m) day

día: al día per day *or* up-to-date

día de ajuste quarter day

día festivo bank holiday

diagrama (m) diagram

diagrama de flujo flow chart *or* flow diagram

diario (m) de bolsillo pocket diary

diario (-ria) daily *or* day-to-day

dictado (m) dictation

dictáfono (m) dictating machine

dictar dictate

diferencia (f) difference *or* discrepancy

diferencial differential (adj)

diferencias (fpl) de precio differences in price

diferente different

diferido (-da) deferred

diferir differ

diferir *[aplazar]* defer *or* adjourn

diferir el pago defer payment

difícil difficult

dificultad (f) difficulty (n)

difundir a través de la red de emisoras network (v)

difusión (f) circulation

dígito (m) digit

dilución (f) del capital dilution of equity

dimensiones (fpl) dimensions *or* size *or* measurements

dimisión (f) resignation

dimitir resign

dinero (m) money

dinero: sin dinero broke (adj)

dinero barato cheap money

dinero efectivo cash (n)

dinero en mano spot cash

dinero escaso tight money

dinero para gastos menores petty cash

dinero para gastos personales spending money

dinero suelto change (n)

diplomado (-da) certificated

dique (m) dock (n)

dirección (f) direction

dirección (f) *[gerencia]* management

dirección (f) *[señas]* address (n)

dirección comercial business address

dirección conjunta joint management

dirección de personal personnel management

dirección de reenvío forwarding address

dirección postal accommodation address

dirección telegráfica cable address

directamente direct (adv)

directiva (f) directive

directivo (-va) managerial

directo (-ta) direct (adj)

director (-ra) director *or* manager

director (-ra) adjunto (-ta) deputy manager

director (-ra) comercial sales manager

director (-ra) de banco bank manager

director (-ra) de una empresa company director

director (-ra) de exportación export manager

director (-ra) de finanzas finance director

director (-ra) de hotel hotel manager

director (-ra) de 'marketing' marketing manager

director (-ra) de planta floor manager

director (-ra) de producción production manager

director (-ra) de proyecto project manager

director (-ra) de publicidad publicity manager

director (-ra) de reclamaciones claims manager

director (-ra) de sucursal branch manager

director (-ra) ejecutivo (-va) executive director

director (-ra) externo (-na) outside director

director (-ra) en funciones acting manager

director (-ra) general general manager

director (-ra) general adjunto (-ta) deputy managing director

director (-ra) gerente managing director (MD)

director (-ra) no ejecutivo (-va) non-executive director

director (-ra) principal senior manager *or* senior executive

director (-ra) regional area manager

directorio (m) directory

directorio comercial classified directory

directriz (f) guideline *or* directive

dirigido (-da) a un mercado popular down-market

dirigir direct (v) *or* channel (v)

dirigir *[gestionar]* manage

dirigir *[llevar]* run (v)

dirigir *[obrar]* operate

dirigir un negocio control a business

disco (m) disk

disco duro hard disk

discrepancia (f) discrepancy *or* variance

disculpa (f) apology

disculparse apologize

discurrir flow (v)

discusión (f) discussion *or* argument

discusión (f) *[debate]* debate

discutir discuss

diseñar design (v)

diseño (m) design (n)

diseño de productos product design

diseño industrial industrial design

diseño registrado registered design

disminución (f) decrease *or* lowering

disminución (f) *[impuestos]* abatement

disminución de valor decrease in value

disminuir decline (v) *or* decrease (v) *or* fall off

disolver dissolve

disolver una sociedad dissolve a partnership

dispararse soar

disponer arrange *or* set out

disponibilidad (f) availability

disponible available *or* vacant

disposición (f) provision

dispositivo (m) device

disquete (m) *o* **diskette (m)** diskette

disquetera (f) disk drive

distinto (-ta) different

distribución (f) distribution

distribución exclusiva distributorship

distribuidor (-ra) distributor *or* stockist

distribuir distribute

distribuir un dividendo pay a dividend

distrito (m) district *or* area

distrito comercial commercial district

disuadir advise against

diversificación (f) diversification

diversificar diversify

dividendo (m) dividend

dividendo: con dividendo cum dividend

dividendo: sin dividendo ex dividend

dividendo final final dividend

dividendo mínimo minimum dividend

dividendo por acción earnings per share *or* earnings yield

dividendo por superávit surplus dividend

dividendo provisional interim dividend

dividir divide *or* share (v)

dividir *[separar]* separate (v)

divisas (fpl) foreign exchange

divisas de reserva reserve currency

división (f) division

divulgación (f) disclosure

divulgar disclose *or* release (v)

doble double (adj)

doble imposición (f) double taxation

doble reserva (f) double-booking

docena (f) dozen

documentación (f) documentation

documental documentary

documento (m) document

documento adjunto enclosure

documento escrito instrument

documento falso forgery

documento no negociable non-negotiable instrument

documentos (mpl) documents *or* papers

documentos falsos faked documents

dólar (m) dollar

domiciliación (f) bancaria direct debit *or* standing order

domicilio (m) domicile

domicilio: a domicilio house to house *or* door to door

domicilio particular home address

domicilio social registered office *or* headquarters (HQ)

dorso (m) back (n)

dotación (f) de personal manning

dpto. (= departamento) dept (= department)

dracma (m) *[moneda]* drachma

dueña (f) proprietress *or* landlady *or* owner

dueño (m) proprietor *or* landlord *or* owner

dumping (m) dumping

duplicación (f) duplication

duplicado (m) duplicate (n)

duplicar duplicate (v) *or* double (v)

duro (-ra) hard

Ee

echar al correo post *or* mail (v)

economía (f) economy *or* economics

economía de libre mercado free market economy

economía de oferta supply side economics

economía dirigida controlled economy

economía estable stable economy

economía madura mature economy

economía mixta mixed economy

economía sumergida black economy

economías de escala economies of scale

económico (-ca) economic *or* economical

economista (mf) economist

economista de mercado market economist

economizar economize (v) *or* save (on)

ecu *o* **ECU (m)** ecu *or* ECU (European currency unit)

edad (f) de jubilación retirement age

edificio (m) building *or* facility *or* premises

edificio principal main building

efectivo (m) ready cash

efectivo: en efectivo cash

efectivo en caja cash in hand

efectivo (-va) effective *or* actual

efecto (m) effect (n) *or* instrument (n)

efecto de favor accommodation bill

efecto indirecto spinoff

efecto negociable bankable paper

efecto secundario knock-on effect

efectos a cobrar receivables

efectos embargados (vendidos a bajo precio) distress merchandise

efectuar effect (v)

eficacia (f) effectiveness *or* efficiency

eficaz efficient

eficiencia (f) efficiency *or* effectiveness

eficiente efficient

ejecución (f) execution *or* implementation *or* enforcement

ejecutar exectute (v) *or* implement (v) *or* enforce (v)

ejecutivo (m) de cuentas account executive

ejecutivo de ventas sales executive

ejecutivo (-va) executive

ejecutivo (-va) auxiliar junior executive *or* junior manager

ejecutivo (-va) en formación management trainee

ejemplar (m) copy (n)

ejercer exercise (v) *or* perform (v)

ejercer derecho de opción exercise an option

ejercicio (m) exercise (n)

ejercicio del derecho de opción exercise of an option

ejercicio económico financial year

ejercicio fiscal tax year

elaboración (f) de datos data processing

elaborar process (v)

elaborar *[producto]* manufacture (v)

elaborar cifras process figures

elasticidad (f) elasticity

elección (f) election *or* choice

elegir elect *or* choose

elemento (m) factor (n)

elevador (m) de granos grain elevator

eludir evade

elusión (f) evasion

elusión de impuestos tax avoidance

embalador (-ra) packer

embalaje (m) packaging *or* packing *or* package

embalaje de exposición display pack

embalaje de plástico tipo burbuja blister pack *or* bubble pack

embalaje hermético airtight packaging

embalaje vacío *o* ficticio dummy pack

embalar pack (v)

embalar *[caja]* case (v) *or* crate (v)

embalar mercancías en cajas de cartón pack goods into cartons

embarcadero (m) wharf

embarcar embark

embarcarse board (v)

embarcarse en embark on

embargador (-ra) sequestrator

embargar seize

embargo (m) embargo *or* seizure *or* sequestration

embarque (m) embarkation

embaucar fiddle (v)

embolsar pocket (v)

embotellamiento (m) bottleneck

emergencia (f) emergency

emisión (f) issue (n)

emisión de acciones share issue

emisión de acciones gratuitas scrip issue

emisión de derechos rights issue

emisión gratuita bonus issue

emisión publicitaria TV commercial

emitir issue (v)

emolumentos (mpl) fee

empaletar palletize

empaquetador (-ra) packer

empaquetar parcel (v) *or* pack (v)

empezar start (v) *or* begin (v)

empezar un negocio a cero cold start

emplazamiento (m) summons

empleado (-da) employee *or* employed

empleado (-da) de oficina office worker *or* clerk

empleado (-da) del servicio de información information officer

empleado (-da) para mantener llenos los estantes shelf filler

emplear employ *or* use (v)

emplear de nuevo re-employ

emplear más personal take on more staff

empleo (m) employment *or* appointment *or* job

empleo: sin empleo unemployed

empleo a tiempo parcial part-time work *or* part-time employment

empleo de la capacidad capacity utilization

empleo eventual temporary employment

empleo fijo staff appointment

empleo seguro secure job

emprendedor (-ra) go-ahead (adj)

emprender undertake

emprender un negocio go into business

empresa (f) enterprise *or* business *or* company *or* undertaking

empresa a pequeña escala small-scale enterprise

empresa comercial commercial undertaking

empresa competidora rival company

empresa con fines de lucro profit-oriented company

empresa conjunta joint venture

empresa de alquiler de maquinaria plant-hire firm

empresa de transporte público common carrier

empresa de transportes haulage contractor *or* carrier

empresa de ventas por correo mail-order business *or* mail-order firm

empresa en ruinas wreck (n)

empresa familiar family company

empresa mediana middle-sized company

empresa privada private enterprise

empresa que comercia con otra trading partner

empresarial entrepreneurial

empresario (-ria) employer *or* entrepreneur *or* businessman *or* businesswoman

empresas (fpl) rivales rival firms *or* competing firms

empréstito (m) loan capital

empuje (m) drive (n) *or* energy

encargado (-da) *[almacén, tienda]* manager

encargado (-da) de compras buyer

encargado (-da) del libro de compras bought ledger clerk

encargado (-da) del libro de ventas sales ledger clerk

encargar *[confiar]* entrust

encargar *[hacer un pedido]* order (v)

encargarse de undertake

encarte publicitario *[de una revista]* magazine insert

encauzar channel (v)

enchufe (m) electric plug *or* connection

enchufe (m) *[influencia]* useful contact

encogimiento (m) shrinkage

encontrar find (v) *or* meet (v)

encontrar: no encontrar miss (v)

encontrarse (con) meet

encubrimiento (m) de activos concealment of assets

encuesta (f) opinion poll *or* questionnaire

endémico (-ca) chronic

endeudado (-da) indebted

endeudarse get into debt *or* run into debt

endosante (mf) endorser

endosar un cheque endorse a cheque

endosatario (-ria) endorsee

endoso (m) endorsement

energía (f) energy

enjuiciar prosecute

enlace (m) tie-up *or* link

enmendar amend

enmienda (f) amendment

ensayo (m) test (n) *or* trial

enseñar show (v) *or* teach (v)

entablar enter into

entablar negociaciones open negotiations

entablar un pleito take legal action

entender understand

entrada (f) entrance *or* admission *or* entering

entrada (f) *[billete]* ticket

entrada (f) *[depósito]* down payment

entrada de favor complimentary ticket

entradas (fpl) receipts

entrar en enter *or* go in

entrar en dársena dock (v)

entrar en vigor operate (v)

entrega (f) delivery

entrega con acuse de recibo recorded delivery

entrega futura future delivery

entrega gratuita free delivery

entrega urgente express delivery

entregado: no entregado undelivered

entregar deliver or hand in or hand over

entregar: para entregar a care of or c/o

entrevista (f) interview (n)

entrevistado (-da) interviewee

entrevistador (-ra) interviewer

entrevistar interview (v)

enumerar list (v)

envasado (-da) al vacío shrink-wrapped

envasar pack (v)

envase (m) *[embalaje]* packing or packaging or pack (n)

envase (m) *[recipiente]* container

envase al vacío shrink-wrapping

envase no retornable non-returnable packing

envases (mpl) devueltos returned empties

enviar send or dispatch

enviar por carga aérea airfreight (v)

enviar por correo post (v) or mail (v)

enviar por correo aéreo airmail (v)

enviar por correo urgente express (v)

enviar por fax fax (v)

enviar por télex telex (v)

enviar un paquete por correo aéreo send a package by airmail

enviar un paquete por vía terrestre o marítima send a package by surface mail

enviar una carga por vía marítima send a shipment by sea

enviar una factura por correo send an invoice by post

envío (m) dispatch (n)

envío (m) *[carga]* shipment

envío (m) *[expedición]* shipping or forwarding

envío (m) *[giro]* remittance

envío (m) *[remesa]* consignment

envío agrupado de mercancías consolidated shipment

envío de publicidad por correo direct mailing or mailing shot

envío de revistas por correo magazine mailing

envío por correo mailing

envíos (mpl) a granel bulk shipments

envoltorio (m) wrapping or wrapper

envolver wrap up or parcel (v)

epígrafes (mpl) de un acuerdo heads of agreement

equilibrar balance (v)

equilibrio (m) balance (n)

equipaje (m) luggage or baggage

equipaje de mano hand luggage

equipaje no reclamado unclaimed baggage

equipar equip

equiparación (f) equalization

equipo (m) equipment

equipo de consumidores consumer panel

equipo de oficina office equipment

equipo de ventas sales team

equipo defectuoso faulty equipment

equipo directivo management team

equipo pesado heavy equipment

equipos (mpl) de oficina business equipment

equitativo (-va) fair (adj)

equivocación (f) mistake or error

equivocado (-da) wrong

erosionar erode

errar miss (v)

erróneo (-nea) erroneous or wrong

error (m) error (n) or slip (n) or mistake (n)

error aleatorio random error

error de cálculo miscalculation

error de copia o de oficina clerical error

error de ordenador computer error

escala (f) scale or range (n)

escala: sin escalas non-stop

escala de rendimiento earning capacity

escala móvil de salarios incremental scale

escala salarial o escala de salarios wage scale

escalar escalate

escalonar stagger

escaparate (m) shop window or window display

escasez (f) shortage

escasez de mano de obra manpower shortage

escaso (-sa) short of

escogido (-da) choice (adj)

escribir write

escribir a alguien correspond with someone

escribir sin abreviar write out (in full)

escrito (m) writing

escrito (-ta) a mano handwritten

escritorio (m) desk

escritura (f) writing or handwriting

escritura (f) [título] deed

escritura de cesión deed of assignment

escritura de constitución articles of association

escritura de convenio deed of covenant

escritura de sociedad deed of partnership

escritura de transferencia deed of transfer

escudo (m) [moneda] escudo

escuela (f) de secretariado secretarial college

escuela empresarial business school

escuela superior de comercio commercial college

esencial essential

esfuerzo (m) effort

espacio (m) space or room

espacio en blanco blank (n)

espacio para oficinas office space

espacio publicitario advertising space

especial special

especialista (mf) specialist

especialización (f) specialization

especializado (-da) [trabajador] skilled

especializar specialize

especificación (f) specification

especificar specify

esperar instrucciones await instructions

espionaje (m) industrial industrial espionage

esquina (f) corner (n)

estabilidad (f) stability or steadiness

estabilidad de los precios price stability

estabilización (f) stabilization

estabilizar los precios peg prices

estabilizar (se) stabilize or level out

estable stable

establecer establish or set (v)

establecerse settle

establecimiento (m) establishment [business]

estación (f) season

estación (f) [tren] train station

estación de ferrocarril railway station

estación de mercancías freight depot

estación de trabajo [de ordenador] computer workstation

estacional seasonal

estadísticas (fpl) statistics

estadístico (-ca) (adj) statistical

estadístico (-ca) statistician

estado (m) [país] state (n) or country

estado (m) [condición] condition or state

estado de cuenta bank balance

estado de cuenta mensual monthly statement

estado de cuentas statement of account

estado de cuentas semestral half-yearly statement

estado de flujo de caja cash flow statement

estadounidense (mf) American

estafa (f) fraud (n)

estafador (-ra) racketeer

estampilla (f) stamp (n)

estancado (-da) stagnant

estancamiento (m) stagnation

estancia (f) stay

estándar standard (adj)

estandarización (f) standardization

estandarizar (normalizar) standardize

estantería (f) shelves or shelving

estantería (f) [vitrina] display unit or display stand

estar de acuerdo agree with

estar en punto muerto be deadlocked

estatal government (adj)

estatutos (mpl) articles of association

estibador (m) stevedore

estimación (f) estimate (n) or estimation

estimado (-da) estimated

estimar estimate (v)

estimular boost (v)

estimular la economía stimulate the economy

estímulo (m) stimulus or boost (n) or incentive

estipulación (f) stipulation or provision

estipular stipulate

estrategia (f) strategy

estrategia comercial business strategy

estrategia de 'marketing' marketing strategy

estratégico (-ca) strategic

estropear spoil

estropearse break down (v)

estructura (f) structure (n)

estructura cuadricular grid structure

estructural structural

estucturar structure (v)

estudiar study (v)

estudio (m) study (n) or survey (n)

estudio de desplazamientos y tiempos time and motion study

estudio de mercado market research

estudios (mpl) sobre el terreno field work

etapa (f) stage (n)

etiqueta (f) label (n)

etiqueta (de señas) address label

etiqueta de correo aéreo airmail sticker

etiqueta de precio price tag or price ticket or price label

etiquetado (m) labelling

etiquetar label (v)

eurocheque (m) Eurocheque

eurodivisa (f) Eurocurrency

eurodólar (m) Eurodollar

euromercado (m) Euromarket

europeo (-a) European

evadir evade

evadir impuestos evade tax

evaluación (f) valuation or evaluation

evaluación de la rentabilidad measurement of profitability

evaluar evaluate

evaluar los costes evaluate costs

evasión (f) evasion

evasión de capital(es) flight of capital

evasión de impuestos tax avoidance or tax evasion

eventual prospective

eventualidad (f) contingency

evitar avoid or prevent

exactamente exactly

exacto (-ta) exact or accurate

examen (m) examination or test

examinar examine

excedencia (f) leave of absence

excedente (m) surplus or excess

excedente de plantilla [despido] redundancy (n)

excedente laboral overmanning

exceder exceed

excelente excellent or first-class

excepcional exceptional

excepto excluding

excepto except

excesivo (-va) excessive

exceso (m) excess or surplus

exceso de capacidad excess capacity

exceso de equipaje excess baggage

exceso de existencias overstocks

excluir exclude

exclusión (f) exclusion

exclusiva sole right

exclusividad (f) exclusivity

exclusivo (-va) sole

excusa (f) apology

exención (f) exemption

exención fiscal tax exemption or exemption from tax

exento (-ta) exempt (adj)

exento de alquiler rent-free

exento de impuestos exempt from tax or tax-exempt

exhibición (f) exhibition or display

exhibidor (-ra) demonstrator

exhibir o exponer display (v)

exigir require or demand (v) or claim (v)

exigir el reembolso ask for a refund

eximir exempt (v)

existencias (fpl) stock or inventory (n)

existencias finales closing stock

existencias iniciales opening stock

éxito (m) success

éxito: con éxito successful

éxito: sin éxito unsuccessful

expandir expand

expansión (f) expansion

expansión industrial industrial expansion

expedición (f) forwarding *or* shipping *or* consignment (n)

expedidor (-ra) shipper

expedidor (-ra) forwarding agent

expediente (m) dossier *or* file *or* record

expedir ship (v) *or* dispatch (v)

experimentado (-da) experienced

experimentar una recuperación stage a recovery

experto (-ta) experienced

expiración (f) expiration *or* expiry

expirar expire

explicación (f) explanation

explicar explain

explorar explore

explotar exploit

exponer exhibit (v) *or* display (v)

exponer *[describir]* describe

exportación (f) export (n)

exportación: de exportación exporting (adj)

exportaciones (fpl) exports

exportador (-ra) exporter *or* exporting (adj)

exportar export (v)

exposición (f) display (n) *or* exhibition *or* show

exposición (f) *[riesgo]* exposure

expositor (-ra) exhibitor

expresar express (v)

expreso (-sa) express (adj)

expropiación (f) forzosa compulsory purchase

extender make out

extender un cheque write out a cheque

extensión (f) telephone extension

exterior external

exterior *[externo]* outside

externo (-na) external *or* outside

extirpar excise (v)

extra extra

extracto (m) de cuentas bank statement

extranjero (m) overseas (n)

extranjero: en el extranjero abroad *or* overseas (adj)

extranjero (-ra) foreign

extraoficial unofficial

extraoficialmente off the record

extraordinario (-ria) extraordinary

extras (mpl) extras

extras (mpl) opcionales optional extras

Ff

fábrica (f) factory

fábrica (f) *[planta]* plant (n) *or* factory

fabricación (f) manufacturing *or* manufacture (n)

fabricante (m) manufacturer *or* producer

fabricar manufacture (v) *or* produce

fabricar en serie mass-produce

fabricar coches en serie mass-produce cars

fácil easy

facilidad (f) facility

facilidad de venta saleability

facilidades (fpl) de crédito credit facilities

facilidades de pago easy terms

factibilidad (f) feasibility

factor (m) factor (n)

factor de riesgo (en una inversión) downside factor

factor del coste cost factor

factor decisivo deciding factor

factor negativo minus factor

factor positivo plus factor

factores (mpl) cíclicos cyclical factors

factores de producción factors of production

factura (f) bill (n) *or* invoice (n)

factura con el IVA VAT invoice

factura de hotel hotel bill

factura detallada itemized invoice *or* detailed account

factura por duplicado duplicate receipt *or* duplicate of a receipt or invoice

factura pro forma pro forma (invoice)

facturación (f) billing *or* invoicing

facturación (f) *[ingresos]* sales revenue

facturar bill (v) *or* invoice (v)

facturar *[el equipaje]* check in *[at airport]*

facturas (fpl) impagadas unpaid invoices

fallar fail *or* not to succeed *or* miss

fallecido (-da) dead (adj)

fallo (m) *[decisión]* ruling (n)

fallo (m) *[defecto]* mechanical fault

falseado (-da) false

falsear fiddle (v)

falsificación (f) falsification *or* forgery *or* fake (n)

falsificado (-da) counterfeit (adj)

falsificar falsify *or* forge *or* fake (v)

falsificar *[embaucar]* fiddle (v)

falsificar dinero counterfeit (v) (money)

falso (-sa) false

falso (-sa) *[falsificado]* counterfeit (adj)

falta (f) fault *or* blame

falta (f) *[escasez]* shortage

falta de entrega non-delivery

falta de fondos lack of funds

fama (f) fame

fase (m) phase *or* stage (n)

favor: de favor complimentary

favorable favourable

fax (m) fax (n)

fe: de buena fe bona fide

fecha (f) date (n)

fecha: con fecha de dated

fecha: en fecha futura forward

fecha: sin fecha undated

fecha de amortización *o* **de rescate** redemption date

fecha de caducidad sell-by date *or* expiry date

fecha de cumplimiento completion date

fecha de entrada en vigor effective date

fecha de entrega delivery date

fecha de lanzamiento launching date

fecha de recepción date of receipt

fecha de vencimiento maturity date

fecha inicial starting date

fecha tope *o* **fecha límite** closing date *or* deadline

fechador (m) date stamp

fechar date (v)

feria (f) show (n) *or* fair

feria comercial trade fair

ferrocarril (m) rail *or* railway (GB) *or* railroad (US)

ferry (m) ferry

ferry roll-on roll-off roll on/roll off ferry

fiabilidad (f) reliability

fiable reliable

fiador (-ra) guarantor *or* surety

fianza (f) guarantee *or* security *or* surety

ficha (f) filing card *or* index card

ficha de ordenador computer file

fichero (m) file (n) *or* card index (n)

fichero (m) *[de ordenador]* computer file

fichero de tarjetas card-index file

fidelidad (f) a la marca brand loyalty

fidelidad a un establecimiento customer loyalty

fiesta (f) civil bank holiday

fiesta oficial statutory holiday

fiesta nacional public holiday

fijación (f) fixing

fijación colectiva de precios common pricing

fijación de los precios pricing

fijación de precios competitivos competitive pricing

fijación de precios marginal marginal pricing

fijar fix *or* arrange *or* set

fijar los daños assess damages

fijar objetivos set targets

fijar una reunión para las 3 de la tarde fix a meeting for 3 p.m.

fijo (-ja) fixed *or* set (adj)

fijo (-ja) *[uniforme]* flat (adj)

filial (adj) affiliated

filial (f) subsidiary (n)

fin (m) end (n)

fin: con fines lucrativos profit-making

fin: sin fines lucrativos non profit-making

fin de mes month end

final (adj) final *or* closing (adj)

final (m) end (n)

finalización (f) completion

finalizar finalize

finalizar *[terminar]* end (v)

financiación (f) funding *or* financing

financiación del déficit presupuestario deficit financing

financiamiento (m) financing

financiar finance (v) *or* fund (v)

financiar una operación finance an operation

financieramente financially

financiero (-ra) financial

finanzas (fpl) finance (n) *or* finances

finanzas públicas public finance

fingir fake (v)

finiquito (m) settlement

firma (f) signature

firma (f) *[empresa]* firm (n)

firma de un contrato completion of a contract

firmante (mf) signatory

firmar sign (v)

firmar como testigo witness (v)

firmar un cheque sign a cheque

firmar un contrato sign a contract

firme firm (adj) *or* strong

fiscal (adj) fiscal (adj)

fiscal (m) prosecution counsel

fletador (-ra) charterer

fletamento (m) chartering

fletamento (m) *[flete]* freightage

fletar charter (v)

fletar *[cargar]* take on freight

fletar un avión charter an aircraft

flete (m) freight *or* freightage

flete aéreo air freight

flete de vuelta homeward freight

flexibilidad (f) flexibility

flexible flexible

flojo (-ja) slack *or* loose

flojo (-ja) *[débil]* weak

florecer flourish

floreciente booming *or* flourishing

florín (m) *[moneda]* guilder

flotación (f) float (n)

flotante floating

flotar una divisa float (v) a currency

fluctuación (f) fluctuation

fluctuante fluctuating

fluctuar fluctuate

fluir flow (v)

flujo (m) flow (n)

flujo de caja cash flow

flujo de caja negativo negative cash flow

flujo de caja positivo positive cash flow

flujo de caja descontado discounted cash flow (DCF)

FMI (Fondo Monetario Internacional) IMF (= International Monetary Fund)

folleto (m) leaflet *or* prospectus

folleto publicitario brochure

folleto publicitario enviado por correo mailing piece

fondo (m) bottom

fondo (m) *[finanzas]* fund (n)

fondo de caja cash float

fondo de comercio goodwill

fondo de pensiones pension fund

fondo para gastos menores petty cash

fondo para imprevistos contingency fund

Fondo Monetario Internacional (FMI) International Monetary Fund (IMF)

fondos (mpl) mutuos *o* **fondos de inversión** unit trust

fondos públicos public funds

formación (f) training (n)

formación (f) de mandos management training

formación en el puesto de trabajo in-house training

formación profesional en el trabajo on-the-job training

formación profesional fuera del trabajo off-the-job training

formal formal

formalidad (f) formality

formalidades aduaneras customs formalities

formar form (v)

formarse train (v) *or* learn

formulario (m) form (n)

formulario de declaración de la renta tax declaration form

formulario de solicitud application form

fórmulas (fpl) judiciales form of words

fotocopia (f) photocopy (n) *or* photocopying

fotocopiadora (f) copier *or* photocopier

fotocopiaje (m) photocopying

fotocopiar photocopy (v)

fracasado (-da) unsuccessful

fracasar fail *or* flop (v)

fracaso (m) failure *or* flop (n)

frágil fragile

franco (m) *[moneda]* franc

franco *[libre]* franco

franco a bordo free on board (f.o.b.)

franco a domicilio carriage paid

franco de porte carriage free

franco en almacén price ex warehouse

franco en fábrica price ex works

franco en muelle price ex quay

franco sobre vagón *o* **franco vagón FF.CC.** free on rail

franquear frank (v) *or* stamp (v)

franqueo (m) postage

franqueo (m) concertado postage paid *or* postpaid

franqueo y embalaje postage and packing (p. & p.)

franquicia (f) franchise *or* franchising

franquiciador (-ra) franchiser

franquiciar franchise (v)

fraude (m) fraud

fraude fiscal tax evasion

fraudulentamente fraudulently

fraudulento (-ta) fraudulent

frecuencia (f) de visitas de un representante call rate

frecuente frequent

frenar plug (v) *or* block (v) *or* stop (v)

freno (m) brake *or* check (n)

frontera (f) border

fuego (m) fire (n)

fuente (f) de ingresos source of income

fuera de control out of control

fuera de horas de oficina outside office hours

fuera de horas punta off-peak

fuerte strong

fuerte competencia keen competition

fuerza (f) strength

fuerza: a la fuerza forced

fuerza mayor act of God *or* force majeure

fuerzas (fpl) del mercado market forces

fuga (f) flight

fuga de capital(es) flight of capital

funcionamiento (m) *[maquinaria]* operating *or* running (n)

funcionamiento (m) *[rendimiento]* performance

funcionario (-ria) official (n) *or* civil servant

funcionario (-ria) de aduanas customs officer *or* customs official

función: en funciones acting

funda (f) cover (n) *or* top (n)

fundamental basic (adj) *or* fundamental

fundar una compañía set up a company *or* float a company

furgoneta (f) de reparto delivery van

fusión (f) merger

fusionar merge

futura: en fecha futura forward

futuros (mpl) futures

Gg

galería (f) comercial shopping mall

gama (f) range (n)

gama de precios price range

gama de productos product line

gama de productos de una compañía product mix

ganancia (f) gain (n) or profit (n) or return (n)

ganancia neta clear profit

ganancias (fpl) earnings

ganancias netas net earnings or net income

ganancias: cuenta de pérdidas y ganancias profit and loss account

ganar gain (v)

ganar [sueldo] earn (v)

ganar dinero make money

ganga (f) bargain (n)

garante (m) backer or guarantor or surety (n)

garantía (f) guarantee or warranty or collateral (n)

garantía (f) [fianza] surety (n) or security

garantizar guarantee (v) or warrant (v)

garantizar el pago underwrite

gasolina a precio reducido cut-price petrol

gastar spend

gastar excesivamente overspend

gastar más de lo presupuestado overspend one's budget

gastar menos underspend

gasto (m) expense or expenditure or outlay

gasto de tramitación handling charge

gastos (mpl) expenses

gastos: sin gastos de franqueo post free

gastos a cobrar a la entrega charges forward

gastos adicionales y complementarios extra charges

gastos administrativos administrative expenses

gastos aparte extras

gastos bancarios bank charges

gastos corrientes running costs or running expenses

gastos de capital capital expenditure

gastos de demora demurrage

gastos de descarga landing charges

gastos de embalaje packing charges

gastos de explotación operating costs or operating expenses

gastos de franqueo postal charges or postal rates

gastos de mantenimiento running costs or running expenses

gastos de producción overheads or overhead costs or expenses

gastos de publicidad publicity expenditure

gastos de transporte freight costs

gastos del consumidor o de consumo consumer spending

gastos generales o gastos de producción overheads or overhead costs or expenses

gastos generales de fabricación manufacturing overheads

gastos iniciales start-up costs

gastos menores petty expenses or incidental expenses

gastos no autorizados unauthorized expenditure

gastos reembolsables out-of-pocket expenses

gastos totales total expenditure

general general or across-the-board

general [completo] full-scale (adj)

género (m) merchandise (n)

genuino (-na) genuine

gerencia (f) management

gerente (mf) manager

gestión (f) management

gestión de cartera portfolio management

gestión de deudas con descuento factoring

gestión lineal line management

gestionar negotiate (v)

gestionar deudas con descuento factor (v)

girar draw (v)

girar (volumen de ventas) turn over (v)

girar en descubierto overdraw

giro (m) *[envío]* remittance

giro (m) *[letra]* draft (n)

giro a la vista sight draft

giro bancario bank draft *or* banker's draft *or* giro system

giro bancario *[letra bancaria]* bank bill (GB)

giro postal postal order *or* money order

giro postal internacional foreign money order

global overall *or* comprehensive

global *[mundial]* worldwide (adj)

gobierno (m) government (n)

gobierno: del gobierno government (adj)

grado: de grado inferior low-level

graduado (-da) graduated

gradual gradual

gráfico (n) *o* **gráfica (f)** graph (n) *or* chart (n)

gráfico circular *o* **gráfico sectorial** pie chart

gráfico de barras bar chart

gráfico de ventas sales chart

gramo (m) gram *or* gramme

gran demanda (f) keen demand

gran gasto (m) heavy expenditure

grande large *or* big

grande *[importante]* heavy *or* important

grandes almacenes (mpl) store (n) *or* large shop *or* department store

grandes costes (mpl) heavy costs *or* heavy expenditure

granel: a granel loose

grapa (f) staple (n)

grapadora (f) stapler

grapar staple (v)

grapar papeles staple papers together

gratificación (f) por méritos merit award *or* merit bonus

gratis gratis *or* free *or* free of charge

gratuitamente gratis *or* free (adv)

gratuito (-ta) free (adj)

gravamen (m) lien

gravamen sobre las importaciones import levy

gravar impose

gravar con un impuesto tax (v)

gremio (m) guild

grúa (f) crane

gruesa (f) gross (n) (= 144)

grupo (m) group

grupo de trabajo working party

grupos (mpl) socioeconómicos socio-economic groups

guardar save (v) *or* store (v)

guardar *[ordenador]* back up (v) *or* save (v)

guardar *[tener]* hold (v) *or* keep (v)

guardia (m) de seguridad security guard

guerra (f) de precios price war *or* price-cutting war

guía (f) comercial commercial directory *or* trade directory

guía telefónica telephone book *or* telephone directory

guía urbana street directory

guía (mf) de turismo courier *or* guide (n)

Hh

haber (m) credit balance *or* credit side

habilidad (f) skill

habitación (f) room

habitaciones (fpl) de hotel hotel accommodation

habitante (mf) inhabitant *or* occupier

habitante (mf) *[residente]* resident (n)

habitual usual *or* routine (adj)

hacer do (v) *or* make (v)

hacer bajar los precios force prices down

hacer cumplir enforce

hacer efectivo encash

hacer falta take (v) *or* need (v)

hacer frente (a) cope (v) (with)

hacer funcionar run (v) *or* work (a machine)

hacer negocios transact business

hacer publicidad con mucho bombo hype (v)

hacer subir los precios force prices up

hacer trabajo eventual temp (v)

hacer un asiento post an entry

hacer un borrador draft (v)

hacer un depósito pay money down

hacer un inventario take stock

hacer un muestreo sample (v)

hacer un pedido order (v)

hacer una lista make a list *or* list (v)

hacerse cargo take over

hacerse un seguro take out a policy

hacia abajo down *or* downward

hacia el centro downtown (adv)

Hacienda (f) Publica the Treasury

hasta up to

hecho a medida *o* **a la orden** custom-built *or* custom-made

hectárea (f) hectare

herramienta (f) implement (n) *or* tool (n)

hipermercado (m) hypermarket *or* superstore

hipoteca (f) mortgage (n)

hipotecar mortgage (v)

historial (m) personal record

hoja (f) de cálculo spreadsheet

hoja de papel sheet of paper

hoja de sueldo *o* **de salario** pay slip

holding (m) holding company

hombre (m) man (n)

hombre de confianza right-hand man

hombre de negocios businessman

honorarios (mpl) fee *or* honorarium

hora (f) hour

hora: por hora hourly *or* per hour

hora de apertura opening time

hora de cierre closing time

hora-hombre (f) man-hour

horario (m) timetable (n)

horario bancario banking hours

horario comercial opening hours

horario de oficina office hours

horario de presentación (en el aeropuerto) check-in time

horas (fpl) de oficina business hours

horas extraordinarias overtime

horas punta peak period *or* rush hour

hotel (m) hotel

hotel homologado graded hotel

hueco (m) gap

hueco de un mercado niche

hueco en el mercado gap in the market

huelga (f) strike (n)

huelga de brazos caídos sit-down strike

huelga de celo go-slow *or* work-to-rule

huelga de protesta protest strike

huelga de solidaridad sympathy strike

huelga general general strike

huelga salvaje wildcat strike

huelguista (mf) striker

hundimiento (m) collapse (n)

hundirse collapse (v) *or* sink (v)

hundirse *[caer en picado]* slump (v)

hurto (m) pilferage *or* pilfering (n)

hurto en las tiendas shoplifting

Ii

I+D (investigación y desarrollo) research and development (R & D)

igual equal (adj)

igualar equal (v)

igualdad (f) equality *or* parity

ilegal illegal

ilegalidad (f) illegality

ilegalmente illegally

ilícito (-ta) illicit

imagen (f) de marca brand image

imagen pública public image

imagen pública de una empresa corporate image

imitación (f) imitation *or* fake (n)

impagado (-da) unpaid

impago (m) de una deuda non-payment

impar odd

impedir prevent

imperfección (f) imperfection

imperfecto (-ta) imperfect

imponer impose (v)

importación (f) import *or* importing (n)

importación-exportación import-export

importaciones (fpl) imports

importaciones (fpl) visibles visible imports

importador (-ra) importer (n) *or* importing (adj)

importancia (f) importance

importante important *or* major

importante *[grande]* heavy

importar import (v)

importar *[valer]* matter (v)

importe (m) amount

importe debido amount owing

importe pagado amount paid

imposible de conseguir unobtainable

imposición (f) *[depósito]* deposit

imposición (f) *[impuesto]* taxation

imposición alta high taxation

imposición directa direct taxation

imposición en efectivo cash deposit

imposición indirecta indirect taxation

impositor (-ra) depositor

imprenta (f) printer

imprescindible essential

impresión (f) printout

impreso (m) form (n)

impreso de solicitud application form

impreso de declaración de aduana customs declaration form

impresora (f) printer *or* computer printer

impresora de líneas line printer

impresora de rueda de margarita daisy-wheel printer

impresora láser laser printer

impresora matricial dot-matrix printer

imprimir print out

impuesto (m) tax (n) *or* taxation (n)

impuesto ad valorem ad valorem tax

impuesto atrasado back tax

impuesto básico basic tax

impuesto de circulación road tax

impuesto de sociedades corporation tax

impuesto de venta purchase tax

impuesto del timbre stamp duty

impuesto directo direct tax

impuesto indirecto indirect tax

impuesto no incluido exclusive of tax

impuesto pagado tax paid

impuesto para financiar la formación profesional training levy

impuesto progresivo graded tax

impuesto progresivo sobre la renta graduated income tax

impuesto sobre el consumo excise duty

impuesto sobre el valor añadido (IVA) value added tax (VAT)

impuesto sobre el volumen de ventas turnover tax

impuesto sobre la renta income tax

impuesto sobre la venta sales tax

impuesto sobre las plusvalías capital gains tax

impuesto sobre las ventas de bienes o servicios output tax

impuestos (mpl) duty

impuestos incluidos inclusive of tax

impuestos retenidos en el origen tax deducted at source

impulsar boost (v)

impulso (m) impulse *or* boost (n)

inalcanzable unobtainable

inalterado (-da) unchanged

inasequible unavailable

inauguración (f) opening (n)

inaugural opening (adj)

incapaz incapable

incautación (f) seizure

incautar seize (v)

incendio (m) fire (n)

incentivo (m) incentive

incluido (-da) inclusive

incluido: no incluido exclusive of

incluir include (v)

incluir incorporate

inclusive *o* **inclusivo (-va)** inclusive

incompetencia (f) *[incapacia]* incompetence (n)

incompetencia (f) *[ineficacia]* inefficiency

incompetente *[incapaz]* incompetent

incompetente *[ineficaz]* inefficient

incondicional unconditional

incorporado (-da) built-in

incorporar incorporate (v)

incorrectamente incorrectly

incorrecto (-ta) incorrect

incremental incremental

incremento (m) increment (n) *or* increase (n)

incumplimiento (m) default (n)

incumplir default (v) *or* break (v)

incumplir los pagos default on payments

incurrir en incur

indemnidad (f) *o* **indemnización (f)** indemnity *or* indemnification

indemnización por daños y perjuicios compensation for damage

indemnizar indemnify

indemnizar *[resarcir]* make good

indemnizar *[compensar]* compensate

indemnizar a alguien por una pérdida indemnify someone for a loss

independiente independent

indexación (f) indexation

indicador (m) indicator *or* index number

indicadores (mpl) económicos economic indicators

indicar show (v) *or* specify (v)

indicar *[citar referencia]* quote (v)

índice (m) index number

índice de crecimiento growth index

índice de ocupación occupancy rate

índice de precios al comsumo retail price index

índice de precios al consumo (IPC) consumer price index

índice de precios al por mayor wholesale price index

índice del coste de vida cost-of-living index

índice ponderado weighted index

indiciación (f) indexation

indirecto (-ta) indirect

indisponibilidad (f) unavailability

industria (f) industry

industria clave key industry

industria con alto coeficiente de capital capital-intensive industry

industria de servicios service industry *or* tertiary industry

industria nacionalizada nationalized industry

industria pesada heavy industry

industria principal staple industry

industria próspera *o* **en pleno auge** boom industry

industria secundaria secondary industry

industria terciaria tertiary industry

industrial industrial

industrial (mf) industrialist (n)

industrialización (f) industrialization

industrializar industrialize

ineficacia (f) inefficiency

ineficaz inefficient

inexplicado (-da) unexplained *or* unaccounted for

inferior lower (adj)

inflación (f) inflation

inflación de costes cost-push inflation

inflacionario (-ria) *o* inflacionista inflationary

influencia (f) influence (n)

influir influence (v)

información (f) information

información de vuelos flight information

información privilegiada insider dealing

información publicitaria sales literature

informar inform (v) *or* report (v)

informar *[advertir]* advise

informar *[dar instrucciones]* brief (v)

informar sobre la marcha report on progress

informático (-ca) computerized

informatizado (-da) computerized

informatizar computerize

informe (m) report (n) *or* survey (n)

informe (m) *[registro]* record (n)

informe anual annual report

informe confidencial confidential report

informe de viabilidad (de un proyecto) feasibility report

informe provisional interim report

informe sobre la marcha de un trabajo progress report

infracción (f) aduanera infringement of customs regulations

infracción fiscal tax offence

infraestructura (f) infrastructure

infringir break (v) *or* infringe (v)

infringir la ley break the law

ingeniero (-ra) de producto product engineer

ingeniero (-ra) de obra site engineer

inglés (-esa) English *or* British

ingresar bank (v) *or* deposit (v)

ingresar en caja take (v)

ingreso (m) revenue

ingreso (m) *[depósito]* deposit (n)

ingreso (m) *[entrada]* entry *or* admission

ingreso fijo regular income

ingreso real real income *or* real wages

ingreso total total revenue

ingresos (mpl) income *or* earnings *or* salary

ingresos (mpl) *[entradas]* receipts

ingresos (mpl) *[recaudación]* take (n) *or* money taken

ingresos brutos gross earnings

ingresos de un negocio takings

ingresos de ventas sales revenue

ingresos invisibles invisible earnings

ingresos libres de impuestos non-taxable income

ingresos netos net receipts *or* net earnings *or* net income

ingresos por publicidad revenue from advertising

ingresos por alquiler rental income

iniciación (f) induction

iniciado (m) insider

inicial initial (adj) *or* starting (adj)

iniciar initiate *or* pioneer (v)

iniciar conversaciones initiate discussions

iniciativa (f) initiative

inicio (m) start (n)

injusto (-ta) unfair

inmediatamente immediately

inmediato (-ta) immediate *or* instant (adj) *or* prompt

inmovilizar capital lock up capital

innovación (f) innovation

innovador (-ra) innovator (n) *or* innovative (adj)

innovar innovate

inquietud (f) concern (n) *or* worry (n)

inquilino (-na) tenant *or* lessee *or* occupant

inquilino (-na) en posesión sitting tenant

inscribir *[registrar]* enter

inscribir (en un registro) register (v)

inscribir una compañía en un registro register a company

inscribirse *[registrarse]* register (v)

inscripción (f) registration

inscripción (f) *[entrada]* entering

insignificante petty *or* negligible

insistir en hold out for

insolvencia (f) insolvency *or* bankruptcy

insolvente insolvent *or* bankrupt

inspección (f) inspection *or* survey (n)

inspección aduanera customs examination

inspección de daños damage survey

inspeccionar inspect *or* survey (v)

inspector (-ra) inspector *or* controller

inspector (-ra) de calidad quality controller

inspector (-ra) de fábrica factory inspector

inspector (-ra) de Hacienda tax inspector

inspector (-ra) de obra surveyor

inspector (-ra) del IVA VAT inspector

instalaciones (fpl) facilities

instalaciones de almacenaje storage facilities

instalaciones portuarias harbour facilities

instalar la maquinaria en una fábrica tool up (v)

instantáneo (-nea) instant (adj) *or* immediate

institución (f) institution

institución financiera financial institution

institucional institutional

instituir institute (v)

instituto (m) institute (n)

instrucción (f) instruction *or* directive

instrucciones (fpl) directions for use

instrucciones de envío forwarding instructions *or* shipping instructions

instrumento (m) instrument *or* implement (n)

instrumento (m) *[medio]* medium (n)

instrumento negociable negotiable instrument

insuficiencia (f) insufficiency *or* shortfall

intangible intangible

integración (f) horizontal horizontal integration

integración vertical vertical integration

intensificar (el control) tighten up on

intercambiable exchangeable

intercambiar exchange (v) *or* swap (v)

intercambio (m) exchange (n) swap (n)

interés (m) interest (n)

interés (m) *[atracción]* appeal (n) *or* attraction

interés acumulado accrued interest

interés acumulativo cumulative interest

interés compuesto compound interest

interés elevado high interest

interés fijo fixed interest

interés personal vested interest

interés simple simple interest

interesar interest (v)

interesar *[atraer]* appeal to (v) *or* attract

intereses (mpl) creados vested interest

interfaz (m) interface (n)

interino (-na) temp (n)

interino (-na) *[en funciones]* acting (adj)

interior internal

interior *[nacional]* domestic *or* inland (GB)

intermediario (-ria) intermediary *or* middleman

intermediario (-ria) *[agente]* broker

internacional international

interno (-na) internal

interno (-na) *[de la casa]* in-house

interpretar interpret

intérprete (mf) interpreter

interrumpir discontinue

interrupción (f) interruption *or* breakdown (n)

intervención (f) audit (n)

intervenir las cuentas audit (v)

interventor (-ra) auditor

introducción (f) introduction

introducir introduce

introducir datos input information

introducir gradualmente phase in

inundación (f) flood (n)

inundar flood (v)

inundar el mercado glut (v) *or* flood (v) the market

invalidación (f) invalidation

invalidar void (v) *or* invalidate

invalidez (f) invalidity

inválido (-da) invalid *or* void (adj)

invariable unchanged *or* constant

inventariar inventory (v) *or* take stock

inventario (m) inventory *or* stocktaking *or* stock list

inventario de posición (en almacén) picking list

inversión (f) investment

inversión (f) *[revocación]* reversal

inversión: gastos de inversión capital expenditure

inversión segura safe investment *or* secure investment

inversión sin riesgo risk-free investment

inversiones de interés fijo fixed-interest investments

inversiones en valores seguros blue-chip investments

inversiones exteriores foreign investments

inversionista (mf) investor

inversor (-ra) investor

inversores (mpl) institucionales institutional investors

invertir invest

investigación (f) investigation *or* research (n)

investigación (f) *[petición de informes]* inquiry

investigación de conflictos problem solving *or* troubleshooting

investigación sobre el consumo consumer research

investigación y desarrollo (I+D) research and development (R & D)

investigador (-ra) researcher *or* research worker

investigar investigate *or* research (v)

investigar *[perseguir]* follow up

invitación (f) invitation

invitar invite

IPC (índice de precios al consumo) consumer price index

ir go

ir a la huelga strike (v) *or* go on strike

ir de compras *o* de tiendas shopping

ir haciendo get along

irregular irregular

irregularidades (fpl) irregularities

irrevocable irrevocable

irse leave (v)

itinerario (m) itinerary

IVA (impuesto sobre el valor añadido) VAT (= value added tax)

izquierdo (-da) left

Jj Kk

jefe (adj) chief (adj)

jefe (-fa) manager *or* head *or* boss

jefe ejecutivo chief executive

jefe (-fa) de almacén stock controller

jefe (-fa) de compras purchasing manager

jefe (-fa) de departamento *o* de sección departmental manager *or* head of department

jefe (-fa) de distribución distribution manager

jefe (-fa) de equipo de ventas field sales manager

jefe (-fa) de oficina chief clerk

jefe (-fa) de publicidad advertising manager

jefe (-fa) de personal personnel manager

jornada (f) day *or* working day

joven young

joven: más joven junior *or* younger

jubilación (f) retirement

jubilarse retire (from one's job)

judicial legal

juego (m) game *or* set (n)

juego completo en caja de presentación boxed set

juez (mf) judge (n)

juicio (m) lawsuit *or* court case *or* trial

juicio (m) *[sentencia]* judgement *or* judgment

junta (f) de directores management *or* managers

junta directiva board of directors

junta general general meeting

junta general anual annual general meeting (AGM)

juntar join (v)

jurídico (-ca) legal

jurisdicción (f) jurisdiction

justificar justify *or* warrant (v)

justificar *[responder]* account for

justo (-ta) fair (adj)

juzgar judge (v)

kilo (m) *o* **kilogramo (m)** kilo *or* kilogram

kilometraje (m) distance *or* mileage (allowance)

Ll

laboral occupational *or* labour

lado (m) side

laguna (f) fiscal tax loophole

lanzamiento (m) launch (n) *or* launching

lanzamiento float (n) *or* flotation (of company)

lanzamiento de una sociedad floating of a company

lanzar launch (v)

lanzar al mercado bring out

largo (-ga) long

largo plazo long-term

largo plazo: a largo plazo long-range

leasing (m) leasing

legal legal *or* lawful *or* statutory

legalizar authenticate

legible por ordenador computer-readable

legislación (f) legislation

legítimo (-ma) rightful

lenguaje (m) burocrático officialese

lenguaje de programación programming language

lenguaje informático *o* **de ordenador** computer language

lento (-ta) slow

letra (f) handwriting

letra (f) *[bancaria]* bill (n) *or* draft

letra a largo plazo long-dated bill

letra al propio cargo note of hand *or* promissory note

letra bancaria bank bill (GB)

letra de cambio bill of exchange

letras (fpl) a cobrar bills receivable

letras a corto vencimiento short-dated bills

letras a pagar bills payable

letras por cobrar bills for collection

letrero (m) notice *or* sign (n)

levantar lift (v) *or* remove

levantar acta minute (v)

levantar un embargo lift an embargo

levantar una sesión close a meeting

ley (f) law

ley de la oferta y la demanda law of supply and demand

ley de prescripción statute of limitations

ley de rendimientos decrecientes law of diminishing returns

ley de sociedades anómimas company law

liberación (f) release (n)

liberalización (f) liberalization *or* deregulation

liberalizar liberalize *or* decontrol

liberar free (v) *or* release (v)

libra (f) pound

libra esterlina pound sterling

librado (-da) drawee

librador (-ra) drawer

libramiento (m) order (n)

libre free (adj) *or* vacant

libre *[franco]* franco

libre cambio *o* **libre comercio** free trade

libre de derechos de aduana free of duty

libre de impuestos duty-free *or* free of tax *or* tax-free

libre: de libre dedicación freelance (adj)

libreta (f) de ahorros bank book

libro (m) book (n)

libro de caja cash book

libro de pedidos order book

libro de registro register (n)

libro de ventas sales book

libro diario *[contabilidad]* journal *or* accounts book

libro mayor ledger

libro mayor de compras purchase ledger *or* bought ledger

libro mayor de resultados nominal ledger

libro mayor de ventas sales ledger

libro registro de accionistas register of shareholders

licencia (f) licence *or* permit

licencia (f) *[autorización]* licensing

licencia de exportación export licence *or* export permit

licencia de importación import licence *or* import permit

licencia por maternidad maternity leave

licenciado (-da) en prácticas graduate trainee

licitación (f) bidding (n)

licitador (m) tenderer *or* bidder

licitar para un contrato tender for a contract

lícito (-ta) lawful *or* legal

líder (m) del mercado market leader

limitación (f) limitation *or* restriction

limitado (-da) limited

limitar limit (v) *or* restrict

limitar el crédito restrict credit

límite (m) limit (n)

límite de crédito credit limit *or* lending limit

límite de descubierto bancario overdraft facility

límite de precios price ceiling

línea (f) line (n)

línea aérea airline

línea de carga load line

línea de productos product line

línea exterior outside line

línea ocupada *[teléfono]* engaged

línea telefónica telephone line

línea de flotación load line

liquidación (f) liquidation *or* winding up

liquidación (f) *[rebajas]* sale (n)

liquidación de una deuda clearing (of a debt)

liquidación de activo realization of assets

liquidación de inventario stocktaking sale

liquidación forzosa compulsory liquidation

liquidación total por cierre closing-down sale

liquidación voluntaria voluntary liquidation

liquidar sell off

liquidar existencias clear (v) *or* liquidate stock

liquidar propiedades realize property

liquidar una compañía liquidate a company

liquidar una cuenta settle an account

liquidar una deuda clear a debt

liquidar una sociedad wind up a company

liquidez (f) liquidity

lira (f) lira

lista (f) list (n)

lista de bultos packing list *or* packing slip

lista de contenidos packing list *or* packing slip

lista de correos poste restante

lista de destinatarios mailing list

lista de direcciones address list

lista de existencias stocklist

lista de precios price list *or* scale of charges

lista de precios fija fixed scale of charges

lista del contenido de un paquete docket

lista negra black list (n)

listado (m) de ordenador computer listing

listo (-ta) ready

litro (m) litre

llamada (f) (phone) call

llamada a cobro revertido reverse charge call or collect call (US)

llamada de fuera incoming call

llamada internacional international call

llamada local local call

llamada rutinaria routine call

llamada telefónica phone call or telephone call

llamadas internacionales directas international direct dialling

llamar (por teléfono) call (v) or phone (v) or telephone (v)

llamar a cobro revertido reverse the charges

llave (f) key

llegada (f) arrival

llegadas (fpl) arrivals

llegar arrive or reach

llegar: que está por llegar due

llegar a un acuerdo reach an agreement

llegar al máximo peak (v)

llenar fill (a gap)

lleno (-na) full

llevar take (v) or carry or transport (v)

llevar [dirigir] run (v) or manage

llevar [producir] bear (v)

llevar a alguien ante los tribunales take someone to court

llevar negociaciones conduct negotiations

llevar un negocio carry on a business

local local (adj)

local (m) [edificio] premises

local comercial business premises

local de exposición (exhibition) stand

local sin vivienda incorporada lock-up premises

logotipo (m) logo

lonja (f) commodity market or commodity exchange

lote (m) batch (n) or lot

lucrativo (-va) money-making or profit-making or profitable

lugar (m) place (n) or site or venue or spot

lugar de trabajo place of work

lugar de reunión meeting place

Mm

macroeconomía (f) macro-economics

magistratura (f) del trabajo industrial tribunal

mal equipado (-da) underequipped

mal pagado (-da) underpaid

mala administración (f) maladministration or mismanagement

mala calidad (f) poor quality

mala compra (f) bad buy

malentendido (m) misunderstanding

maleta (f) case (n) or suitcase

maletas (fpl) baggage or luggage

maletín (m) briefcase

malgastar waste (v)

malversación (f) misappropriation or embezzlement

malversador (-ra) embezzler

malversar misappropriate or embezzle

mandante (m) principal (n)

mandar por correo post (v) or mail (v)

mandar trabajo fuera farm out work

mandato (m) mandate or writ

mandato (m) [campo de aplicación] terms of reference

mandato (m) [periodo] tenure

mando (m) control (n)

mando a distancia remote control

mandos (mpl) intermedios middle management

manejable manageable

manejar handle (v) or manage or operate

manejo (m) handling

manejo: de fácil manejo user-friendly

manejo de materiales materials handling

manera (f) means *or* ways

manifiesto (m) manifest

manipulación (f) handling

mano: de segunda mano secondhand

mano: en manos de los tribunales sub judice

mano: escrito a mano handwritten

mano (f) de obra manpower *or* workforce *or* labour force

mano de obra barata cheap labour

mano de obra cualificada skilled labour

mano de obra local local labour

mantener maintain *or* keep up

mantenimiento (m) maintenance

mantenimiento de relaciones maintenance of contacts

mantenimiento de suministros maintenance of supplies

manual (adj) manual (adj)

manual (m) manual (n)

manual de funcionamiento operating manual

manual de mantenimiento service manual

manufacturar manufacture (v)

manzana (f) *[edificios]* block (n)

maqueta (f) mock-up *or* model (n)

máquina (f) machine

máquina de cambio change machine

máquina franqueadora franking machine

maquinaria (f) plant (n) *or* machinery

maquinaria pesada heavy machinery

maquinista (mf) machinist *or* operator

marca (f) brand

marca (f) *[señal]* mark (n)

marca comercial trademark *or* trade name *or* brand name

marca registrada registered trademark

marcador (m) marker pen

marcar mark (v)

marcar *[teléfono]* dial (v)

marcar directamente dial direct

marcar un número dial a number

marcha (f) progress (n)

marcha: en marcha going

marcharse leave (v) *or* go away

marco (m) frame (n)

marco alemán mark (n) *or* Deutschmark

margen (m) margin

margen de beneficio profit margin *or* mark-up

margen de beneficio bruto gross margin

margen de cobertura backwardation

margen de error margin of error

margen neto net margin

marginal marginal

marina (f) mercante merchant navy

marino (-na) marine

marítimo (-ma) maritime

más more *or* plus

masa (f) mass

master (m) en administración de empresas Master's degree in Business Administration (MBA)

material (m) de embalaje packaging material

material de exposición display material

materias (fpl) primas raw materials

matrícula (f) registration (fee)

matriz (f) *[de un talonario]* counterfoil *or* cheque stub

maximización (f) maximization

maximizar maximize

máximo (m) maximum (n)

máximo (-ma) maximum (adj)

mayor *[importante]* major

mayor *[principal]* main

mayor *[superior]* senior

mayoría (f) majority

mayorista (mf) wholesale dealer *or* wholesaler

mechera (f) shoplifter

media (f) mean (n)

media ponderada weighted average

media docena (f) half a dozen *or* a half-dozen

mediación (f) mediation

mediador (-ra) mediator

mediador de conflictos problem solver *or* troubleshooter

mediana (f) median

mediano (-na) medium *or* medium-sized *or* average (adj)

mediar mediate

medición (f) de la rentabilidad measurement of profitability

medida (f) de tiempo timing

medida de volumen *o* **de capacidad** cubic measure

medida: hecho a la medida custom-built *or* custom-made

medidas (fpl) measures *or* measurements

medidas de precaución safety precautions

medidas de seguridad safety measures

medidas de seguridad (en una oficina) office security

medidas fiscales fiscal measures

medio (m) medium (n)

medio (m) *[manera]* means

medio (-dia) *[mitad]* half (adj)

medio (-dia) mean (adj) *or* average (adj) *or* medium (adj)

mediocre mediocre *or* low-quality

medios (mpl) *[instalaciones]* facilities

medios (mpl) *[recursos]* means

medios de comunicación mass media

medios de transporte transport facilities

medios fraudulentos false pretences

mejor (el, la) best

mejor postor highest bidder

mejora (f) upturn *or* improvement

mejorar recover *or* get better

memorandum (m) memo *or* memorandum

memoria (f) (computer) memory

memoria (f) *[informe]* report (n)

mencionar mention *or* refer to

menor junior (adj) *or* younger

menos minus *or* less

menos de under *or* less than

menos de lo necesario *[escaso]* short of

mensaje (m) message

mensajero (-ra) messenger *or* courier

mensual monthly (adj)

mensualmente monthly (adv)

mercadeo (m) merchandizing

mercado (m) market (n) *or* marketplace

mercado (m) *[salida]* outlet

mercado a futuros forward market

mercado alcista bull market

mercado bajista bear market

mercado cautivo captive market

mercado cerrado closed market

Mercado Común Europeo Common Market

mercado de compradores buyer's market

mercado de divisas foreign exchange market

mercado de valores stock market

mercado de vendedores seller's market

mercado débil weak market

mercado interior home market *or* domestic market

mercado libre open market

mercado limitado limited market

mercado mundial world market

mercado nacional home market *or* domestic market

mercado negro black market

mercado potencial potential market

mercado previsto target market

Mercado Unico Europeo Single European Market

mercados (mpl) extranjeros overseas markets

mercados monetarios money markets

mercadotecnia (f) marketing

mercancía (f) commodity

mercancías (fpl) goods *or* merchandise (n)

mercancías a precio reducido cut-price goods

mercancías con impuestos aduaneros pagados duty-paid goods

mercancías dañadas por un incendio fire-damaged goods

mercancías en tránsito goods in transit

mérito (m) merit

mermas (fpl) leakage

mes (m) month

mes: del presente mes instant (adj)

mes civil calendar month

mesa (f) de despacho desk

meta (f) target (n)

mezclado (-da) mixed

microeconomía (f) micro-economics

microordenador (m) microcomputer

miembro (m) member

miembros: los miembros membership

mil millones (mpl) billion

millón (m) million

millonario (-ria) millionaire

mínimo (m) low (n) *or* minimum (n)

mínimo (-ma) minimum (adj)

ministerio (m) (government) department

ministerio (m) de Hacienda Exchequer

ministro (m) del gobierno secretary *or* government minister

minoría (f) minority

minorista (mf) retail dealer *or* retailer

minusvalías (fpl) capital loss

minuto (m) minute (n)

misceláneo (-nea) miscellaneous

misión (f) comercial trade mission

mitad (f) half (n)

mitad de precio half-price sale

mixto (-ta) mixed

modelo (m) model (n) *or* standard (n)

modelo a escala model (n) *or* mock-up

modelo de prueba demonstration model

modelo económico economic model

modem (m) modem

moderado (-da) moderate (adj)

moderar moderate (v)

moderno (-na) modern *or* up to date

moderno: muy moderno state-of-the-art

modificación (f) alteration

modificar alter

modo (m) mode

modo de empleo directions for use

modo de pago mode of payment

moneda (f) coin *or* currency

moneda bloqueada blocked currency

moneda convertible convertible currency *or* hard currency

moneda de curso legal legal currency *or* legal tender

moneda débil soft currency

moneda estable stable currency

moneda extranjera foreign currency

moneda fuerte strong currency

moneda inflacionista inflated currency

moneda suelta change (n) *or* small change

monetario (-ria) monetary

monopolio (m) monopoly *or* corner (n)

monopolio absoluto absolute monopoly

monopolización (f) monopolization

monopolizar monopolize

montacargas (m) goods elevator

montaje (m) assembly

moratoria (f) moratorium

moroso *([extra charge]* slow payer

mostrador (m) counter

mostrador de facturación check-in counter

mostrar (el funcionamiento de algo) demonstrate

mostrar show (v)

mostrar un beneficio show a profit

motivación (f) motivation

motivado (-da) motivated

motor (m) drive (n)

movilidad (f) mobility

movilizar mobilize

movilizar capital mobilize capital

movimiento (m) movement

movimientos (mpl) de capital movements of capital

movimientos de existencias stock movements

mudanza (f) move *or* removal

mudar(se) move (house, office)

muebles (mpl) accesorios fittings

muebles de oficina office furniture

muelle (m) quay *or* dock (n) *or* wharf

muerto (-ta) dead (adj)

muestra (f) (trial) sample

muestra aleatoria random sample

muestra de inspección check sample

muestra gratuita free sample

muestra pequeña swatch

muestreo (m) sample *or* sampling

muestreo aleatorio random sampling

muestreo de aceptación acceptance sampling

muestreo por áreas sampling

mujer (f) de negocios businesswoman

multa (f) fine (n)

multar fine (v)

multicopista (f) copying machine

multilateral multilateral

multinacional (f) multinational (n)

múltiple multiple (adj)

multiplicación (f) multiplication

multiplicar multiply

multitud (f) crowd *or* multitude *or* mass of people

mundial worldwide (adj)

mundialmente worldwide (adv)

mundo (m) world

mutua (f) de seguros mutual (insurance) company

mutuo (-tua) mutual (adj)

muy cualificado (-da) *o* **muy capacitado (-da)** highly qualified

Nn

nación (f) más favorecida most-favoured nation

nacional national *or* domestic

nacional: de ámbito nacional nationwide

nacionalización (f) nationalization

nada (f) nothing

naufragar wreck (v)

naufragio (m) wreck (n)

nave (f) de carga loading bay

necesario (-ria) necessary

necesidad (f) need

necesitar need (v)

negar(se) refuse (v)

negarse a cumplir un acuerdo repudiate an agreement

negarse a pagar dishonour

negativa (f) refusal

negligencia (f) negligence

negociable negotiable

negociación (f) bargaining *or* negotiation

negociaciones (fpl) conjuntas joint discussions

negociaciones salariales wage negotiations

negociador (-ra) negotiator

negociar negotiate (v) *or* bargain (v)

negociar en deal in (v)

negocio (m) bargain (n) *or* deal (n)

negocio (m) *[empresa]* business *or* concern (n)

negocio descuidado neglected business

negocio deshonesto (pero no ilegal) sharp practice

negocio duro hard bargain *or* hard bargaining

negocio ilícito racketeering

negocio suplementario sideline

negocios (mpl) business

negocios: por asuntos de negocios on business

neto (-ta) net (adj)

nivel (m) level

nivel: de bajo nivel low-level

nivel de existencias stock level

nivelarse level off *or* level out

niveles (mpl) de dotación de personal manning levels

niveles de salarios wage levels

noche (f) night

nombramiento (m) appointment

nombramiento de administrador judicial letters of administration

nombrar appoint

nombrar por coopción co-opt someone

nombre (m) name

nombre: en nombre de on behalf of

nombre (m) comercial brand name *or* trademark *or* trade name

norma (f) norm *or* standard (n)

norma (f) *[regla]* rule (n)

normal *[estándar]* normal *or* standard (adj)

normal *[corriente]* regular *or* usual

normalización (f) standardization

normalizar standardize

normas (fpl) regulations

normas de conducta code of practice

normas de producción production standards

normas de seguridad safety regulations

nota (f) note (n)

nota de abono credit note

nota de adeudo debit note

nota de aviso advice note

nota de cobertura cover note

nota de crédito credit note

nota de envío o de expedición shipping note or consignment note or dispatch note

notable outstanding or exceptional

notario (m) notary public

noticia (f) news or item

notificación (f) notice (n) or notification

notificación de despido o de dimisión notice

notificación de renovación renewal notice

notificar notify

novedad (f) novelty or (new) departure

nuevo nombramiento (m) reappointment

nuevo pedido (m) reorder (n)

nulo (-la) null or void

numerar number (v)

numérico (-ca) numeric or numerical

número (m) number (n)

número (m) [ejemplar] copy (n) or issue (n)

número de apartado de correos box number

número de cheque cheque number

número de cuenta del Girobank giro account number

número de factura invoice number

número de llamada gratuita toll free number (US)

número de lote batch number

número de pedido order number

número de referencia reference number

número de registro o número de matrícula registration number

número de serie serial number

número de teléfono phone number or telephone number

números (mpl) impares odd numbers

Oo

obedecer obey or comply with

objetivo (m) objective (n) or target (n) or aim (n)

objetivo: cumplir un objetivo meet a target

objetivo: no cumplir un objetivo miss a target

objetivo de producción production targets

objetivo de ventas sales target

objetivos (mpl) a largo plazo long-term objectives

objeto (m) de una OPA takeover target

objetos (mpl) salvados salvage (n)

obligación (f) obligation or duty

obligación perpetua irredeemable bond

obligación redimible callable bond

obligaciones (fpl) loan stock

obligaciones (fpl) [respnsabilidades] responsibilities

obligaciones a corto plazo current liabilities

obligacionista (mf) debenture holder

obligatorio (-ria) compulsory or binding

obrero (m) workman or (manual) worker

obreros (mpl) cualificados skilled workers

obreros semicualificados semi-skilled workers

obsequiar give or present (v)

obsequio (m) (free) gift or present (n)

obsequio publicitario premium offer

obsolescencia (f) obsolescence

obsolescente obsolescent

obsoleto (-ta) obsolete

obtener obtain *or* get

obtener beneficios brutos gross (v)

obtener beneficios netos net (v)

obtener el título de qualify as

obtener la libertad de alguien bajo fianza bail someone out

ocupación (f) *[empleo]* occupation *or* employment

ocupación (f) *[posesión]* tenure *or* occupancy

ocupación temporal temporary employment

ocupado (-da) busy *or* engaged

ocupante (mf) occupant *or* occupier

ocupar un vacío fill a gap

ocuparse de attend to

oferta (f) offer (n)

oferta (f) *[puja]* bid (n)

oferta (f) *[suministro]* supply (n)

oferta (f) *[trabajo]* tendering *or* tender

oferta de adquisición disputada *o* **rebatida** contested takeover

oferta de lanzamiento introductory offer

oferta de ocasión bargain offer

oferta de venta offer for sale

oferta en metálico cash offer

oferta especial special offer

oferta final closing bid

oferta inicial opening bid

oferta monetaria money supply

oferta pública de adquisición (OPA) takeover bid

oferta y demanda supply and demand

ofertas (fpl) bidding

ofertas de trabajo appointments vacant *or* situations vacant

ofertas lacradas sealed tenders

oficial official (adj)

oficial: no oficial unofficial

oficina (f) office

oficina: de oficina clerical

oficina central head office

oficina central de correos general post offfice

oficina de colocación employment agency *or* employment bureau

oficina de distribución modificable open-plan office

oficina de expedición dispatch department

oficina de información information bureau

oficina de informática computer bureau

oficina de reclamaciones complaints department

oficina del registro civil registry office

oficina general general office

oficina principal main office

oficinas (fpl) de alquiler offices to let

oficinista (mf) clerk

oficioso (-sa) unofficial

ofrecer offer (v)

OIT (Organización Internacional del Trabajo) ILO (= International Labour Organization)

omisión (f) omission

omitir omit

opción (f) de compra option to purchase

opcional optional

OPEP (Organización de los Países Exportadores de Petróleo) OPEC (= Organization of Petroleum Exporting Countries)

operación (f) operation *or* transaction

operación al contado cash transaction

operación en multiples divisas multicurrency operation

operación fraudulenta fraudulent transaction

operación llaves en mano turnkey operation

operacional operational

operaciones (fpl) en bolsa dealing (on the Stock Exchange)

operador (-ra) de cambios foreign exchange broker *or* foreign exchange dealer

operador (-ra) de teclado keyboarder

operario (-ria) operator *or* worker

operativo (-va) operative (adj)

opinión (f) pública public opinion

oportunamente duly

oportunidad (f) opportunity

oportunidades de mercado market opportunities

optar *[decidir]* decide

optar por una línea de conducta decide on a course of action

optativo (-va) optional

orden (mf) order (n)

orden (f) *[mandato]* writ *or* warrant (n)

orden (f) de compra purchase order

orden (f) de domiciliación (bancaria) banker's order

orden (f) de expedición delivery order

orden (f) de pago bank mandate *or* money order

orden (m) alfabético alphabetical order

orden (m) cronológico chronological order

orden (m) del día agenda

ordenador (m) computer

ordenador (m) personal personal computer (PC)

ordenar order (v) *or* arrange *or* put in order

ordinario (-ria) ordinary *or* regular

organigrama (m) organization chart *or* flow chart

organismo (m) organization

organismo paraestatal quango

organización (f) organization

organización lineal line organization

Organización de los Países Exportadores de Petróleo (OPEP) Organization of Petroleum Exporting Countries (OPEC)

Organización Internacional del Trabajo (OIT) International Labour Organization (ILO)

organización y métodos organization and methods

organizar organize *or* arrange

organizativo (-va) organizational

órgano (m) administrativo administrative body *or* authority

órgano decisorio decision-making body

órganos (mpl) de gestión managerial posts

origen (m) origin

original original (adj)

oro (m) en lingotes bullion

oscilación (f) fluctuation

oscilar *[fluctuar]* fluctuate

oscilar *[variar]* range (v)

otorgar grant (v) *or* award (v)

Pp

pactar *[convenir]* covenant (v)

pacto (m) covenant (n) *or* agreement (n)

padrino (m) sponsor (n)

paga (f) pay (n)

paga de vacaciones holiday pay

paga extraordinaria de Navidad Christmas bonus

pagadero (-ra) payable

pagadero a la entrega payable on delivery

pagadero a la vista payable on demand

pagadero a sesenta días payable at sixty days

pagadero por adelantado payable in advance

pagado (-da) paid

pagado: muy bien pagado highly-paid

pagado (-da) por adelantado prepaid

pagador (-ra) payer

pagar pay (v) *or* pay out

pagar: sin pagar unpaid

pagar (costes) bear (v) (costs)

pagar *[devolver]* repay

pagar a plazos pay in instalments

pagar al contado *o* **en efectivo** pay cash

pagar con cheque pay by cheque

pagar con tarjeta de crédito pay by credit card

pagar intereses pay interest

pagar la cuenta y marcharse check out

pagar los intereses de una deuda service a debt

pagar por adelantado prepay *or* pay in advance

pagar una cuenta pay a bill

pagar una deuda discharge a debt *or* redeem a debt

pagar una factura pay an invoice *or* settle an invoice

pagar una reclamación settle a claim

pagaré (m) accommodation bill *or* promissory note *or* note of hand

pagaré (m) *[vale]* IOU (= I owe you)

pagaré (m) de interés fijo debenture

páginas (fpl) amarillas yellow pages

pago (m) payment *or* repayment

pago (m) *[de una deuda]* discharge (n)

pago (m) *[finiquito]* settlement

pago a cuenta interim payment *or* payment on account

pago a destajo payment by results

pago al contado cash terms *or* spot cash

pago anticipado advance payment

pago anual yearly payment

pago aplazado deferred payment

pago atrasado back payment

pago en efectivo cash payment *or* payment in cash

pago en especie payment in kind

pago en exceso overpayment

pago en metálico payment in cash

pago íntegro full payment

pago mediante cheque payment by cheque

pago mínimo minimum payment

pago parcial partial payment

pago por adelantado prepayment *or* money up front

pago simbólico token payment

pago total de una deuda full discharge of a debt

pago único lump sum

pagos (mpl) a cuenta progress payments

pagos de la hipoteca mortgage payments

pagos mensuales monthly payments

pagos por etapas staged payments

pagos semestrales half-yearly payment

país (m) country *or* state

país de origen country of origin

país en vías de desarrollo developing country

países (mpl) exportadores de petróleo oil-exporting countries

países productores de petróleo oil-producing countries

países subdesarrollados underdeveloped countries

palabras (fpl) de agradecimiento speech of thanks

paleta (f) pallet

panel (m) panel

pantalla (f) monitor (n) *or* screen

papel (m) carbón carbon paper

papel carbón: sin papel carbón carbonless

papel continuo continuous stationery

papel de envolver wrapping paper

papel de estraza brown paper

papel reciclado recycled paper

papeleo (m) paperwork

papeleo (m) *[burocracia]* red tape

papeles (mpl) *[documentos]* papers

paquete (m) parcel (n) *or* pack (n) *or* packet

paquete (m) *[acciones]* block (n) (of shares)

paquete de cigarrillos packet of cigarettes

paquete de sobres pack of envelopes

par par

parada (f) stop (n)

parado (-da) unemployed

paraíso (m) fiscal tax haven

parar stop (v) *or* check (v)

parar: sin parar non-stop

parecer appear *or* seem

paridad (f) parity

paro (m) stoppage *or* stopping

paro (m) *[desempleo]* unemployment

paro estructural structural unemployment

paro técnico work-to-rule

parte (f) part *or* party

parte (f) *[proporción]* proportion

parte acusadora prosecution

parte contratante contracting party

parte superior top (n)

parte (m) de baja doctor's certificate

participación (f) share (n)

participación de beneficios equity

participación en los beneficios profit-sharing

particular private

partida (f) batch (n)

partida (f) *[de un balance]* item (n)

partidas (fpl) excepcionales exceptional items *or* extraordinary items

pasado (-da) de moda old-fashioned

pasaje (m) fare

pasaje sencillo one-way fare

pasante (mf) junior clerk

pasar *[tiempo]* spend

pasar a cuenta nueva carry over a balance *or* carry forward

pasar información a un fichero card-index (v)

pasar modelos model (v)

pasar por la criba screen (v)

pasarse a switch over to

pasivo (m) liabilities

pasivo a largo plazo long-term liabilities

pasivo circulante current liabilities

paso (m) de información a un fichero card-indexing

patentado (-da) patented

patentar un invento patent an invention

patente (f) patent

patente de invención letters patent

patente solicitada *o* **patente en tramitación** patent applied for *or* patent pending

patrimonio (m) capital *or* net worth *or* heritage

patrocinado (-da) por el Estado government-sponsored

patrocinador (-ra) sponsor (n)

patrocinar sponsor (v)

patrocinio (m) sponsorship

patrón (m) standard (n)

peaje (m) toll

pedido (m) order (n)

pedido (-da) on order

pedido cursado al representante comercial journey order

pedido no servido *o* **por servir** unfulfilled order

pedido por correo mail-order

pedido suplementario repeat order

pedido urgente rush order

pedidos (mpl) pendientes back orders *or* outstanding orders

pedidos (mpl) por servir dues *or* back orders

pedir ask *or* ask for

pedir *[solicitar]* request (v)

pedir información inquire (v)

pedir más detalles ask for further details *or* particulars

pedir perdón apologize (v)

pedir prestado borrow (v)

peligro (m) de incendio fire risk

pena (f) penalty

penalizar penalize (v)

pendiente outstanding *or* pending

penetración (f) en el mercado market penetration

penetrar un mercado penetrate a market

pensión (f) pension

pequeño (-ña) small

pequeñas empresas (fpl) small businesses

pequeño empresario (m) small businessman

pequeño hurto (m) pilferage *or* pilfering

pequeños accionistas (mpl) minor shareholders

per *[a, por]* per

per cápita per capita

perder lose (something)

perder *[tren, avión]* miss (v)

perder dinero lose money

perder un depósito forfeit a deposit

perder un pedido lose an order

perder valor depreciate *or* lose value

pérdida (f) loss *or* wastage

pérdida de clientela loss of customers

pérdida de ejercicio trading loss

pérdida de trabajadores por jubilación natural wastage

pérdida de un pedido loss of an order

pérdida de valor depreciation *or* loss of value

pérdida neta net loss

pérdida parcial partial loss

pérdida sobre el papel paper loss

pérdida total write-off *or* dead loss

pérdidas (fpl) leakage

pérdidas de capital capital loss

perecedero (-ra) perishable

pericia (f) expertise

periféricos (mpl) peripherals

periódico (m) newspaper

periódico (-ca) periodic *or* periodical (adj)

periodo (m) period

periodo de conservación de un producto shelf life of a product

periodo de preaviso period of notice

periodo de prueba probation *or* trial period

periodo de reembolso payback period

periodo de reflexión cooling off period

periodo de validez period of validity

permanecer stay (v)

permanencia (f) stay (n)

permiso (m) permit (n) *or* permission *or* leave (n)

permiso de exportación export licence *or* export permit

permiso de residencia residence permit

permiso de trabajo work permit

permitir permit *or* allow

permitirse un gasto afford

perseguir chase *or* follow up

persona: por persona per head

persona (f) autorizada licensee

persona dedicada a las relaciones públicas public relations man

personal personal

personal (m) personnel *or* staff (n)

personal administrativo office staff *or* managerial staff

personal clave key personnel *or* key staff

personal de atención al público counter staff

personal de oficina clerical staff

personal de ventas sales force *or* sales people

personal de ventas muy motivado highly motivated sales staff

personal del hotel hotel staff

personal eventual temporary staff

personal fijo regular staff

personal reducido al mínimo skeleton staff

personalidad (f) jurídica legal status

perspectivas (fpl) prospects

pertenecer belong to

pertinente relevant

pesado (-da) heavy

pesar weigh

pesar en exceso be overweight

peseta (f) peseta

peso (m) weight

peso (m) *[moneda]* peso

peso bruto gross weight

peso escaso false weight

peso máximo weight limit

peso muerto deadweight

peso neto net weight

petición (f) request (n)

petición: a petición on request

petición de informes inquiry

petición de informes sobre crédito status inquiry

petición de pago (de acciones) call (n)

petróleo (m) oil

petrolero (m) oil tanker

PIB (Producto Interior Bruto) GDP (= gross domestic product)

pieza (f) piece

pieza de recambio *o* **pieza de repuesto** spare part

piloto (mf) pilot (n)

pionero (-ra) pioneer (n)

piso (m) floor

piso (m) *[apartamento]* flat (n) *or* appartment (US)

plan (m) plan (n) *or* project (n)

plan (m) *[sistema]* arrangement

plan de emergencia contingency plan

plan de pensiones pension scheme

plan de trabajo de una empresa corporate plan

plan general overall plan

plan periódicamente actualizado rolling plan

plan remunerativo money-making plan

planear plan (v)

planes de contingencia standby arrangements

planificación (f) planning

planificación a largo plazo long-term planning

planificación de la mano de obra manpower planning

planificación económica economic planning

planificación empresarial corporate planning

planificación estratégica strategic planning

planificador (-ra) planner

planificar plan (v)

planificar las inversiones plan investments

plano (m) plan (n) *or* drawing (n)

planta (f) floor plan

planta (f) *[fábrica]* plant (n) *or* factory

plantear raise (v)

plantilla (f) staff *or* establishment

plata (f) en lingotes bullion

plaza (f) (job) vacancy *or* position (n)

plaza (f) *[mercado]* market (n)

plaza del mercado marketplace *or* square

plazo (m) term *or* notice *or* instalment

plazo (m) *[límite]* time limit

plazo (m) *[periodo]* period

plazo: a plazo forward

plazo de entrega delivery time

plazo de espera lead time

plazo de tiempo límite time limitation

plazo límite deadline

plazo medio medium-term

pleito (m) lawsuit

plena: en plena dedicación full-time

pluriempleado (-da) moonlighter

pluriempleo (m) moonlighting

plus (m) de carestía de vida cost-of-living bonus

plusvalía (f) capital gains

PNB (Producto Nacional Bruto) GNP (= gross national product)

poder (m) power

poder (m) *[procuración]* proxy

poder adquisitivo purchasing power *or* spending power

poder de negociación bargaining power

poder notarial *o* **poderes (mpl)** power of attorney

poderhabiente (mf) proxy

política (f) policy

política comercial de reciprocidad arancelaria fair trade

política crediticia credit policy

política de precios pricing policy

política de precios flexibles flexible pricing policy

política presupuestaria budgetary policy

póliza (f) de seguros insurance policy *or* assurance policy

póliza (f) a todo riesgo all-risks policy

póliza provisional cover note

ponderación (f) weighting

poner put (v) *or* place (v)

poner a la venta release (v)

poner al día update (v)

poner el sello stamp (v)

poner en contenedores containerize (v)

poner en la lista negra blacklist (v)

poner en libertad free (v)

poner en práctica un acuerdo implement an agreement

poner en una caja case (v) *or* put in a box

poner la dirección *o* **las señas** address (v) (a letter, a parcel)

poner las iniciales a initial (v)

poner por escrito put in writing

poner precio a price (v)

poner término a un acuerdo terminate an agreement

poner un negocio set up in business

popular popular

por via

porcentaje (m) percentage

porcentaje de aumento percentage increase

porcentaje de comisión cost plus

porcentaje de descuento percentage discount

porcentaje fijo flat rate

pormenores (mpl) particulars

portacontenedores container ship

portador (-ra) bearer *or* payee

portátil portable

porte (m) carriage *or* freight

porte debido carriage forward *or* freight forward

porte pagado carriage paid *or* postpaid *or* postage paid

poseedor (-ra) holder

poseer possess (v) *or* own (v)

posesión (f) possession *or* ownership *or* tenure

posfechar postdate

posibilidad (f) possibility

posibilidad de comparación comparability

posible possible

posible comprador (-ra) prospective buyer

posición (f) position *or* place (n)

posición (f) *[status]* status

positivo (-va) positive

posponer postpone *or* hold over

postal postal

postal (f) card *or* postcard

postor (m) bidder *or* tenderer

postura (f) position

postura (f) negociadora bargaining position

potencial potential (adj)

potencial (m) potential (n)

practicar el 'dumping' dump goods on a market

prácticas (fpl) comerciales justas fair dealing

prácticas restrictivas restrictive practices

práctico (-ca) handy

precauciones (fpl) safety precautions

precintar seal (v)

precinto (m) seal (n)

precinto de aduana customs seal

precio (m) price (n) *or* charge (n)

precio (m) *[tarifa]* rate (n) *or* tariff

precio: a precio reducido cut-price

precio a destajo piece rate

precio acordado *o* **precio convenido** agreed price

precio actual current price

precio al cierre closing price

precio al contado cash price

precio al detallista trade price

precio al por mayor wholesale price

precio al por menor retail price

precio competitivo competitive price

precio con entrega de artículo usado trade-in price

precio de apertura opening price

precio de catálogo list price *or* catalogue price

precio de compra purchase price

precio de conversión conversion price *or* conversion rate

precio de coste cost price

precio de descuento discount price

precio de entrada admission charge

precio de entrega delivered price

precio de entrega inmediata spot price

precio de fábrica factory price

precio de intervención intervention price

precio de mercado market price *or* market rate

precio de ocasión bargain price

precio de oferta offer price *or* supply price

precio de reventa resale price

precio de subvención support price

precio de transporte freight rates

precio de venta selling price

precio de venta recomendado manufacturer's recommended price (MRP)

precio del crudo *o* **del petróleo** oil price

precio en fábrica price ex works

precio en firme firm price

precio excesivo overcharge (n)

precio facturado invoice price

precio fijo set price

precio inicial starting price *or* upset price

precio irrisorio bargain price

precio justo fair price

precio máximo maximum price

precio máximo autorizado ceiling price

precio medio average price

precio mínimo aceptable reserve price

precio módico moderate price

precio neto net price

precio por unidad unit price

precio reducido cut price *or* reduced rate

precio simbólico token charge

precio sin descuento full price

precio todo incluido inclusive charge *or* all-in price

precio tope ceiling price

precio umbral threshold price

precio vigente going rate

precios (mpl) competitivos keen prices

precios estables stable prices

precios exagerados inflated prices

precios flexibles flexible prices

precios mínimos *o* precios de saldo knockdown prices

precios populares popular prices

precios reventados rock-bottom prices

precipitarse rush (v)

precisar specify

predecir forecast (v)

preempaquetar prepack *or* prepackage

preferencia (f) preference *or* choice (n)

preferencial *o* preferente preferential

preferir prefer

prefijo (m) dialling code

prefinanciación (f) pre-financing

pregunta (f) question (n)

preguntar ask (v) *or* inquire (v) *or* question (v)

premio (m) award (n)

prensa (f) press (n)

preocupación (f) concern (n) *or* worry

preparación (f) de pedidos order processing

preparación de presupuestos budgeting

preparado (-da) ready

preparar train (v)

preparar *[elaborar]* process (v)

preparar *[redactar]* draw up

preparar un contrato draw up a contract

preparar un horario timetable (v)

preparar una factura raise an invoice

prepararse train (v)

prescribir prescribe (v)

preselección (f) shortlist (n)

preseleccionar shortlist (v)

presentación (f) presentation *or* production

presentación (f) *[introducción]* introduction

presentar present (v) *or* produce (v)

presentar *[entregar]* hand in

presentar *[introducir]* introduce

presentar *[organizar]* stage (v) *or* organize

presentar *[petición, demanda]* file (v) (a petition)

presentar excusas apologize

presentar una cuenta *o* una factura render an account

presentar una letra a la aceptación present a bill for acceptance

presentar una letra al pago present a bill for payment

presentar una reconvención counter-claim (v)

presentarse report (v) (to a place)

presentarse a una entrevista report for an interview

presente present (adj)

presente: del presente mes instant

presidente (-ta) chairman

presidente y director gerente chairman and managing director

prestamista (mf) (money)lender

préstamo (m) borrowing *or* loan

préstamo a corto plazo short-term loan

préstamo a largo plazo long-term loan

préstamo a plazo fijo term loan

préstamo bancario bank loan

préstamo garantizado secured loan

préstamo sin interés soft loan

préstamos (mpl) bancarios bank borrowings

prestar lend (v) *or* loan (v)

prestatario (-ria) borrower *or* debtor

prestigio (m) prestige

presupuestar budget (v)

presupuestario (-ria) budgetary

presupuesto (m) budget (n)

presupuesto (m) *[cotización]* quote (n) *or* quotation *or* estimate

presupuesto de explotación operational budget *or* operating budget

presupuesto de gastos generales overhead budget

presupuesto de promoción promotion budget

presupuesto de publicidad advertising budget

presupuesto de ventas sales budget

presupuesto del Estado (government) budget

presupuesto provisional provisional budget

presupuesto publicitario publicity budget

pretender *[alegar]* claim (v)

prevención (f) prevention

prevenir prevent *or* pre-empt

preventivo (-va) preventive

prever forecast (v) *or* foresee *or* anticipate

prever *[estipular]* provide for

previo (-via) previous *or* prior

previsión (f) forecast *or* forecasting

previsión a largo plazo long-term forecast

previsión de mano de obra manpower forecasting

previsión de mercado market forecast

previsión de ventas sales forecast

previsión provisional de ventas provisional forecast of sales

previsto (-ta) projected

prima (f) bonus (n)

prima al comisionista del credere

prima de incentivo incentive bonus *or* incentive payments

prima de productividad productivity bonus

prima de renovación renewal premium

prima de riesgo risk premium

prima de seguros (insurance) premium

prima por ausencia de siniestralidad no-claims bonus

primario (-ria) primary

primer trimestre first quarter

primera opción first option

primeras entradas, primeras salidas first in first out (FIFO)

primero (-ra) first

primero (-ra) *[inicial]* initial (adj)

primero (-ra) *[principal]* prime

principal principal (adj) *or* chief *or* main

principal (m) *[capital]* principal (n)

principio (m) principle

principio (m) *[inicio]* start (n)

prisa (f) rush (n)

privado (-da) private

privatización (f) privatization

privatizar privatize

privilegio (m) fiscal tax concession

probar sample (v) *or* test (v)

probatorio (-ria) probationary

problema (m) problem

proceder proceed

procedimiento (m) process (n) *or* procedure

procedimiento de selección selection procedure

procedimientos (mpl) judiciales judicial processes

procesamiento (m) prosecution *or* legal action

procesamiento por lotes batch processing

procesar prosecute

proceso (m) *[juicio]* trial *or* court case *or* lawsuit

proceso de datos data processing

proceso judicial legal proceedings

procesos (mpl) decisorios decision-making processes

procesos industriales industrial processes

procuración (f) proxy

procurador (-ra) attorney

producción (f) production *or* output

producción en serie mass production

producción interior *o* **producción nacional** domestic production

producción total total output

producir produce (v) *or* make *or* bring in

producir *[devengar]* carry (v)

producir *[ordenador]* output (v)

producir a gran escala mass-produce

producir en exceso overproduce

productividad (f) productivity

productivo (-va) productive *or* profitable

producto (m) product

producto defectuoso reject (n)

producto destinado a un mercado de masas mass-market product

producto derivado by-product

producto ficticio dummy

producto final end product

Producto Interior Bruto (PIB) gross domestic product (GDP)

Producto Nacional Bruto (PNB) gross national product (GNP)

producto prestigioso prestige product

producto principal staple product

producto sensible a los cambios de precio price-sensitive product

productor (-ra) producer

productos (mpl) produce (n)

productos acabados finished goods

productos competitivos competitive products

productos de marca propia own label goods *or* own brand goods

productos de primera calidad high-quality goods

productos devueltos sin vender returns *or* unsold goods

productos en competencia competing products

productos manufacturados manufactured goods

productos perecederos perishables

productos semiacabados semi-finished products

profesional (adj) professional (adj)

profesional (mf) professional (n)

programa (m) programme *or* program

programa de investigación research programme

programa de ordenador computer program

programa informático software

programa piloto pilot scheme

programación (f) scheduling

programación de ordenador computer programming

programador (-ra) de ordenadores computer programmer

programar un ordenador program a computer

progresar progress (v)

progresivo (-va) progressive *or* gradual

progreso (m) progress (n)

prohibición (f) ban (n) *or* embargo (n)

prohibición de hacer horas extras overtime ban

prohibición de importar import ban

prohibir ban (v) *or* forbid *or* embargo (v)

prohibitivo (-va) prohibitive

prolongación (f) extension

prolongar extend

promedio (m) average (n) *or* mean (n)

promedio ponderado weighted average

promesa (f) promise (n) *or* undertaking

prometer promise (v)

promoción (f) promotion *or* publicity

promoción: en *o* de promoción promotional

promoción de un producto promotion of a product

promoción de ventas sales promotion *or* sales drive

promocionar promote *or* advertise

promocionar la imagen pública de una empresa promote a corporate image

promocionar un nuevo producto promote a new product

pronosticar forecast (v) *or* tip (v)

pronóstico (m) forecast (n)

pronto (-ta) prompt

pronto early *or* soon

pronto pago (m) prompt payment

propicio (-cia) favourable

propiedad (f) ownership (n) *or* property (n)

propiedad colectiva collective ownership *or* common ownership

propiedad conjunta multiple ownership

propiedad inmobiliaria real estate

propiedad privada private property *or* private ownership

propietaria (f) proprietress *or* landlady

propietario (m) proprietor *or* landlord

propietario (-ria) owner

propietario (-ria) legítimo (-ma) rightful owner

propietario (-ria) único (-ca) sole owner

propina (f) tip (n)

proponer propose

proponer una enmienda move an amendment

proponer(se) propose to

proponerse *[aspirar a]* aim (v)

proporción (f) proportion

proporcional proportional

proposición (f) proposition *or* proposal *or* suggestion

propósito (m) aim (n)

propuesta (f) proposal *or* proposition

prorrata pro rata

prórroga (f) renewal *or* extension

prorrogar extend *or* renew

prorrogar un arrendamiento renew a lease

proseguir continue

prospecto (m) prospectus *or* leaflet

prosperar flourish *or* boom (v)

próspero (-ra) prosperous *or* flourishing *or* booming

protección (f) protection *or* defence

protección (f) *[cobertura]* hedging *or* hedge

protección al consumidor consumer protection

proteccionista protective *or* protectionist

protector (-ra) protective

proteger protect *or* safeguard *or* defend

protesta (f) protest (n)

protestar (contra algo) protest (v) (against something)

protestar una letra protest a bill

protesto (m) protest (n)

prototipo (m) de contrato model agreement

proveedor (-ra) supplier

proveer provide (v) *or* supply (v)

provisión (f) de fondos provision *or* allocation of funds

provisional provisional

próximo (-ma) close to

proyectado (-da) projected

proyectar project (v) *or* plan (v) *or* design (v)

proyecto (m) project *or* plan

proyecto (m) *[borrador]* draft (n) *or* rough plan

proyecto de ley bill (n)

prueba (f) proof

prueba (f) *[ensayo]* trial *or* test

prueba: a prueba on approval

prueba: de prueba probationary

prueba documentada documentary proof

prueba gratuita free trial

pruebas (fpl) documentales documentary evidence

publicación (f) asistida por ordenador desk-top publishing (DTP)

publicación (f) periódica periodical (n)

publicar *[anunciar]* advertise

publicar *[divulgar]* release (v) *or* make public

publicidad (f) publicity *or* advertising

publicidad a escala nacional national advertising

publicidad en el punto de venta point of sale material (POS material)

publicidad exagerada hype (n)

publicidad por correo direct-mail advertising *or* mail shot

publicidad sin interés (por correo) junk mail

público (-ca) public (adj)

público (-ca) *[común]* common

puente-báscula (m) weighbridge

puerta (f) door

puerta: de puerta en puerta door-to-door

puerto (m) port *or* harbour

puerto de contenedores container port

puerto de embarque port of embarkation

puerto de escala port of call

puerto de registro port of registry

puerto distribuidor entrepot port

puerto franco free port

puesta (f) en marcha (de un negocio) start-up

puesta al día updating

puesta en práctica implementation

puesto (m) post (n) *or* position *or* job *or* place (n)

puesto aduanero customs entry point

puesto clave key post

puesto de trabajo *[empleo]* job

puesto de trabajo *[informática]* workstation

puja (f) bid (n)

pujar más alto outbid
punto (m) point
punto (m) *[discusión]* item (on agenda)
punto de partida starting point
punto de referencia benchmark
punto de reunión venue
punto de venta point of sale (p.o.s. *or* POS)

punto decimal decimal point
punto máximo peak (n)
punto muerto breakeven point *or* deadlock (n)
punto porcentual percentage point
puntos (mpl) de venta electrónicos electronic point of sale (EPOS)
PYME (pequeña y mediana empresa) small and middle-sized businesses

Qq

quebrado (m) bankrupt (n)
quebrado no rehabilitado undischarged bankrupt
quebrado rehabilitado certificated bankrupt
quebrar crash (v) *or* fail
quedar remain *or* be left
quedarse stay (v) *or* remain
quedarse atrás fall behind
queja (f) complaint

quejarse complain (about)
querellante (mf) plaintiff
quiebra (f) bankruptcy
quiebra: en quiebra bankrupt (adj)
quiebra comercial commercial failure
quitar remove
quitar *[rebajar]* take off *or* deduct
quórum (m) quorum

Rr

racionalización (f) rationalization
racionalizar rationalize
radicar base (v)
rama (f) branch (n)
rampa (f) de carga loading ramp
rápidamente rapidly *or* fast (adv)
rápido (-da) rapid *or* prompt *or* fast (adj)
rápido (-da) *[urgente]* express (adj)
ratero (-ra) de tiendas shoplifter
ratificación (f) ratification
ratificar ratify
raya (f) line (n)
razón (f) *[motivo]* reason
razón (f) *[relación]* ratio
razón social corporate name

reacción (f) feedback *or* response
reactivación (f) recovery *or* turnround *or* upturn
reajustar adjust *or* readjust
reajuste (m) adjustment *or* readjustment
real real *or* actual
realización (f) fulfilment
realizar realize
realizar activos realize assets
realizar un proyecto *o* **un plan** realize a project *or* a plan
realizar una operación de cesión-arrendamiento lease back
reanudar resume
reanudar las negociaciones resume negotiations

reasegurador (-ra) reinsurer

reasegurar reinsure

reaseguro (m) reinsurance

rebaja (f) rebate *or* discount *or* reduction

rebaja (f) *[recorte]* cut (n)

rebajar mark down *or* deduct *or* reduce

rebajar un precio reduce a price

rebajas (fpl) de fin de temporada end of season sale

rebajas a mitad de precio half-price sale

rebajas de precios price reductions

recadero (m) deliveryman

recado (m) message

recargar mark up

recargo (m) surcharge (n) *or* overcharge (n)

recargo de importación import surcharge

recaudación (f) takings *or* take (n)

recaudación de impuestos levy (n) *or* tax collection

recaudador (-ra) collector

recaudador (-ra) de impuestos tax collector

recaudar levy (v)

recepción (f) reception (desk)

recepcionista (mf) receptionist *or* reception clerk

recesión (f) recession

rechazar reject (v) *or* turn down

rechazo (m) rejection *or* refusal

recibir receive *or* take (v) *or* get

recibir una llamada take a call

recibo (m) receipt

recibo de aduana customs receipt

recibo de depósito deposit slip *or* paying-in slip

reciclaje (m) profesional retraining

reciclar recycle *or* retrain

recipiente (m) container

reciprocidad (f) reciprocity

recíproco (-ca) reciprocal

reclamación (f) claim (n)

reclamación de pago demand (n) (for payment)

reclamar claim (v) *or* demand (v)

recobrar recover (v) *or* repossess (v)

recoger collect (v)

recogida (f) collection

recomendación (f) recommendation

recomendar recommend

reconciliación (f) reconciliation

reconocer a un sindicato recognize a union

reconocer una firma honour a signature

reconocimiento (m) recognition

reconocimiento de un sindicato union recognition

reconvención (f) counter-claim (n)

récord (adj) record *or* record-breaking

récord (m) record (n)

récord de ventas record sales

recordar remind *or* remember

recordatorio (m) reminder

recortar cut (v)

recorte (m) cut (n)

rectificación (f) rectification *or* correction

rectificar rectify *or* correct (v)

recuperable recoverable

recuperación (f) recovery *or* retrieval

recuperación (f) *[precios]* rally (n)

recuperación de datos data retrieval

recuperar *[recobrar]* recover *or* repossess

recuperar *[rescatar]* retrieve *or* get back

recuperarse *[mejorar]* recover

recuperarse *[precios]* rally (v)

recursos (mpl) resources *or* means

recursos financieros financial resources

recursos naturales natural resources

red (f) network (n)

red de distribución distribution network

redactar draft (v) *or* draw up

redactar un contrato draft a contract *or* draw up a contract

redactar una carta draft a letter

redimir pay off *or* redeem (v)

redistribuir redistribute

rédito (m) interest (n) *or* rate of interest

redondear por defecto round down

redondear por exceso round up

reducción (f) reduction *or* decrease (n) *or* lowering *or* shrinkage

reducción (f) *[desaceleración]* slowdown

reducción de costes cost-cutting

reducción de empleos job cuts

reducción de gastos retrenchment

reducción de los impuestos tax reductions

reducir reduce

reducir *[desacelerar]* slow down

reducir a escala scale down

reducir gradualmente phase out

reducir drásticamente *[los precios]* slash prices

reducir gastos reduce expenditure *or* cut down on expenses

reducir los precios lower prices

reducir un precio reduce a price

redundante redundant

reelección (f) re-election

reelegir re-elect

reembolsable refundable *or* repayable

reembolsar refund (v) *or* repay *or* pay back

reembolsar *[redimir]* pay off

reembolso (m) repayment

reembolso (m) *[reintegro]* reimbursement *or* rebate *or* refund (n)

reembolso de gastos reimbursement of expenses

reembolso total full refund

reemplazar replace

reemplazo (m) replacement

reempleo (m) re-employment

reestructuración (f) restructuring

reestructuración de la compañía restructuring of the company

reestructurar restructure

reexportación (f) re-export (n)

reexportar re-export (v)

referencia (f) reference

referente a relating to

referirse refer

referirse a apply to

refinanciación (f) de un préstamo refinancing of a loan

refinanciar un crédito *o* **una deuda** roll over credit *or* a debt

refrendar countersign

refugio (m) shelter

regalar give (away)

regalar *[obsequiar]* present (v)

regalo (m) present (n) *or* gift

regatear haggle (v) *or* bargain (v)

región (f) region *or* area

regional regional

regir rule (v) *or* run *or* be in force

registrado (-da) registered

registrador (-ra) registrar

registrar record (v) *or* register (v)

registrar una marca comercial register a trademark

registrar una propiedad register a property

registrarse *[inscribirse]* register (v) *or* check in

registro (m) register (n) *or* registry

registro (m) *[informe]* record

registro (m) *[inscripción]* registration

registro (m) *[inspección]* examination *or* inspection

registro de compañías companies' register

Registro Marítimo de Lloyd Lloyd's register

Registro Mercantil Registrar of Companies

regla (f) law *or* rule (n)

reglamentación (f) regulation

reglamentar regulate

reglamentario (-ria) statutory

reglamento (m) regulations

reglamento sobre incendios fire regulations

regreso (m) return (n)

regulación (f) regulation

regulado (-da) por el Estado government-regulated

regular (adj) regular (adj)

regular regulate (v)

rehusar refuse (v)

reimportación (f) reimport (n)

reimportar reimport (v)

reintegro (m) reimbursement *or* withdrawal

reinversión (f) reinvestment

reinvertir reinvest (v)

reivindicación (f) claim (n)

reivindicación salarial wage claim

relación (f) relation *or* connection

relación (f) *[lista]* list (n)

relación (f) *[razón]* ratio

relación: con relación a further to

relación de directivos de una empresa register of directors

relación de gastos statement of expenses

relación precio-ganancias price/earnings ratio (P/E ratio)

relacionar connect

relaciones (fpl) relations

relaciones laborales industrial relations

relaciones públicas public relations (PR)

relativo a regarding *or* relating to

rematar knock down (v) *or* reduce

remate (m) distress sale

remesa (f) *[envío]* consignment

remesa (f) *[partida]* batch (n)

remite (m) return address

remitente (mf) sender *or* consignor

remitir remit (v) *or* refer

remitir adjunto enclose

remitir por cheque remit by cheque

remontarse soar

remuneración (f) remuneration *or* payment

remunerar remunerate

remunerativo (-va) money-making

rendimiento (m) *[actuación]* performance

rendimiento (m) *[capacidad]* (production) capacity

rendimiento (m) *[producción]* output (n) *or* throughput

rendimiento (m) *[rentabilidad]* yield (n) *or* return

rendimiento bruto gross yield

rendimiento corriente current yield

rendimiento de la inversión return on investment (ROI)

rendimiento efectivo effective yield

rendimiento máximo peak output

rendimiento neto net yield

rendir yield (v) *or* bear (v)

rendir cuentas a alguien report to someone

renovación (f) renewal

renovación de existencias restocking

renovación urbana redevelopment *or* urban renewal

renovar redevelop *or* renew

renovar existencias restock

renovar un abono *o* una suscripción renew a subscription

renovar un pedido reorder (v) *or* repeat an order

renta (f) *[alquiler]* rent (n)

renta (f) *[ingresos]* income (n)

renta (f) *[rendimiento]* yield (n)

renta bruta gross income

renta de inversiones investment income

renta fija fixed income

renta imponible taxable income

renta nominal nominal rent

renta personal personal income

renta por alquiler rental income

renta que no llega a cubrir los costes uneconomic rent

renta real real income *or* real wages

renta total total income

renta vitalicia life interest

rentabilidad (f) profitability *or* cost-effectiveness

rentabilidad del dividendo dividend yield

rentable paying (adj) *or* cost-effective

rentable *[lucrativo]* profit-making *or* profitable

renuncia (f) renunciation *or* resignation

renuncia (f) *[abandono de responsabilidad]* disclaimer

renuncia (f) *[desistimiento]* waiver

renunciar a abandon

renunciar a un pago waive a payment

reorganización (f) reorganization

reorganizar reorganize

reparación (f) repair (n)

reparar repair (v)

repartir distribute (v) *or* share out

repartir *[entregar]* deliver (v)

repartir un riesgo spread a risk

reparto (m) distribution (n) *or* delivery (n)

reparto de mercancías delivery of goods

repercusión (f) knock-on effect

repertorio (m) index (n) *or* list (n)

repetir repeat

repetirse: que se repite recurrent

reponer replace (v)

repostar restock

representación (f) exclusiva sole agency

representante (mf) representative

representante (mf) *[vendedor]* salesman *or* sales representative

representante a comisión commission rep

representante exclusivo sole agent

representar represent

representativo (-va) representative (adj)

repudiar repudiate

repuesto (m) replacement

reputación (f) reputation *or* standing

requerimiento (m) de pago demand (n) for payment

requerir require *or* need

requisitos (mpl) requirements

resarcir repay (v) *or* indemnify (v) *or* compensate (v)

resarcirse de las pérdidas recoup one's losses

rescatable redeemable

rescatador (-ra) de empresas white knight

rescatar retrieve (v)

rescatar una póliza surrender a policy

rescatar una prenda redeem a pledge

rescate (m) retrieval *or* recovery *or* salvage (n)

rescate (m) *[póliza]* surrender (n) (of insurance policy)

rescate (m) *[préstamo]* redemption (of a loan)

rescindir rescind

rescindir un contrato cancel a contract

reserva (f) booking *or* reservation

reserva (f) *[almacén]* reserve *or* store (n)

reserva (f) *[provisión]* supply (n) *or* provision

reserva anticipada advance booking

reserva en bloque block booking

reserva en dólares dollar balance

reservar reserve (v) *or* book (v)

reservar con exceso overbook

reservar la misma plaza a dos personas double-book

reservas (fpl) reserve (n) *or* reserves *or* supplies *or* stockpile

reservas: con reservas qualified

reservas de divisas currency reserves

reservas de caja cash reserves

reservas de materias primas stock of raw materials

reservas ocultas hidden reserves

reservas para imprevistos emergency reserves

resguardo (m) slip (n) *or* receipt (n)

residencia (f) residence

residente resident (adj)

residente (mf) resident (n)

residuos (mpl) waste (n)

resignar resign

resolución (f) resolution

resolver resolve (v)

resolver un problema solve a problem

respaldar back up (v) *or* support

respaldo (m) financiero financial backing

respetar respect (v)

responder answer (v) *or* reply (v) *or* respond (v)

responder de account for

responsabilidad (f) responsibility *or* liability

responsabilidad contractual contractual liability

responsabilidad ilimitada unlimited liability

responsabilidad limitada limited liability

responsabilidades (fpl) responsibilities

responsable responsible (for)

responsable de liable for

responsable (mf) de la capacitación training officer

responsable (mf) del progreso de un trabajo progress chaser

responsable (mf) de relaciones públicas public relations officer

respuesta (f) reply (n) *or* answer (n) *or* response (n)

respuesta (f) *[reacción]* feedback

resto (m) rest *or* remainder

restricción (f) restraint *or* restriction

restricción a las importaciones import restrictions

restricción comercial restraint of trade

restrictivo (-va) restrictive

restringir restrict (v)

resultado (m) result (n)

resultados (mpl) (company) results

resultar result in

resultar de result from

retención (f) de impuestos en origen withholding tax

retención fiscal tax deductions

retener keep back *or* withhold

retirada (f) withdrawal

retirar withdraw

retirar gradualmente phase out

retirar una oferta withdraw an offer

retirar una oferta de adquisición withdraw a takeover bid

retirarse *[jubilarse]* retire (v)

retirarse (de una elección) stand down

retiro (m) withdrawal

retiro (m) *[jubilación]* retirement *or* pension

retornable returnable

retrasar hold up (v) *or* delay

retrasarse fall behind

retraso (m) hold-up (n) *or* delay

retraso: con retraso late (adv)

retroactivo (-va) retroactive

reunión (f) meeting *or* assembly

reunión de ventas sales conference

reunión del consejo de administración board meeting

reunión de personal staff meeting

reunir recursos pool resources

reunirse meet (v)

revaluación (f) revaluation *or* reassessment

revaluar revalue *or* reassess

revelación (f) disclosure

revelación de información confidencial disclosure of confidential information

revelar disclose

revelar una información disclose a piece of information

reventa (f) resale

reverso (m) back (n)

revertido (-da) reverse (adj)

revés (m) setback

revisar revise (v) *or* inspect (v)

revisar *[máquina]* service (v)

revisar las cuentas audit the accounts

revisión (f) *[máquina]* service (n)

revisión de sueldos salary review

revista (f) magazine *or* journal *or* periodical (n)

revista profesional especializada trade magazine *or* trade journal

revocar revoke *or* reverse (v) *or* countermand

riesgo (m) risk (n) *or* exposure

riesgo financiero financial risk

rincón (m) corner (n)

ritmo (m) de producción rate of production

robo (m) theft

rollo (m) publicitario sales pitch

romper las negociaciones break off negotiations

romper un acuerdo break an agreement

romperse break down (v)

rotación (f) turnover

rotación de existencias stock turnover

rotulador (m) marker pen

rótulo (m) sign (n)

roturas (fpl) breakages

rubricar initial (v)

ruego (m) request (n)

ruptura (f) breakdown (n)

ruta (f) habitual run (n) *or* regular route

rutina (f) routine (n)

rutinario (-ria) routine (adj)

Ss

sacar *[dinero]* draw *or* withdraw *[money]*

sacar el título de qualify as

saco (m) bag

sala (f) room

sala de conferencias conference room

sala de embarque departure lounge

sala de exposición showroom

sala de exposiciones exhibition hall

sala de juntas boardroom

sala de subastas auction rooms

sala de tránsito transit lounge

salario (m) salary *or* wage

salario inicial starting salary

salario interesante attractive salary

salario mínimo minimum wage

salario mínimo interprofesional guaranteed minimum wage

salario neto net income *or* net salary

saldar balance (v)

saldar una cuenta settle an account

saldo (m) balance (brought down *or* brought forward)

saldo (m) *[rebajas]* sale (n)

saldo a cuenta nueva balance carried down *or* carrried forward

saldo acreedor *o* saldo a favor credit balance

saldo a (nuestro) favor balance due to us

saldo de caja cash balance

saldo deudor debit balance

saldo final closing balance *or* bottom line

saldo inicial opening balance

saldo insuficiente insufficient funds (US)

salida (f) departure

salidas (fpl) departures

saliente retiring *or* outgoing

salir go (out)

salón (m) de exposiciones exhibition hall

salón VIP (salón de personalidades) VIP lounge

saltarse la cola jump the queue

saltarse un plazo miss an instalment

salud (f) health

saluda (m) compliments slip

salvamento (m) salvage (n)

salvar salvage (v)

salvedad (f) proviso

salvo except

salvo error u omisión errors and omissions excepted (e. & o.e.)

sancionar penalize (v)

satisfacción (f) satisfaction

satisfacción del cliente customer satisfaction

satisfacción laboral job satisfaction

satisfacer satisfy (v) *or* meet (v)

satisfacer una demanda meet a demand *or* satisfy a demand

satisfacer la demanda keep up with the demand

saturación (f) saturation

saturar saturate

saturar el mercado saturate the market

se admiten ofertas open to offers

sección (f) section *or* division

sección (de tienda) department

sección de 'marketing' marketing division

sección de compras purchasing department

sección de ventas sales department

secretario (-ria) secretary

secretario (-ria) de una empresa company secretary

secretario (-ria) eventual temp (n)

secreto (m) secret (n)

secreto (-ta) secret (adj)

sector (m) sector

sector primario primary industry

sector privado private sector

sector público public sector

sector terciario *o* sector de los servicios tertiary sector

secuestrar sequester *or* sequestrate *or* seize

secundario (-ria) subsidiary (adj) *or* secondary

sede (f) headquarters (HQ)

seguir follow *or* proceed

según depending on *or* according to *or* under

según contrato contractually

según factura as per invoice

según muestra as per sample

según nota de expedición as per advice

segundo (-da) second (adj)

segunda solicitud (f) reapplication

segundo trimestre (m) second quarter

seguridad (f) safety *or* security

seguridad de empleo security of employment

seguridad en el empleo job security

seguridad social social security

seguro (m) insurance

seguro (m) *[de vida]* life assurance

seguro (-ra) safe (adj)

seguro a todo riesgo comprehensive insurance

seguro contra incendios fire insurance

seguro contra terceros third-party insurance

seguro corriente de vida whole-life insurance

seguro de automóviles motor insurance

seguro de enfermedad health insurance

seguro de la vivienda house insurance

seguro de vida life assurance

seguro general general insurance

seguro marítimo marine insurance

seguro temporal term insurance

selección (f) selection *or* choice (n)

selección de artículos para preparar un pedido order picking

seleccionar candidatos (-tas) select *or* screen candidates

selecto (-ta) choice (adj)

sellar stamp (v)

sellar *[precintar]* seal (v)

sello (m) stamp (n)

semana (f) week

semana: a mediados de semana mid-week

semanalmente weekly

semestre (m) half-year

señal (f) sign (n) *or* mark (n)

señal (f) *[entrada]* deposit (n)

señal de comunicar engaged tone

señal de línea dialling tone

señalar mark (v)

señas (fpl) address (n)

señas: poner las señas address (v)

sencillo (-lla) single

sentada (f) sit-down protest

sentencia (f) *[fallo]* award (n)

sentencia (f) *[juicio]* judgement *or* judgment

separado (-da) separate (adj)

separado: por separado under separate cover

separar separate (v)

ser despedido get the sack

ser distinto differ (v)

ser igual a equal (v)

ser responsable ante alguien be responsible to someone

ser válido *[regir]* run (v) *or* be in force

serie (f) *[remesa]* batch (n)

servicio (m) service (n)

servicio de contestación answering service

servicio de fotocopias photocopying bureau

servicio de habitaciones de un hotel room service

servicio de mantenimiento service department

servicio de paquetes postales parcel post

servicio de post-venta *o* **servicio posventa** after-sales service

servicio de recortes de prensa clipping service

servicio deficiente poor service

servicio rápido prompt service

servicios (mpl) de informática computer services

servir serve

servir un pedido deal with an order

signatario (-ria) signatory

signatario colectivo joint signatory

significado (m) content

signo (m) de calidad quality label

símbolo (m) symbol *or* token

símbolo de prestigio status symbol

sindicalista (mf) trade unionist

sindicato (m) (trade) union

síndico (m) liquidator *or* (official) receiver

síndrome del fénix phoenix syndrome

sinergia (f) synergy

siniestro (m) total dead loss

sistema (m) system

sistema (m) *[organización]* setup

sistema de ordenador a tiempo real real-time system

sistema de recuperación retrieval system

sistema económico economy *or* economic system

sistema informático computer system

Sistema Monetario Europeo (SME) European Monetary System (EMS)

sistema operativo operating system

sistema tributario tax system

sistemas (mpl) de control control systems

sitio (m) *[lugar]* site *or* place (n)

situación (f) situation *or* position

situación financiera financial position

situado (-da) situated

S.L. (= sociedad limitada) Ltd (= limited company)

SME (Sistema Monetario Europeo) EMS (= European Monetary System)

sobornar bribe (v)

soborno (m) bribe (n) *or* backhander

sobre (m) abierto unsealed envelope

sobre cerrado sealed envelope

sobrecapacidad (f) overcapacity

sobrecontratación (m) overbooking

sobregiro (m) overdraft

sobrepasar exceed

sobreprima (f) additional premium

sobreproducción (f) overproduction

sobrepujar *[pujar]* outbid

sobresaliente outstanding (adj)

sobrestimar *[sobrevalorar]* overestimate (v) *or* overvalue (v)

sobretasa (f) surcharge

sobretasa de importación import surcharge

sobrevalorar overvalue *or* overestimate (v)

social social

sociedad (f) society

sociedad (f) *[asociación]* partnership

sociedad (f) *[compañía]* company

sociedad anónima (S.A.) Public Limited Company (Plc)

sociedad comercial trading company

sociedad cooperativa cooperative society

sociedad cotizada en bolsa quoted company

sociedad de cartera holding company *or* proprietary company (US)

sociedad de responsabilidad limitada (S.R.L.) limited (liability) company (Ltd)

sociedad en comandita limited partnership

sociedad ficticia (para la compra de acciones) shell company

sociedad financiera finance company

sociedad hipotecaria *o* de crédito hipotecario building society

sociedad limitada (S.L.) private limited company

sociedad matriz parent company

sociedad mercantil corporation

sociedades (fpl) industriales industrialized societies

socio (-cia) *[asociado]* partner *or* associate

socio (-cia) *[miembro]* member

socio comanditario *o* socio en comandita sleeping partner

socio (-cia) principal senior partner

socio subalterno *o* de menor antigüedad junior partner

socios: los socios membership

solar (m) site (n)

solicitación (f) de votos canvassing

solicitar apply for *or* ask for *or* request (v)

solicitar pedidos solicit orders

solicitar votos canvass (votes)

solicitar por escrito apply in writing

solicitar un trabajo apply for a job

solicitar una patente file a patent application

solicitud (f) application *or* request (n)

solicitud de empleo *o* **de trabajo** job application *or* application for a job

solución (f) solution

solucionar un problema solve a problem

solvencia (f) solvency

solvente solvent *or* credit-worthy

someter a prueba test (v)

sondeo (m) de opinión opinion poll

soporte (m) holder

soslayar get round (a problem)

sostener keep up *or* maintain

S.R.L. (= sociedad de responsabilidad limitada) Ltd (= limited company)

stand (m) stand (n)

status (m) status

statutario (-ria) statutory

sub judice sub judice

subalterno (-na) junior (adj)

subarrendador (-ra) sublessor

subarrendar sublease (v) *or* sublet (v)

subarrendatario (-ria) sublessee

subarriendo (m) sublease (n)

subasta (f) auction (n) *or* bidding (n)

subastar auction (v)

subcontratar subcontract (v)

subcontratista (mf) subcontractor

subcontrato (m) subcontract (n)

subdirector (-ra) assistant manager *or* deputy manager

subida (f) rise (n) *or* increase *or* appreciation

subir climb *or* increase (v) *or* raise (v) *or* mount up

subir *[avanzar]* rise (v)

subir *[en valor]* appreciate

subir de precio increase (v) in price

subproducto (m) by-product

subsidiario (-ria) subsidiary (adj)

subsidio (m) subsidy *or* benefit (n)

subsidio de carestía de vida cost-of-living allowance

subsidio de paro *o* **desempleo** unemployment pay

subvención (f) subvention *or* subsidy

subvención (f) *[beca]* grant (n)

subvencionado: no subvencionado unsubsidized

subvencionar subsidize

suceder succeed

sucursal (f) branch (office) *or* division

sucursal *[tienda]* chain store

sueldo (m) wage *or* salary

sueldo bruto gross salary

sueldo neto net income *or* net salary

sueldo por hora hourly wage

suelo (m) floor

suelto (-ta) loose (adj)

suelto (-ta) *[desparejado]* odd

suficiente sufficient

sufragar defray

sufrir daños suffer damage

sugerencia (f) suggestion (n)

sujetapapeles (m) paperclip

sujetar attach (v)

sujeto (-ta) a liable to *or* subject to

sujeto (-ta) a impuesto taxable

suma (f) sum *or* addition

suma global lump sum

suma total grand total

sumar add up *or* total (v)

sumar una columna de cifras add up a column of figures

suministrador (-ra) supplier

suministrar supply (v)

suministro (m) supply (n)

superar exceed (v) *or* top (v)

superávit (m) surplus (n)

superficie (f) area *or* surface

superficie útil floor space

superior superior (adj) *or* senior (adj) *or* top (adj)

supermercado (m) supermarket

supervisar supervise

supervisión (f) supervision

supervisión: de supervisión supervisory

supervisor (-ra) supervisor

suplemeneto (m) de póliza endorsement

suplementario (-ria) supplementary

suplemento (m) supplement

suplemento por el servicio service charge

suplente (mf) deputy (n)

suprimir delete *or* remove *or* lift (v)

suprimir *[extirpar]* excise (v) *or* cut out

suprimir controles decontrol (v)

surtido (m) choice (n) *or* range (n) *or* selection

suscribir una opción take up an option

suspender suspend *or* cancel

suspender *[interrumpir]* discontinue

suspender un acuerdo call off a deal

suspender pagos stop payments

suspender una cuenta stop an account

suspendido (-da) off *or* cancelled

suspensión (f) suspension *or* stoppage (n)

suspensión de entregas suspension of deliveries

suspensión de pagos suspension of payments *or* stoppage of payments

sustituir replace (v) *or* take over

sustituir a alguien deputize for someone

sustituto (-ta) replacement *or* substitute (n)

Tt

tablas (fpl) actuariales *o* tablas de mortalidad actuarial tables

tablero (m) panel

tablero de hojas sueltas flip chart

tabulación (f) tabulation

tabulador (-ra) tabulator

tabular tabulate

tachar cross out *or* cross off

tacógrafo (m) tachograph

talla (f) corriente stock size

talla muy grande outsize (OS)

taller (m) workshop

talonario (m) de cheques cheque book

talonario de recibos receipt book

tamaño (m) size

tamaño corriente stock size

tamaño normal regular size

tangible tangible

tanteo (m) trial and error

tanto (m) alzado flat rate

tanto por ciento percentage

taquilla (f) booking office

taquillero (-ra) booking clerk

tara (f) tare (n)

tara (f) *[defecto]* defect (n) *or* fault (n) *or* imperfection (n)

tarado (-da) damaged

tarde late (adv)

tarea (f) assignment *or* task *or* job

tarifa (f) tariff *or* rate

tarifa de horas extras overtime pay

tarifa de mercado market rate

tarifa horaria hourly rate *or* time rate

tarifa nocturna night rate

tarifa por horas time rate

tarifa postal postage

tarifa preferente *o* tarifa preferencial preferential duty *or* preferential tariff

tarifa reducida cheap rate *or* reduced rate

tarifas (fpl) de carga aérea air freight charges *or* rates

tarifas de flete freight rates

tarifas de seguros insurance rates

tarifas diferenciadas differential tariffs

tarifas postales postal charges *or* postal rates

tarifas publicitarias advertising rates

tarifas publicitarias regresivas graded advertising rates

tarjeta (f) card *or* business card

tarjeta de cajero automático *o* tarjeta de dinero cash card

tarjeta de crédito credit card *or* charge card

tarjeta de desembarque landing card

tarjeta de embarque embarkation card *or* boarding card *or* boarding pass

tarjeta de saludo compliments slip

tarjeta inteligente smart card

tarjeta oro gold card

tarjeta postal card *or* postcard

tasa (f) rate (n)

tasa de amortización depreciation rate

tasa de cambio exchange rate

tasa de conversión conversion price *or* conversion rate

tasa de crecimiento growth rate

tasa de descuento discount rate

tasa de errores error rate

tasa de impuestos normal standard rate (of tax)

tasa de inflación rate of inflation

tasa de interés interest rate

tasa de rendimiento rate of return

tasación (f) valuation (n)

tasación de acciones stock market valuation

tasador (-ra) valuer

tasar value (v)

tasas (fpl) de aeropuerto airport tax

techo (m) ceiling

techo crediticio credit ceiling

tecla (f) key

tecla de control control key

tecla de mayúsculas shift key

teclado (m) keyboard (n)

teclado numérico numeric keypad

tecleado (m) keyboarding

teclear keyboard (v)

tecleo (m) keyboarding

técnica (f) skill *or* technique

técnicas (fpl) de 'marketing' marketing techniques

técnicas de dirección de empresas management techniques

técnicas de sondeo canvassing techniques

técnico asesor *o* **técnica asesora** consulting engineer

telefax (m) fax (n)

telefonear telephone (v) *or* phone (v)

telefonista (mf) telephonist

teléfono (m) telephone (n) *or* phone (n)

teléfono celular cellular telephone

teléfono de conferencias conference phone

teléfono de tarjeta card phone

teléfono interno internal telephone

teléfono móvil mobile phone

teléfono público pay phone

teletarjeta (f) phone card

télex (m) telex (n)

tema (f) subject (n)

temporada (f) season

temporada baja off-season

temporero (-ra) casual worker

temprano early

tendencia (f) trend

tendencia alcista upward trend

tendencias (fpl) del mercado market trends

tendencias económicas economic trends

tendero (-ra) shopkeeper

tenedor (-ra) holder

tenencia (f) tenure

tenencia de acciones shareholding

tener hold (v) *or* have *or* own

tener: sin tener en cuenta regardless of

tener como objetivo target (v)

tener en existencia carry *or* have in stock

tener existencias stock (v)

tener éxito succeed (v)

tener lugar take place

tener tiempo afford (the time)

tener una discusión hold a discussion

tercer trimestre (m) third quarter

tercero (m) third (n) *or* third party

terminación (f) termination *or* expiration

terminado (-da) finished

terminal terminal (adj)

terminal (f) de aeropuerto air terminal

terminal de contenedores container terminal

terminal del aeropuerto airport terminal

terminal (m) de ordenador computer terminal

terminar end (v) *or* terminate (v) *or* wind up

terminar de trabajar knock off *or* stop work

término (m) time limit *or* term

término: por término medio on average

términos (mpl) terms

terna (f) shortlist (n)

territorio (m) territory

Tesoro (m) treasury

testigo (mf) witness (n)

texto (m) text *or* wording

tiempo (m) time

tiempo: a tiempo on time

tiempo: a tiempo completo full-time

tiempo: a tiempo parcial part-time

tiempo: de hace tiempo long-standing

tiempo de preparación (de una máquina) make-ready time

tiempo invertido por el ordenador computer time

tiempo libre spare time

tiempo muerto down time

tienda (f) shop

tienda de barrio corner shop

tienda de fábrica factory outlet

tienda de rebajas cut-price store *or* discount store

tienda de regalos gift shop

tienda de una cadena chain store

tienda libre de impuestos duty-free shop

tiendas (fpl) al detall retail outlets

tierra (f) land (n)

timador (-ra) racketeer

timo (m) fiddle (n) *or* racket (n)

tipo (m) base de interés bancario bank base rate

tipo de cambio rate of exchange *or* exchange rate

tipo de cambio actual current rate of exchange

tipo de cambio cruzado cross rate

tipo de cambio desfavorable unfavourable exchange rate

tipo de cambio estable stable exchange rate

tipo de cambio para operaciones a plazo forward rate

tipo de descuento discount rate

tipo de gravamen tax rate

tipo de interés interest rate *or* rate of interest

tipo impositivo tax rate

tipo preferencial de interés bancario prime rate

tipos (mpl) de cambio flotantes floating exchange rates

tipos de interés money rates

tirada (f) circulation

tirar: de usar y tirar disposable

titulado (-da) certificated

título (m) deed

título (m) *[acción]* unit *or* share certificate

título (m) *[bono]* government bond

título al portador bearer bond

títulos (mpl) equities *or* securities

títulos del Estado government stock *or* gilt-edged securities

títulos profesionales professional qualifications

todo incluido all-in

todos los gastos pagados all expenses paid

toma (f) de decisiones decision making

tomar take (v)

tomar la iniciativa take the initiative

tomar medidas act (v) *or* take steps *or* make provision for

tomar nota take note *or* minute (v)

tomar posesión take over

tomar prestado borrow

tomar una decisión reach a decision

tomarse tiempo libre (durante el trabajo) take time off work

tonelada (f) ton

tonelada métrica tonne

toneladas (fpl) de peso muerto deadweight tonnage

tonelaje (m) tonnage

tonelaje bruto gross tonnage

total total (adj)

total (m) total (n) *or* sum (n)

total acumulado running total

total parcial subtotal

totalidad (f) total (n)

totalizar total (v)

trabajador (-ra) working (adj)

trabajador (-ra) worker *or* employee

trabajador (-ra) a domicilio homeworker

trabajador (-ra) a tiempo parcial part-timer

trabajador (-ra) eventual casual worker

trabajador (-ra) por libre freelance (n) *or* freelance worker

trabajadores (mpl) pagados por horas hourly-paid workers

trabajar work (v)

trabajo (m) labour *or* work (n) *or* job

trabajo: sin trabajo unemployed *or* out of work

trabajo a contrata contract work

trabajo a destajo piecework

trabajo a tiempo completo full-time employment

trabajo bien remunerado well-paid job

trabajo de campo field work

trabajo de oficina clerical work

trabajo en curso work in progress

trabajo eventual casual work

trabajo manual manual work

trabajo por horas part-time work *or* part-time employment

trabajo por turnos shift work

trabajo rutinario routine work

trabajo urgente rush job

traducción (f) translation

traducir translate

traductor (-ra) translator

traer bring

tramitación (f) procedure

tramitación del pago de un cheque clearance of a cheque

tramitar process (v)

tramitar el pago de un cheque clear a cheque

trámite (m) formality *or* procedure

trampa (f) fiddle (n)

transacción (f) deal (n) *or* (business) transaction

transacción en efectivo cash deal

transacción global package deal

transbordador (m) ferry

transbordo (m) transfer (n)

transferencia (f) transfer (n)

transferencia bancaria bank transfer

transferencia de fondos transfer of funds

transferible transferable

transferir transfer (v)

transigir compromise (v)

tránsito (m) transit

transmisión (f) de títulos de propiedad conveyancing

transportar transport (v) *or* carry

transportar en contenedores containerize

transporte (m) transport (n) *or* freight *or* carriage

transporte en contenedores containerization

transporte por carretera (road) transport *or* road haulage

transporte por carretera o por vía marítima surface transport

transporte por ferrocarril rail transport

transporte público public transport

Transporte Internacional por Carretera TIR (= Transports Internationaux Routiers)

transportista (mf) road haulier *or* carrier *or* shipper

trasladar transfer (v) *or* move to new place

trasladar temporalmente second (v) (member of staff)

trasladar(se) move (house, office)

traslado (m) transfer (n)

traslado (m) *[mudanza]* removal *or* move

traspaso (m) premium *or* transfer fee *or* key money

traspaso de bienes assignment *or* cession

tratamiento (m) de textos word-processing

tratante (mf) dealer

tratar handle (v)

tratar con alguien deal with someone

trato (m) bargain (n) *or* deal

trato difícil hard bargaining

tren (m) train (n)

tren de mercancías freight train *or* goods train

tren de mercancías de contenedores freightliner

tribunal (m) court

tribunal de arbitraje arbitration board *or* arbitration tribunal

tribunal de arbitraje laboral industrial arbitration tribunal

tribunal de justicia adjudication tribunal

tribunal de rentas rent tribunal

tribunales (mpl) de justicia law courts

tributación (f) progresiva progressive taxation

trimestral quarterly (adj)

trimestralmente quarterly (adv)

trimestre (m) quarter *or* three months *or* term

triple triple (adj)

triplicado: por triplicado in triplicate

triplicar triple (v) *or* treble (v)

trocar barter (v)

trozo: en trozos pequeños fine (adv) *or* very small

trueque (m) barter (n) *or* bartering (n)

turno (m) shift (n)

turno de día day shift

turno de noche night shift

Uu

UE (= Unión Europea) EU (= European Union)

último (-ma) last *or* latest

último (-ma) *[final]* final

último requerimiento (m) de pago final demand

último trimestre last quarter

últimos en entrar, primeros en salir last in first out (LIFO)

umbral (m) threshold

único (-ca) *[exclusivo]* sole

único (-ca) *[fuera de serie]* one-off

único (-ca) *[sencillo]* single

unidad (f) unit

unidad de almacenaje storage unit

unidad de producción production unit

unidad monetaria monetary unit

uniforme flat (adj) *or* uniform

unilateral unilateral

unión (f) aduanera customs union

Unión Europea (UE) European Union (EU)

unir join *or* unite

urgente urgent

urgente *[correo]* express (adj)

usado (-da) *[de segunda mano]* secondhand

usar use (v)

usar: de usar y tirar disposable

uso (m) use (n) *or* utilization

uso: de fácil uso user-friendly

uso: en uso used *or* employed

usual usual

usuario (-ria) user

usuario final end user

usufructo (m) vitalicio life interest

útil useful *or* handy

utilización (f) utilization

utilizado (-da) employed *or* used

utilizar use (v) *or* run (v)

utilizar capacidad ociosa use up spare capacity

Vv

vacaciones (fpl) reglamentarias statutory holiday

vacante (f) vacancy

vacante (adj) free (adj) *or* vacant

vaciar empty (v)

vacío (m) gap

vacío (-cía) empty (adj)

vagón (m) (de ferrocarril) railway wagon *or* truck

vale (m) voucher

vale de caja cash voucher

vale para un regalo gift voucher

valedero (-ra) valid

valer cost (v)

validez (f) validity

válido (-da) valid

valla (f) publicitaria hoarding

valor (m) value (n) *or* worth (n)

valor: sin valor worthless

valor a la par par value

valor actual present value

valor contable book value

valor de activo asset value

valor de escasez *o* **valor de exclusividad** scarcity value

valor de mercado market value

valor de reposición replacement value

valor de rescate surrender value

valor declarado declared value

valor neto net worth

valor nominal face value *or* nominal value

valor total de factura total invoice value

valoración (f) valuation *or* assessment *or* estimation

valoración (f) *[apreciación]* appreciation

valoración de daños assessment of damages

valoración de existencias stock valuation

valoración de resultados performance rating

valorar value (v) *or* assess *or* estimate (v)

valorar *[apreciar]* appreciate

valores (mpl) securities

valores convertibles en acciones convertible loan stock

variación (f) variation *or* variance

variaciones estacionales seasonal variations

vehículo (m) vehicle

vehículo de transporte carrier

vencer mature (v) *or* fall due *or* expire (v)

vencido (-da) overdue *or* due

vencimiento (m) expiration (n) *or* expiry (n)

vendedor (-ra) salesman *or* seller *or* vendor

vendedor (-ra) a domicilio door-to-door salesman

vendedor (-ra) de seguros insurance salesman

vender sell (v) *or* market (v)

vender: sin vender unsold

vender a futuros sell forward

vender a precio más bajo que un rival undercut a rival

vender con entrega aplazada sell forward

vender las existencias sobrantes dispose of excess stock

vender más barato undersell

vender un bono redeem a bond

vender un negocio sell out *or* sell one's business

vender(se) al por menor retail (v)

vendible saleable *or* marketable

vendido: más vendido top-selling

vendido: no vendido unsold

venirse abajo fall through

venta (f) sale (n) *or* selling (n)

venta: a la venta on sale

venta: en venta for sale

venta a domicilio house-to-house selling *or* door-to-door selling

venta a prueba *o* **en depósito** sale or return *or* see-safe

venta agresiva hard selling

venta al contado cash sale

venta al por menor *o* **al detalle** retail (n)

venta con tarjeta de crédito credit card sale

venta directa direct selling

venta en la bolsa bargain (n) (on Stock Exchange)

venta en subasta sale by auction

venta forzosa forced sale *or* distress sale

venta por correo direct mail

venta sin presionar al cliente soft sell

ventana (f) window

ventanilla (f) counter

ventas (fpl) sales

ventas a plazo forward sales

ventas bajas low sales

ventas estimadas estimated sales

ventas nacionales domestic sales *or* home sales

ventas netas net sales

ventas por teléfono telesales

ventas previstas projected sales

ventas registradas book sales

verbal verbal

verdadero (-ra) real *or* true

verificación (f) verification

verificado: no verificado unaudited

verificar verify

vetar una decisión veto a decision

vía via

viabilidad (f) feasibility

viable viable

viajar travel (v)

viajar diariamente al trabajo commute (v)

viaje (m) voyage (n) *or* journey (n) *or* trip (n)

viaje de negocios business trip

viaje de regreso homeward journey

viajero diario *o* **viajera diaria** commuter

viejo (-ja) old

vigente ruling (adj)

vigilante (m) security guard

vigor (m) energy *or* strength

vigoroso (-sa) strong

vinculante binding

vínculo (m) connection *or* link

violación (f) de contrato breach of contract

violación de garantía breach of warranty

violación de patente infringement of patent

violar violate *or* infringe

violar una patente infringe a patent

visado (m) visa

visado de entrada entry visa

visado de entradas múltiples multiple entry visa

visado de tránsito transit visa

visita (f) visit (n) *or* call (n)

visita comercial sin cita previa cold call

visita de negocios business call

visitar visit (v) *or* call on

vista (f) sight

vitrina (f) display case *or* showcase

vitrina de exposición display unit *or* display stand

volumen (m) volume *or* bulk

volumen comercial volume of trade

volumen de ventas volume of sales *or* sales volume *or* turnover

volumen de negocios volume of business

voluminoso (-sa) bulky

volver a comprar buy back

volver a nombrar reappoint

volver a presentarse reapply

volver a telefonear *o* **volver a llamar** phone back

voto (m) de calidad casting vote

voto de gracias vote of thanks

voto por poderes proxy vote

vuelo (m) flight (n)

vuelo chárter charter flight

vuelo de correspondencia connecting flight

vuelo de larga distancia long-haul flight *or* long-distance flight

vuelo regular scheduled flight

vuelta (f) *[cambio]* change (n)

vuelta (f) *[regreso]* return (n)

Zz

zona (f) zone *or* area *[of town]*

zona comercial peatonal shopping
    precinct

zona de libre cambio free trade area

zona del dólar dollar area

zona franca free (trade) zone

zona industrial industrial estate

BILINGUAL DICTIONARIES

A range of comprehensive, up-to-date bilingual business dictionaries. The dictionaries cover all aspects of business usage: buying and selling, office practice, banking, insurance, finance, stock exchange, warehousing and distribution.

Each dictionary includes:

over 50,000 entries

clear and accurate translations

example sentences

grammar notes

Ideal for any business person, teacher or student

Business French	ISBN 0-948549-64-5	600pp	h/b
Business German	ISBN 0-948549-50-5	650pp	h/b
Business Spanish	ISBN 0-948549-90-4	736pp	h/b
Business Chinese	ISBN 0-948549-63-7	534pp	h/b
Business Romanian	ISBN 0-948549-45-9	250pp	h/b
Business Swedish	ISBN 0-948549-14-9	420pp	h/b

Available from all good bookshops.

For further details, please contact:
Peter Collin Publishing Ltd
1 Cambridge Road, Teddington, TW11 8DT, UK
fax: +44 181 943 1673   email: info@pcp.co.uk   www.pcp.co.uk